LIFE-GIVING LOVE

Life-Giving Love

Embracing God's Beautiful Design for Marriage

KIMBERLY KIRK HAHN

CHARIS

Servant Publications
Ann Arbor, Michigan

Charis Books is an imprint of Servant Publications especially designed to serve Roman Catholics.

All Scripture quotations, unless otherwise indicated, are taken from the Revised Standard Version of the Bible (RSV), the Catholic Edition of the New Testament, copyright 1965, the Catholic Edition of the Old Testament, incorporating the Apocrypha, copyright 1966 by the Division of Christian Education of the National Council of the Churches of Christ in the USA. Used by permission.

Excerpts from the English translation of the *Catechism of the Catholic Church* for use in the United States of America © 1994, United States Catholic Conference, Inc.-Libreria Editrice Vaticana. Used with permission. Excerpts from the English translation of the *Catechism of the Catholic Church: Modifications from the "Editio Typica"* © 1997, United States Catholic Conference, Inc.-Libreria Editrice Vaticana. Used with permission.

The personal stories and testimonies in this book are true. Real names have been used where permission was granted. However, names and identifying characteristics in some stories have been changed to protect the privacy of those involved.

NIHIL OBSTAT: Reverend James Dunfee
                Censor Liborum
IMPRIMATUR: Most Reverend Gilbert I. Sheldon
                Bishop of Steubenville
                August 10, 1999

The NIHIL OBSTAT and IMPRIMATUR are a declaration that a book or pamphlet is considered to be free from doctrinal or moral error. It is not implied that those who have granted the NIHIL OBSTAT and IMPRIMATUR agree with the contents, opinions, or statements expressed.

Servant Publications
P.O. Box 8617
Ann Arbor, MI 48107

Cover design by Paul Higdon, Minneapolis, Minn.

03 04 10 9 8 7 6

Printed in the United States of America
ISBN 1-56955-292-4

Library of Congress Cataloging-in-Publication Data

Hahn, Kimberly.
    Life-giving love : embracing God's beautiful design for marriage / Kimberly Kirk Hahn.
        p. cm.
    Includes bibliographical references.
    ISBN 1-56955-292-4 (alk. paper)
      1. Human reproduction—Religious aspects—Christianity. 2. Marriage—Religious aspects—Catholic Church. 3. Catholic Church—Doctrines. I. Title.
    BX1795.H84 .H34 2002
    248.4'82—dc21

                                                      2001007670

CONTENTS

What this book teaches is true. It's challenging. And it's life-changing. I know all this because I've had the joy and the privilege of discovering its truth, its challenge, and its transformation alongside the author, who is my wife, Kimberly.

What the Church teaches about love, sex, and marriage is true. That should be apparent by now, as nothing else seems to bring lasting happiness to families. Pundits deride the popes as out of touch with reality and out of step with the times. But it is actually society's sexual "liberation" that has proven to be unworkable in the real world—breaking up homes and hearts, burdening bodies with disease and souls with sin.

The Church's teaching works in the real world because it is based upon our nature. The moral law comes from the God who created the real world, human nature, and our human bodies. He knows us better than we know ourselves. He loves us better than we can love ourselves or love each other. So his law does not constrain us so much as perfect us and guide us along right paths. It is no more repressive than a map is for a traveler.

The Church's teaching makes sense, and it works, unlike any of the alternatives. That should be enough to recommend it; but there are more and even better reasons behind it. For this doctrine is based not only on the natural law known to reason but also on the divine law confirmed by faith.

All Christians, throughout all of history, saw this matter clearly until the late twentieth-century sexual revolution muddled many minds. The ancient world was well acquainted with birth control, divorce, homosexuality, adultery, abortion, premarital sex, and divorce. In many parts of the Roman Empire, these practices were as common and as socially acceptable as they are in America today.

Yet Christians unanimously condemned these actions. And the Protestant Reformation accepted this tradition. Indeed, Protestants and Catholics unanimously shared a sexual ethic for four hundred years after the Reformation. In matters of love, sex, and marriage, Christian tradition spoke with one voice until the 1930s. Since then, Protestant denominations have broken ranks one by one, but the Church's Magisterium has remained steadfast.

Why did the Church hold fast to this teaching? Not to be authoritarian or retrograde, but to be true and to be loving. Let all the rest of the world declare war on human nature and the human body. The Church would rather help us find salvation, peace, and good health in happy homes.

Is it always easy to do what's right? Of course not. Whether you're married or not, you may look at this doctrine and wonder how anyone can live it.

Well, no one can live it—without dedicated human effort and the supernatural help of the Holy Spirit. It may not be easy, but it is a relatively simple matter to follow the path of prayer, sacrifice, and self-discipline that Christian tradition has clearly spelled out for us. Again, it is the alternatives that are hopelessly difficult, and complicated, and ultimately lonely.

We moderns have a mania for planning and control. We think we can make matters simpler and make life easier by dictating the fine details of our lives. Many people do this in marriage, too, and that's why they place such hope in "family *planning*" and "birth *control.*" Life, however, rarely turns out the way we plan it. In the words of the popular song, life is what happens while we're busy making other plans.

The Church's teaching is life-changing, and that scares many people—because God's plan for us might upset our own dreams for our life, career, and home. I can testify to this reality. I had my whole career mapped out when Kimberly and I stopped using contraceptives. I was all ready to set sail for a prestigious doctoral program in Aberdeen, Scotland.

But God's plan is always better for us than our wildest dreams would have been. By becoming a father, I learned what no doctoral program could have taught me. Indeed, fatherhood taught me more about my profession—which is theology—than I ever could have learned in a classroom. By practicing fatherhood, I came to know God's fatherhood in deeper ways. By the time I did get my doctorate—on God's schedule, not mine—I was living what I was learning.

God's ways are not always life-changing in the way we want but rather in the way we need. By following the perennial Christian truth in matters of love and sex, Kimberly and I gained a much deeper reverence and gratitude for each other and for the mystery of marriage as it's expressed in sexual love. We have also discovered that we're not alone. In the last two decades, we've encountered hundreds and even thousands of families who have been similarly transformed. We personally know hundreds of wonderful children who wouldn't exist if not for their parents' changed lives and changed minds. These kids are the bearers of a message.

This book bears the same message. It comes from an author who knows it to be true, and challenging, and life-changing. She has received it lovingly from the Author of life.

Scott Hahn

DEDICATION

I dedicate this book to Jesus, the life-giving Lover of my soul, and to my beloved soulmate, Scott, who chose me for his wife and who cooperated with God to bestow motherhood upon me. How grateful I will ever be for the truth we have found and had the privilege to live for more than twenty years together.

Many thanks to each of our children, who are part of the civilization of love in our home, the consequences of our life-giving love. For our children yet on earth who inspire our hearts with their love, prayers, and acts of service: Michael, Gabriel, Hannah, Jeremiah, Joseph, and David. And for our children who have gone before us for their love and prayers that we faithfully spread truth: Raphael, Noel Francis, and Angelica Frances.

INTRODUCTION

What was conceived years ago is finally delivered—this manuscript. Years of presentations, conversations, and fledgling articles, with intermittent attempts at a full-length book, have reached fruition. Since living the message is more important than writing about it, several sabbaticals from this work were necessary to prepare for and welcome new little ones.

Thank you for allowing me the privilege of unpacking the Church's teaching on the act of marriage and on openness to life in the following pages. In love, God called us into being—male and female—to image his life-giving love. My heart's desire is to invite you into a fuller participation in God's divine life and love.

Sometimes people approach others in a blunt way: "Here's the Church's teaching. Tough it out. Others did!" This approach makes us feel bound in chains from which there is no escape. That is not the way of truth spoken in love. Rather than binding us, truth liberates us to be all we were created to be. That is why Jesus said, "You will know the truth, and the truth will make you free" (Jn 8:32).

Just as a groom pulls back his bride's veil to reveal her beauty, so the Lord unveils his Church to reveal the splendor of her beauty: the truth lived by the children of God. Openness to life occurs in the context of our life with God; it's not simply a command to be obeyed, but it's truth to be lived. My earnest hope and prayer is that we will all come to a deeper knowledge of and appreciation for God's design for the marital covenant and the part it plays in our call to holiness.

I.

THE BEAUTY OF GOD'S DESIGN: PROCREATION AND UNION

CHAPTER ONE

MY TESTIMONY

I am one of five children, happy consequences of a marriage overflowing with love. My parents planned on a certain number of children; however, they acknowledged God had a better plan and treasured us whether or not we were *planned*. It was so much fun growing up in a big family that I hoped my future spouse would want a lot of children. My desire was not rooted so much in a conviction about openness to life as in wanting to imitate my family's example.

Scott and I fell in love while attending Grove City College in Grove City, Pennsylvania. We had a sense of a call to serve Christ together. I realized one day as we were talking in a hall on campus that though we were already engaged, we had never discussed whether or not we would have children or how many we would have. I picked my timing carefully.

"Scott, you do want to have children, don't you?"

He quickly rejoined, "Sure, but not too many."

I thought, *Oh, no. I'm marrying a ZPGer and didn't know it!* (A "ZPGer" is a person who wants Zero Population Growth, so he limits his family to two children to maintain the current population level instead of causing the population to grow.) I took a deep breath, yet tried to appear casual. "How many is not too many?"

"I think we ought to keep it down to five or six."

Now I had to appear casual for a different reason. "Yes, let's think small: no more than five or six," I said, suppressing a smile.

Months later, premarital counseling with my father, who was also my Presbyterian pastor, included a discussion about contraception—not whether or not to use it, but what kind we were going to use. We all believed that Christian stewardship involved careful family planning, especially since we were heading off to seminary with few finances to support a family. Contraception was obviously the prudent choice.

My father said, "What are you going to do for birth control?"

I said, "I am going to take the Pill."

To which he replied, "As your pastor, I have no difficulty with that, but as your father, I have some concerns."

I allayed his fears with some supposed facts the gynecologist had given us, and we moved on to another topic. End of discussion. Dad knew that as our marital love grew, our desire for children would grow. For now the focus was on us as a couple and our marriage ceremony.

Our wedding was a wonderful celebration of God's call on our lives to form a new family in service to him. But, to the best of my knowledge, children were never mentioned as part of the ceremony. (This is in contrast to a Catholic wedding, in which the couple commits publicly to receive children from God and to educate them for God.)

Three weeks later, Scott and I journeyed to New England for Scott to attend Gordon-Conwell Theological Seminary. After I worked full time for a year while Scott studied, we were both able to get onto an educational track. This time of study together proved life-changing for both of us.

My first project in seminary was to study the issue of abortion and develop a presentation for teens. The more I presented the truth about life, the more I saw teens appreciate the beauty of life. At the same time, they felt anger at the lies they had been told at school about abortion.

Oddly enough, as I spoke about abortion, many people asked questions about contraception. At first it bothered me. I would say, "We're getting off the topic—we need to stick with the issue of abortion," until a few people pointed out how some forms of contraception, the IUD and occasionally the Pill, can be abortive.

Some people, I learned, even rely on abortion as their fail-proof birth control. I was horrified to discover that one of every five women having abortions is married.[1] Perhaps there was more of a connection between abortion and contraception than I had originally thought.

On a personal note, I experienced difficult side effects with the Mini-Pill recommended by my gynecologist. When I approached a new doctor with questions, he asked me, "Did you know that some forms of the Pill, mainly the Mini-Pill, are abortive? They don't suppress ovulation; they just alter the lining of the uterus so that a baby cannot implant."

I was shocked and grieved. I had had no idea that I potentially was placing our children in such danger. I was thankful it was only our third month of marriage; I pray today that no harm was done. We immediately changed to a barrier form of contraception.

A class on Christian ethics at an evangelical Protestant seminary, taught by Dr. Jack Davis, gave me the opportunity to explore these issues further. Our assignments included picking a current topic of interest for research and making a presentation in a small group. Since I saw some connection between abortion and contraception, I thought it would be worth studying issues related to contraception in greater depth.

Seven of us signed up for the topic of contraception. When we met in the back of the class, one man, acting as self-appointed chairman, said, "Let's rule out anything that's abortive. But barrier methods of contraception should be OK. The only people who think that contraception is completely wrong are Catholics." It was as if he were concluding the study before we began. Was there really nothing more to study?

"Why," I wondered out loud, "do Catholics oppose contraception?" I didn't even know Catholics opposed contraception; no Catholic friend had ever mentioned that fact.

"There are only two reasons," he quipped, with a note of authority. "First, the pope isn't married. He doesn't live with the consequences! And second, Catholics are just out to make all the new Catholics they can!"

Surely there are reasons more substantial than that, I thought to myself. Then I said, "I doubt Catholics would put it that way."

"Well, why don't you study what they think?" he challenged. "But I already know what I think."

"I sure will," I replied. And I did.

Over supper that night Scott and I discussed our classes. He was amazed that I had selected contraception as my topic and that several others had as well. The previous year, no one had opted for that issue. As the course progressed, his amazement grew. I began to share the reasonable argument in opposition to artificial contraception not only from Catholic authors but from Scripture as well.

I too was amazed at the simple yet profound explanation of the act of marriage in the context of Christian faith that I discovered in Pope Paul VI's encyclical *Humanae Vitae*, required reading for class. Though I was not a Catholic, *Humanae Vitae* spoke to my heart, capturing a splendid vision of how our marriage could better reflect truth and love. In the few years since its promulgation, the prophetic nature of this document could already be seen.

Noted chastity speaker Molly Kelly calls it "the most prophetic document of the century because Pope Paul VI told us that the contraceptive mentality would lead to the abortion mentality—because when the child is *not* perceived as a gift but rather as something to put off, prevent, or if all else fails, abort—then our children are *not gifts* but burdens. And 3.6 million abortions have resulted because *Humanae Vitae* was rejected or never taught!"[2]

One day I spoke with a good friend who challenged me to consider these things more deeply. He could tell from my responses that I seemed convinced that contraception was wrong.

"Kimberly, you sound convicted against contraception. Are you still using it?"

That stopped me in my tracks. "It's not that easy," I answered. "It reminds me of the old story about the chicken and the pig.

"The chicken and the pig were walking down the road one day when the chicken commented to the pig about the generosity of the farmer.

"'Let's do something special for Farmer Brown,' said the chicken.

"'Like what?' asked the pig.

"'Let's give him a ham-and-eggs breakfast.'

"'That's fine for you,' said the pig. 'For you, that's just a donation. For me, that's total commitment.'

"My point is, as a single seminarian you don't have the consequences I might face should I throw out contraception tonight. But you're right to challenge me to live what I believe."

I left the library knowing I was persuaded, but there were two people in our marriage. I needed to have a thorough talk with Scott about all that I had discovered.

Scott and I talked and talked. We prayed. We sought counsel from others. We read and prayed and researched some more. Finally, we believed that God's design for marital love has at its heart a marital embrace unencumbered by devices or selfish designs. Our act of self-donating love was to be nothing less than an imitation of God's total self-donation.

To delay obedience is disobedience. Once we were convicted about the truth regarding openness to life, we brought our practice into conformity with our conviction. On April 1, 1981, we threw out artificial contraception for good.

No more drugs, plugs, jams, or jellies! That year, April Fool's Day meant no longer playing the fool with contraception but embracing the role of a fool for Christ. I wrote in my journal, "God be praised, we are now honoring him more in seeking to be consistent. Lord, your will be done in terms of timing."

Scott and I were impressed that the Roman Catholic Church alone,[3] with more than one billion members, took such a courageous (and, dare I say, biblical) stand against our culture in proclaiming the truth about openness to life. We were impressed but not moved toward the Church at that time. Nevertheless, I believe that seeds planted through studying this issue and living the truth opened our hearts years later to the fullness of the Christian faith in the Church.

Compelling Reasons

The reasonableness of the Catholic position on openness to life and the Scriptures that supported it amazed us. Perhaps that was why Protestants unanimously affirmed the same view as the Catholic Church until 1930. What a revelation!

Scores of Protestant church leaders and theologians since the Reformation can be quoted to demonstrate their strong convictions against the use of birth control.[4] Did Protestants simply fail to eradicate the last vestiges of "Romanism" in the area of sexual ethics until 1930? Or did Protestants through the centuries affirm basic truths that must govern all Christian marriages, Catholic or otherwise, for each of us to reflect the vision of the life-giving love of the Trinity in our families?

After all, marriage is not a man-made institution. It is God's work according to God's plan. Fundamentally, this is not a Catholic-versus-Protestant issue but a Christian-versus-non-Christian issue. That is why so many more non-Catholics are returning to the once nearly universal Christian understanding of the power, beauty, and truth of living marital love God's way.

I knew from research on abortion that Planned Parenthood was the single largest abortion provider in the country. What I did not know was that as early as 1917, the American radical activist Margaret Sanger had advocated contraception and abortion through the Birth Control League, which later became Planned Parenthood. As former feminist Mary Pride has observed, "It's no accident that the very organization that calls itself Planned Parenthood has been the driving force behind abortion's popularity in this country."[5]

In 1930, the Anglican's Lambeth Conference in England became the first official Christian body to approve use of contraception in the most severe cases. In response, a Jesuit, Fr. David Lord, wrote the following analysis.

1. Birth control destroys the difference between prostitutes and respectable women by eliminating the ideal of motherhood and substituting the ideal of personal pleasure and self-gratification.
2. Birth control leads to infidelity by destroying self-restraint and self-discipline. For unmarried folk it banishes fear of consequences.
3. Birth control prevents noble faculty by refusal to co-operate with God in creation of children and substitutes for it, pleasure.
4. Birth control affects the future. Substituting self-gratification for children, [those using it] strike at the very source of human life.[6]

Since 1930, every major Protestant denomination has relinquished its stand against contraception, and today most even allow abortion. There is a demonstrable connection between the contraceptive mentality promoted in the 1930s and the abortion and death industry mentality of the present day. The Catholic Church alone stands in continuity with Christian teaching throughout the centuries on the sanctity of the act of marriage.

Initially, to Scott and me, the Church's authority and magisterial teachings were nothing more than helpful input, since we had no interest in becoming Catholic. (In fact, Scott did not think that an intelligent Christian would remain in the Catholic Church!) However, the Church intrigued us with her willingness to take a stand obviously unpopular in today's culture and to proclaim it to the world, whether or not the world wanted to hear the message, simply because she believed it to be true.

The Scriptures, on the other hand, compelled us to take a second look at the prevailing Protestant acceptance of contraception. Could it be that most Protestant denominations had capitulated to our culture on abortion because they had first failed to understand why all Christians had affirmed what now only the Catholic Church was declaring on contraception?

The Importance of *Humanae Vitae*

On July 25, 1968, shortly after the close of the Second Vatican Council, Pope Paul VI promulgated a much-anticipated encyclical entitled *Humanae Vitae*. Historically, it was a time of much confusion: the sexual revolution was in full swing, the Pill was being hailed as the long-awaited perfect contraceptive to cure the social ills related to overpopulation, and even Catholic clergy advised the pope to reconcile the Church with the times in response to the report of the commission established by Pope John XXIII.

Pope Paul VI recognized the service of the commission, though he set aside their conclusion. He reiterated the responsibility of the teaching authority of the Church, the Magisterium, to interpret faithfully the current situation in the light of Scripture and Tradition. In a very few pages, he explained God's design for Christian marriage and the Church's view on contraception, sterilization, and abortion in the context of the sanctity of marriage.[7]

This wasn't the message many within or outside the Church wanted to hear. Initially, many (even some Catholic theologians and priests) scoffed at what they saw as an antiquated Church attempting to reign in free-thinking people who understood the times. However, in the light of more than thirty years' hindsight, this document has proven to be prophetic in its explanation of the cultural death awaiting those who would reject the beautiful vision of life and love set forth by our Lord in the Catholic Church.

This was the first encyclical Scott and I ever read as Protestants. Its direct yet pastoral approach to such a difficult subject amazed us. Its teachings are not time-bound; they reveal timeless truths with which we may regain our cultural footings.

A mother from Haslett, Michigan, wrote us about the importance of *Humanae Vitae* in her marriage:

My husband was the more convinced about the Church's teaching. The issue of aesthetics helped me to reject contraception. I was repulsed by condoms, jellies, and the hazards of messing up my body with a pill. Eventually my heart was changed through reading and understanding *Humanae Vitae.*

Sadly enough, many Catholics have never read this brief but beautiful teaching.

Humanae Vitae Ignored

Family members do not always encourage obedience on this issue. Sometimes a family member tries to assure a loved one that Catholics don't have to follow the Church on this issue, if they do not agree with the Church. One woman recalled:

> We used artificial contraception when we got married until my sister called from Indonesia, crying on the phone and begging my forgiveness. Since we have been blessed with a great relationship, I was confused as to what she could have done to me from overseas. She knew she suggested for me to use the Pill when I first got married since it seemed to be working for her and many people she knew. Since then, she had come to learn that it could cause an abortion. She would send information about this as well as information on NFP and what the Church teaches.

Though her sister misled her initially, she also helped her return to truth.

Sometimes parents urge their children not to have a lot of children due to the hardships they themselves have experienced. One newlywed couple from Wilmington, Delaware, felt this kind of pressure: "Family and doctors all said, 'You don't want to get pregnant now; you just got married!'"

Inaccurate advice of friends or family members has often encouraged errant thinking and practice in their loved ones' marriages. As one young mother recounted, "My mother taught me that the Church was wrong in her teaching about contraception and I believed my mother. There is so much misinformation about both NFP and contraception." Though friends and family intend to be helpful, in reality, they sometimes mistake worldly wisdom for godly wisdom. A mother from Washington commented:

What we really needed was good scriptural encouragement and direction for God's best for us, which was to let God be God and let him plan our family. It's amazing how the world's standards have filtered into Church people today and so many Christians aren't even aware of it.

Brenda, from a small town in Ohio, said she and her husband were influenced to contracept through pressure from "parents and middle-class values of having to be prepared financially, career-wise, etc., before having children. [We reevaluated our use of contraception when we] came to desire God to control the timing rather than us."

Sometimes people are not aware of the Church's teaching, while others do know, and yet are unwilling to submit to the Church's authority, such as Leila:

I came of age in the 1980s, and contraception was a given—as normal and necessary as brushing your teeth. I had even heard some of the Church's arguments against artificial contraception, and they made sense to me. I thought the Church was probably right on this issue (how magnanimous of me!), but of course I could never be expected to actually go along with this teaching. I did plan to learn Natural Family Planning one day, sure, but certainly not now, in my young married years. After all, God understands!

Later, I began to study my faith (Catholicism) and realized that the Church spoke for Christ. I fell in love with the One True Church. [NFP] renewed our marriage and deepened our attraction to one another. As I tell people now, God rewards faithfulness! [My husband] was an agnostic Jew who was awestruck to find his Messiah! He knew that Orthodox Jews oppose artificial birth control, and the Church's teaching made perfect sense to both of us.

The most amazing consequence of submitting to Church teaching is the desire—wholly unexpected—to have more children! We had a fourth child in February whom we consider our miracle "Catholic baby." (We were *done* after three kids and had plans for my husband to get a vasectomy eventually.) We are *so* grateful to God for our new baby, Paul Joseph, and we have a strong desire for more! We have been *blessed* by the Church's teaching, and our entire worldview has changed.

For this couple, the beauty of the Church's teaching has not only brought them new life in their son but also new spiritual life in the conversion of a spouse.

Perhaps a priest's instruction for a couple to follow their conscience implies that a couple should do what they want, because life can be difficult. Suzanne acknowledged: "The priest who married us in 1968 said it was OK. After Vatican II, many Catholics received confusing advice." A wife from Richfield, Minnesota, agreed:

Too many people today have adapted the Church's teachings to fit their own needs rather than remain faithful. In 1966, when my husband was in school, we got caught up in adapting the teaching on birth control to fit our need. We already had two babies, a one-year-old and a three-month-old. Needless to say, we weren't anxious to have another one soon, as I was working and my husband was in school full time.

We talked to a priest at the Newman Center who instructed us to form our own opinion as the "Church" didn't really know if it was a sin or not. He said a lot of the college kids were coming to Communion on Sunday even though they were on the Pill. He didn't refuse them because he claimed the Church was no longer sure. While deep down inside we basically knew the right answer, we talked ourselves into believing that if the Church was unsure, then it couldn't really be a sin for us.

Some Catholics say they tried to live the Church's teaching without understanding why the Church teaches what she does. A mother from Crestline, California, relates her experience:

I have been a Catholic all my life. I learned my prayers, my catechism, and all of the rules. I followed the rules—not because I understood them as wise and loving guides from God but because I was afraid if I didn't follow them I would go to hell. When my husband and I experienced some severe marital strain, my fear was not enough. I began to resent God for burdening me with NFP. I did not regard my five children as blessings. I kept thinking that God was trying to break me. Perhaps he was.

About eight weeks into counseling we talked about NFP. The counselor, a Christian, asked me about the Church's stand on birth control. I knew the rule but not the reason. He said that he would like me to explain to him the Church's belief and would I look it up. Lo and behold, I finally—after two years—listened to "Life-Giving Love" [audiotapes]. I am now a Catholic in my heart. From the bottom of my soul, I thank God that he [was willing to wait] so long for me to listen and understand what he was trying to say. I won't be afraid to announce another child when God chooses to bless me again.

The more we comprehend the reasons for Church teaching, the more we obey from the heart, especially when difficulties come.

A survey of Catholic couples that we conducted noted other influences to use contraception: the secular press, nursing school teachers, not knowing or understanding the Church's teachings, pressure from friends, not having a prayer life, lack of faith, lack of instruction at Pre-Cana classes, and even classes at a Catholic college. These negative influences must be counterbalanced by our growth in faith and in knowledge of the faith.

Blessings of Obedience

Others have experienced the joy of living this truth from the beginning of their marriage. One mother gave this testimony: "I grew up when it was 'normal' not to contracept. We needed to take joint responsibility for when to abstain—not just my saying no. It has helped us come to greater trust of God in all areas of our life."

A mother of four, ages eight to sixteen months, concurred: "I'm so glad we've never had contraception come between us."

Nancy, from Evergreen, Colorado, shared about the blessing that comes from beginning marriage without contraception: "We totally left the timing of our children in God's heart. Starting our marriage that way enabled us to trust in his will for us. It certainly helped us to focus on our love for each other by sacrifice and self-denial."

A couple from Greeley, Colorado, agrees: "Being open to life has taught us lessons in generosity and love. It has proven that God is better at planning our family than we could ever be."

A mother in Steubenville, Ohio, summed up the benefits of living the Church's teaching: "No guilt and many beautiful children."

The Fear Factor

Perhaps tnis joy seems elusive in the context of anxiety about how many children might be conceived. One mother reported the following:

[We used artificial contraception] because of our fear of our fertility. In hindsight I see that using artificial contraception caused many burdens in our marriage. [In switching to NFP] I learned about sacrificial love. It was pivotal in my reconversion to my faith and led eventually to my husband's joining the Church.

Laurie, from Louisville, Kentucky, echoed the same concern:

My big fear was that if we didn't use contraception we'd have a baby every year. Then I read *Breastfeeding and Natural Child Spacing* by Sheila Kippley. I realized that God had everything worked out if we will just follow *his* plan. I was vaguely aware of Church teaching on contraception (but I "knew" no one followed this teaching anymore).

Then I practiced ecological breastfeeding and experienced firsthand delayed menstruation and return to fertility. (My cycles returned when my baby was about fifteen months old.) We threw away all contraceptives, and our marriage has been completely open to new life ever since. This has added a sacredness to our marital relations that wasn't there when we were contracepting.

Sometimes the Lord uses dramatic events to awaken our consciences. One father from Quartz Hill, California, recounted the wake-up call he and his wife received:

My wife, our five-year-old son, and I were leaving a restaurant near our home en route to a conference when near tragedy struck. A Brinks armored truck was pulling away from the restaurant. We were walking in the same direction as the truck, and my son was walking along the curb looking at the truck and not at his feet. The curb curved; he didn't see it. He tripped, and his legs and lower back rolled into the path of the rear wheels of the truck.

He was rushed to the hospital by ambulance, and (this is the miracle) the X rays showed no broken bones! A bulletproof truck runs over our son's legs and he has no injuries but a series of bruises on his left leg and lower back!

[We] realize that the children [God] sends us are really his, and that we are but custodians chosen by him. The message was clear. Suppose our child had tripped the other way, and his upper torso had been in the path of those wheels? I shudder when I think of that, but I think of it as often as I can. Our son was two feet from death, and I don't *ever* want to forget that lesson.

He is our only child. We have been married thirteen years and have either practiced abstinence or used condoms both before and after his birth, afraid of the financial burden of more children. We also only have an eight-hundred-square-foot house. These were the only reasons we opted not to have more children, and we now see that we have been selfish and guilty of an extreme lack of faith.

Whether or not this couple is blessed with more children, they are trying to live God's priorities for their family.

One Protestant couple understood contraception as an act of stewardship, much as Scott and I had. They wrestled with this issue before being received into the Church.

We were influenced by the idea that contraception, limiting family size, timing of children, etc., was good Christian stewardship. My husband

and I did not come to agreement on Church teaching at the same time. It was one of the first things that made sense to me, one of the last for him. He has really changed, though. He is 100 percent in agreement with the Church.

Likewise, a mother in Rochester, New York, said, "Our deepening faith caused us to reevaluate our use of artificial contraception."

In fact, one man's strong commitment to the Church's teaching impressed rather than scared off his soon-to-be wife:

My husband influenced our decision. I've been blessed with a husband who has a very strong faith. He made it clear to me before we were married that he put God and his Catholic faith first and he would not waiver on this. His faith made the Catholic Church (and him) even more attractive to me before my conversion.

Some people do not realize that their contraceptive use makes a difference until after they have reexamined their use. Brenda from Houston, Texas, wrote, "While we contracepted, I don't think we felt a difference. It was in hindsight that we could see what we had missed. When we switched, we felt a stronger bond with each other and a happiness and joy because of our openness to life."

Upon further reflection, some people can see how contraception was a cause for some of their marital problems. Theresa, from Illinois, wrote:

We had many problems in the early years of marriage: much quarreling and selfishness concerning sexual issues and other issues as well. Looking back, I feel that the arguments over nonsexual issues probably were compounded by the lack of respect for each other sexually.

A fifty-year-old woman from Boston, Massachusetts, observed an even deeper impact of contraception on her marriage when she wrote: "We were quite self-centered, and the marriage ended in divorce. I believe not being open to life contributed to the breakup of my marriage."

A woman from Chicago, Illinois, noted her frustration over the lack of instruction on the Church's teaching: "I really felt cheated [for not having been taught earlier], when God finally helped me to see that his plan in Scripture is meant to bring stability and great peace, love, and joy."

The Challenge at Hand

If until now you have not heard the truth about the Church's teaching on openness to life, I urge you not to try to figure out "whose fault" it is. Instead, I invite you prayerfully to read this book with as much of an open heart as you can muster, and carefully weigh your response. Our Lord and his Church challenge us—you and me—with the truth that sets our hearts free to love and serve him faithfully in our marriages.

What began as a small group discussion and position paper has led to life-changing decisions and this book. Our Lord desires our marriages to be successful and fruitful; we desire nothing less. Let's look now at his design for marriage.

CHAPTER TWO

TRIUNE FAMILY: LIFE-GIVING LOVERS AND LIFE-LOVING GIVERS

An elderly priest once visited a second-grade classroom and asked, "Who can tell me what the Trinity is?"

A young girl in the back of the class, when called on, quietly answered, "Father, Son, and Holy Spirit."

The priest, whose hearing was impaired, leaned toward her and replied, "I'm sorry, I don't understand."

"You're not supposed to," she quickly rejoined. "It's a mystery."

So much about the Trinity is a mystery to us. How can we imagine Someone who has no beginning or who has no end? How do we understand the Being who knows everything, who is everywhere, who has all power?

How has God revealed himself? God is a communion of Persons: Father, Son, and Holy Spirit. Each Person of the Godhead is fully God: holy, wise, just, true, love—so how do we tell them apart?

We are able to differentiate the Father, Son, and Holy Spirit by their relations. From all eternity, the Father fathers the Son in self-donating love. The Son, in imitation of the Father, pours himself back to the Father in self-donating love. And the bond between them is more than a spirit of love; it constitutes the very Person of the Holy Spirit.

God's inner life of total self-donation creates an intimate communion of love and life. God is not just loving; he is the very *essence of love* (see 1 Jn 4:8). He is the source of all life.

Man and Woman Created in God's Image

Three Persons—Father, Son, and Holy Spirit—in one God, this Family of love and life, called man and woman into existence in his image.

Then God said, "Let us make man in our image, and after our likeness." So God created man in his own image, in the image of God he created him, male and female he created them. And God blessed them, and God said to them, "Be fruitful and multiply, and fill the earth and subdue it; and have dominion over the fish of the sea and over the birds of the air and over every living thing that moves upon the earth."

GENESIS 1:26-28

So man and woman were created in the image of the Triune God, unlike any other creature. They were blessed and commanded to be fruitful—to image God by becoming life-giving lovers.

God did not create man and woman because he was lonely, for "God in his deepest mystery is not a solitude, but a Family, since he has in himself fatherhood, sonship, and the essence of the family, which is love."[1] Rather, as an expression of his life-giving love, the Triune God created us for the joy of creating us and making us life-giving lovers like himself.

As the Vatican II fathers have expressed it, "Man, who is the only creature on earth which God willed for itself, cannot fully find himself except through a sincere gift of himself."[2] Man and woman were made to reflect God's inner life and love. He graced the first man and woman to reflect his image, both as individuals and in their marriage.

Each time God completed a day of creating living creatures, the refrain was repeated: "And God saw that it was *good*" (see Gn 1:12, 18, 25, emphasis added)—until he created man. After he created Adam, the response became, "And God saw everything that he had made, and behold, it was *very good*" (Gn 1:31, emphasis added).

Next the Scriptures record, "Then the Lord God said, 'It is *not good* that the man should be alone; I will make him a helper fit for him'" (Gn 2:18, emphasis added). So God created Eve as a helpmate for Adam, a friend and companion in the Garden, man's match.

God gave man and woman to each other in the covenant of marriage. A covenant is not a contract. A contract is an exchange of goods or services to which both parties agree; when the contract has been fulfilled, the relationship does not need to continue. A covenant, on the other hand, is an exchange of persons: I give myself to you, and you give yourself to me. A contract varies as much from a covenant as a man hiring a prostitute differs from a husband marrying a wife.

God always covenants himself with his people: "I ... will be your God, and you shall be my people" (Lv 26:12). When God establishes man and woman in the covenant bond of marriage, he blesses them with the command to give themselves completely to each other: "Be fruitful and multiply, and fill the earth and subdue it" (Gn 1:28). In essence, God says to his people, "You have been made in our trinitarian image; now do what we have done. Use the life-giving power of love you have received to be cocreators with us in new life."

Marriage is, after all, God's idea. The Second Vatican Council fathers insisted: "The intimate partnership of married life and love has been established by the Creator and qualified by his laws ... God himself is the author of matrimony."[3]

The one-flesh union of persons in the act of marriage is so powerful—the two becoming one—that, as my husband puts it, "Nine months later you might have to give it a name."[4] It constitutes an entirely new person. The two persons have become three persons in one family, reflecting the three-in-one Trinity. This is an unspeakable privilege: God invites us into the inner sanctum of who he is as life-giving Lover, to reflect the communion of trinitarian love in our human family, imaging the total self-donation of love that called us into being and now allows us to participate in a new being's creation.

Adam and Eve needed to respect the way God had designed them and the estate of marriage. As the Congregation for the Doctrine of the Faith has noted: "The gift of life which God the Creator and Father has entrusted to man calls him to appreciate the inestimable value of what he has been given and to take responsibility for it."[5]

Unlike all the creatures that copulate based merely on animal instinct, the response of spouses in openness to life is based on a rational and respectful act in obedience to God and in love for each other. People do not differ from the animals because they can *plan* conception; rather they differ from animals because they can use their rational faculties and their souls to comprehend the covenantal meaning of marriage. They can embrace all that the act of marriage involves in the giving and receiving of persons.

Do the Rules Change After the Fall?

We may be tempted to think, *Surely the rules in marriage changed once sin entered the picture, from the ideal of the Garden of Eden to the reality of life after the Fall.* When everything was perfect, it was easy for Adam and Eve to be open to life and to trust God to take care of things. But a fallen world, replete with fallen people, presented a new set of circumstances (see Gn 3:16-19): It was more difficult to provide for the family (weeds), it was more difficult to produce children without trauma (pain increased in childbearing), and there were more marital conflicts over leadership. In fact, over many years, sin became so rampant that God wiped out everyone except for Noah, his wife, their sons, and their sons' spouses.

After the Flood, the door opened to a renewed world, a fresh start. What were the first words out of God's mouth to the four married couples in this *new* creation? "And God blessed Noah and his sons, and said to them, 'Be fruitful and multiply, and fill the earth'" (Gn 9:1).

Just as with Adam and Eve, the first blessing/command shows how procreation is the primary end of marriage. The *Catechism* adds this note of explanation: "After the fall, marriage helps to overcome self-absorption, egoism, pursuit of one's own pleasure, and to open oneself to the other, to mutual aid and to self-giving."[6]

Old Testament passages refer to other blessings from the act of marriage in addition to procreation: unification (see Gn 2:24) and pleasure (see the Song of Solomon). These blessings are distinguishable but not separable. Pope John Paul II writes: "The two dimensions of conjugal union, the unitive and the procreative, cannot be artificially separated without damaging the deepest truth of the conjugal act itself."[7] Together these two dimensions form an unbreakable union in the act of marriage.

If God Were to Create a Society ...

If God were to create a society, what would it look like? We need only look at the ancient Israelites. When they were wandering in the desert, God gave them a number of laws to regulate their lives, some of which touched on openness to life. Though these laws were descriptions of how the Israelites were to live under Moses rather than a prescription for obedience today, these commands give us insight into keys for holy living.

For instance, a couple was not to participate in the act of marriage until one week after the woman's menses, to avoid being ritually unclean (see Lv 12:2, 5; 15:19, 25, 28). At what time of the woman's monthly cycle would they resume relations? At ovulation! Is it a mere coincidence that couples resumed relations when she was likely to be most fertile and he would have had a higher sperm count?

Another law stated that a man was not to go to war immediately after his wedding: "When a man is newly married, he shall not go out with the army or be charged with any business; he shall be free at home one year, to be happy with his wife whom he has taken" (Dt 24:5).

Why? Was this so the couple could get to know each other? Yes, in the biblical sense, for *to know* another person in Hebrew often meant to have intimate relations from which could come a new person (see Gn 4:1). Presumably, the new husband was to enjoy his first year of married life before military service so that he could raise up offspring in case he died at war. (This clearly does not reflect the current notion that it is better to get to know each other without children for a few years.)

God established his law and revealed it through covenants with his people, whereby they were blessed when obedient and cursed when disobedient. In Deuteronomy 28, Moses listed the national blessings of covenantal faithfulness: fruitfulness of the people as well as their lands and flocks. When he listed covenantal curses for the nation, he included miscarriages, stillbirths, and infertility of the people as well as of their flocks. These verses repeated earlier promises, admonitions, and warnings (see Gn 12:2-3; 17:2; 20:18; 30:22-23; 35:11; 49:25; Lv 26:3-9, 21-22). In response to his people's obedience or lack thereof, the Lord opened or closed the womb (see Gn 20:18; 29:31; 30:22; Job 1:21).

Real wealth was understood in terms of covenantal blessings: land and descendants. What a contrast with our culture! Today, people would say that someone who is *not* having children or is having few is the one who is blessed. Others might say a couple with many children is practically cursed. Yet we need to be able to say with the psalmist, "Your wife will be like a fruitful vine within your house; your children will be like olive shoots around your table. Lo, thus shall the man be blessed who fears the Lord" (Ps 128:3-4).

Please understand these passages in context: The people of God as a group turned away from righteousness and as a group they suffered the curses. Today, our land is polluted with innocent blood through abortion, and some who claim the name of Christ are turning away from him. Perhaps the increase in miscarriage and infertility rates can be correlated with our society's unfaithfulness to God, but covenantal blessings and covenantal curses are applied for corporate, not individual, sins. (For instance, my miscarriages were not God's curses on me for my sins.) However, we cannot ignore our corporate responsibility for the unrighteousness in our culture.

God's Marital Relationship With Israel

God's relationship to Israel was frequently described as a marital covenant. For example, the prophet Isaiah said, "As the bridegroom rejoices over the bride, so shall your God rejoice over you" (Is 62:5). In fact, young men in Israel were not allowed to read the description of God's love for Israel in Ezekiel 16 until they were a certain age because of its semi-erotic imagery of lovers.

Frequently in the Old Testament, the prophets called the Israelites back to faithfulness to God (see Jer 3:11-12). Even in the face of Israel's faithlessness, the prophets described God as having exclusive and faithful married love for her. God went so far as to command the prophet Hosea to buy a harlot and marry her, and when she left him, to redeem her from her prostitution and return her to his home (see Hosea chapters 1–3). Why? God used Hosea as a living example of how he viewed Israel's harlotry after false gods and his ongoing faithfulness and mercy toward Israel, his bride.

Another prophet, Malachi, chastised the people for faithlessness to their spouses. "And what does he desire? Godly offspring. So take heed to yourselves, and let none be faithless to the wife of his youth. 'For I hate divorce,' says the Lord the God of Israel" (Mal 2:15-16). In other words, God desires faithfulness between spouses so that their children will know and love him.

Today, God still desires fidelity in marriage. How can God's people intend childless marriages, if the primary purpose of marriage is godly offspring?

The Church Is the Bride of Christ

St. Paul sees the mystical union of the marital embrace as a reflection of the union between Christ and his Church, between God and his people: "'For this reason a man shall leave his father and mother and be joined to his wife, and the two shall become one flesh.' This mystery is a profound one, and I am saying that it refers to Christ and the church" (Eph 5:31-32).

From beginning to end, Jesus' ministry has a nuptial theme. Jesus' first miracle took place at a wedding where he changed water into wine (see Jn 2:1-11). And the climax of the new heaven and the new earth culminates in the "marriage supper of the Lamb," when the Lord will receive his bride, the Church (see Rv 19:7-9).

In the New Testament God elevates marriage to the level of a sacrament. The husband and wife are ministers of the sacrament of marriage. They become channels of sacramental grace to each other. Fr. Henry Sattler states it this way:

> The experience of unique, total, exclusive, permanent, unconditional, and creative love as both given and received is made paradigmatically and sacramentally present in Christian coitus, which has been raised from a natural to a supernatural sign of total, mutual, and exclusive surrender, to Christ and in the name of Christ.[8]

Christian matrimony is a total surrender of one person to another person, and of both to Christ.

Since Scott and I were validly baptized, though not Catholics, we still had a sacramental marriage recognized by the Church. We understood (as best as one can understand such an all-encompassing pledge) the vow we were taking. We freely consented to the gift of ourselves to each other. We believed we were not simply agreeing to contractual obligations and benefits; we were exchanging persons.

Once we had done that, we were free to express the unity we now possessed through the act of marriage. Any offspring we might have would be a constant reminder of our indissoluble union, for how could a child ever be divided into the two from which he came?

It is this faithful marital love that enables us, as Vatican II says, to "manifest to all men Christ's living presence in the world, and the genuine nature of the Church. This the family will do by the mutual love of the spouses, by their generous fruitfulness, their solidarity and faithfulness, and by the loving way in which all members of the family assist one another."[9] We have the opportunity to image for the world the loving, sacrificial, mutual self-donation between Christ and the Church.[10] This is a powerful testimony.

St. Paul reminds us about the covenantal nature of marriage: an exchange of persons, not an exchange of goods or services, replete with a prenuptial agreement.

> The husband should give to his wife her conjugal rights, and likewise the wife to her husband. For the wife does not rule over her own body, but the husband does; likewise the husband does not rule over his own body, but the wife does. Do not refuse one another except perhaps by agreement for a season, that you may devote yourselves to prayer; but then come together again, lest Satan tempt you through lack of self-control.
>
> 1 CORINTHIANS 7:3-5

When we wed, we literally give ourselves to each other. We are—and continue to be—one, a completely new entity.

Both husband and wife are called to give ourselves completely to our spouse in love. We recognize and submit ourselves to the rights, privileges, and responsibilities enjoined by matrimony. Through the marital act we renew the marriage covenant and become cocreators with God of new human beings who never would have existed otherwise.

How to Have a Successful Marriage

I overheard several college students respond to the question, "Do you have a vocation?" with the reply usually, "Oh, no. I want to get married."

I wasn't Catholic at the time, but I remember asking Scott, "Is that a Catholic answer? That doesn't sound like a Catholic answer."

"No," Scott assured me, "that's not a Catholic answer."

A vocation is a call to holiness in a specific state in life. Either we submit our sexuality to the Lord in chastity through singleness, consecrated life, or Holy Orders—or we submit our sexuality to him in chastity within marriage. There's no double standard. God is holy, and he wants his children to be holy, too.

Marriage is a sacrament, in part, because we need extra grace to live this vocation in a way that pleases God. Some people mistakenly think that cohabitation (living together as if they were husband and wife before they truly are husband and wife sacramentally) is a helpful test of a relationship. They set themselves up for failure in at least two ways.

First, since they are not married, the couple lacks the very sacramental grace of matrimony that they need to be successful. Second, since it is mortal sin to experience the act of marriage apart from marriage, they block the sacramental graces of Confession and Holy Communion to which they do have access.

Does a relationship failure after cohabitation prove that a marriage would not work? No, it only proves that nonsacramental cohabitation does not work.

No one gets married expecting to fail. We all want successful marriages and happy, healthy families. The psalmist gives us the key:

Unless the Lord builds the house, those who build it labor in vain. Unless the Lord watches over the city, the watchman stays awake in vain. It is in vain that you rise up early and go late to rest, eating the bread of anxious toil; for he gives to his beloved sleep.

PSALM 127:1-2

To *build one's house* is a poetic reference to establishing a family. The Lord himself is the One who builds each family so that it can withstand the storms of life. He is the rock on which we must build rather than on the shifting sands of public opinion and pop culture. Otherwise, our work to have a strong family will be in vain. The Designer of marriage has a blueprint and a way to build that will work. He has all of the resources needed to complete the *house*.

Immediately after these verses, the psalmist speaks of the blessing of children (see Ps 127:3-5). God's gift of children to us is critical to building our house solidly. Marriage and the act of marriage are his idea, after all.

God shares his divine life with us, enabling us to experience communion as spouses and then extending that communion to include children. The goal of each family is thus to be, as Pope John Paul II calls it, "a civilization of love."[11]

Since marriage is a sacrament, we receive power to grow in holiness even through the most mundane activities we do each day. Sometimes I am jealous of the nun blissfully kneeling in prayer before the Blessed Sacrament for an hour before supper, while for me, dinner is late, the children are whiny, the phone is ringing, and Scott is late from work. Yet God wants me to be holy just as much as he does that sweet nun. He has built into my vocation many opportunities to die to selfishness, to serve my spouse and children sacrificially.

The Vatican II fathers remind us that the Lord doesn't leave out married folk when it comes to holiness: "The constant fulfillment of the duties of this Christian vocation demands notable virtue. For this reason, strengthened by grace for holiness of life, the couple will painstakingly cultivate and pray for steadiness of love, largeheartedness and the spirit of sacrifice."[12]

Growth in virtue does not happen automatically. But by the grace of God, it can happen. Love leads to life, and life leads to sacrificial service.

Part of that sacrifice is a call to generosity. The Church calls us to give generously of our time, talents, treasure, and, yes, our bodies in order to build up the kingdom of God within our families, in the Church, and throughout the world—and in that order. When we are generous toward God, we discover a basic principle: We cannot outgive God. As St. Paul says, what you sow you shall surely reap (see 2 Cor 9:6-15). This generosity, in turn, strengthens our witness to our children about the trustworthiness of God to provide for our needs and to use us to provide for the needs of others.

Parenthood As Sacrificial Service

A priest once came into a second-grade CCD class to see what the children had learned. When he asked the children what Jesus said about marriage, there was an uncomfortable silence. Then a little girl in the front row raised her hand and ventured: "Jesus said, 'Father, forgive them. They know not what they do.'"

We smile at her innocence. Yet, in fact, most of us did not deeply comprehend what we were entering when we walked down the aisle and took our vows before God.

Every Catholic wedding includes a pledge of openness to life by both the husband and wife. St. Paul teaches, "Yet woman will be saved through bearing children, if she continues in faith and love and holiness, with modesty" (1 Tm 2:15). Given other scriptural texts, this passage applies only to married women, for openness to life is an integral part of a life of obedience to God for those women who are married.

If a married woman is open to life and God has not yet blessed her with a child, she is still sanctified through her obedience and the suffering of waiting. Note the conditional clause: It is not enough to produce children; salvation results from ongoing faith, love, and holiness, of which bearing children is only a part.

St. Paul urges young widows to remarry and to establish households: "So I would have younger widows marry, bear children, rule their households, and give the enemy no occasion to revile us" (1 Tm 5:14). Rather than being gossips who waste time giving Satan opportunities, women who are busy in the affairs of the married state strengthen the body of Christ.

In Titus 2:3-5, St. Paul instructs older women to teach the younger women how to love their children and husbands, so that the Word of God will not be discredited. These passages highlight the role of the service of motherhood, not only for the benefit of the family but also to limit opportunities for sin.

Motherhood is the fullest expression of a woman's femininity as she collaborates with God to create and sustain life. Pope John Paul II declares that of all titles that Mary has received, her most important is *Mother,* for "to serve means to reign."[13] By the mercy of God, Mary was faithful to her call to be the mother of the Savior of the world. Likewise, by the mercy of God, we can be faithful to God's call on our lives to bear and guide godly offspring.

The Sovereignty of God

Our culture is fixated on the idea that a *planned* baby is most valued. Yet many people who do not intend to conceive are thrilled with their unplanned child. They find that they had struggled with the *idea* of another child, not with the actual child. Though we want to have an attitude of heartfelt openness toward each child, we may have to wrestle with the Lord in prayer if his plan differs from ours.

A young teen once ran from her birthday dinner in tears when she realized that her parents had conceived her before they married, a fact they had never told her. Though they had not intended to conceive before marriage, they misjudged how many years they could date and remain pure. They were wrong, but they loved each other deeply, and they loved her. She was still a very wanted child, though the circumstances of her conception were difficult.

Whether or not your parents *planned* to conceive you—or you *planned* each of your children—God did. No one is an *accident.* Consider these words of St. Paul:

> Blessed be the God and Father of our Lord Jesus Christ, who has blessed us in Christ with every spiritual blessing in the heavenly places, even as he chose us in him before the foundation of the world, that we should be holy and blameless before him. He destined us in love to be his sons through Jesus Christ, according to the purpose of his will, to the praise of his glorious grace which he freely bestowed on us in the Beloved.... In him, according to the purpose of him who accomplishes all things according to the counsel of his will, we who first hoped in Christ have been destined and appointed to live for the praise of his glory.
>
> EPHESIANS 1:3-6, 11-12

Let's unpack some of these truths with regard to the openness to life.

Before the world was created, each one of us was a thought in the mind of God. He chose us in Christ to be his children. Just as he blessed Adam and Eve with a blessing that requires obedience to his commands, he blesses us to be holy. God lavishes grace on us so that we can live in a way that gives him honor and glory. *He* will act in and through us to fulfill his will because he accomplishes what he plans to do.

Is it possible to conceive a child God has *not* planned? For a young Pittsburgh couple, three miscarriages followed three normal pregnancies.

A friend of the wife offered the following explanation: "Sue, don't you get it? God does not intend you to have a fourth child. You need to stop trying."

Sue asked me whether it was possible for couples to conceive children that God takes in miscarriage because *he* didn't plan those children. I assured her it was not. Every conception is a unique act of God in cooperation with the parents. As the psalmist says, "Thy eyes beheld my unformed substance; in thy book were written, every one of them, the days that were formed for me, when as yet there was none of them" (Ps 139:16). God's plan includes all our children, no matter how few are their days of life.

These are profound mysteries, and it is beyond the scope of this book to do anything more than peer into them as they apply to this topic. Our heavenly Father has chosen us to be his children and to lead fruitful lives, faithful to his call. For those of us in the vocation of marriage, this means giving him our marital relationship and those children who result from it so that he is glorified in our family. For he is the eternal Father, "from whom every family in heaven and on earth is named" (Eph 3:15).

God our Father can be trusted to plan our families. We have a past that reveals the trustworthiness of God in countless ways. And we have a future.

Jeremiah the prophet records God's words to Israel after they returned to faithfulness to him: "For I know the plans I have for you, says the Lord, plans for welfare and not for evil, to give you a future and a hope. Then you will call upon me and come and pray to me, and I will hear you. You will seek me and find me; when you seek me with all your heart" (Jer 29:11-13). These promises apply to us as well.

If we seek him with all our hearts, he will provide the faith we need to entrust this area of our lives to him. One couple, Jim and Nancy from Omaha, Nebraska, experienced the fragility of their fertility and God's faithfulness to them in response to their faithfulness to him.

When Jim and I got married five years ago, we had *no* idea that I had polycystic ovary disease. We got pregnant with Michael on our honeymoon, and Kolbe was born two years later. We are so very grateful to God for the Catholic Church's teaching on this and in many other areas.

It was only when Kolbe was seventeen months old and we tried to get pregnant again that we found out through our Ob-Gyn that I have that disease. We are still praying and hoping that God blesses us with many more children. Thank God we didn't use any birth control, as we may have never been able to get pregnant at all later. It was the grace of prayer and being open to life, allowing God's will to be done in our lives, that enabled us to conceive the two precious children we have now.

Recently, this couple was blessed with a third child.

The Vatican II "Pastoral Constitution on the Church in the Modern World" (*Gaudium et Spes*) declares: "Thus, trusting in divine Providence and refining the spirit of sacrifice, married Christians glorify the Creator and strive toward fulfillment in Christ when with a generous human and Christian sense of responsibility they acquit themselves of the duty to procreate."[14] The Lord gives us hope that this vision is a part of his plan for our lives. And he pours out his love in and through us to whatever precious souls he places in our care.

For one couple, Molly and Jim, it was not just a matter of trusting the Lord when they were being greatly blessed with children. Molly also had to entrust those children to the Lord in a new way after Jim died in an accident.

We began our marriage open to life, and we were blessed with eight children in twelve years. Jim was killed when our oldest was in seventh grade and our youngest was fourteen months. Our children are living testimonies to our forever love. People ask, had I known that Jim would die, would I have had fewer? I say, I would have had more; for every child reflects a different part of Jim.

God alone knows what the future holds. What we know is that he has a plan for our lives and that we can trust him.

The Lordship of Jesus Christ

People tend to view law as negative: restrictions we do not want with consequences we fear. But that is not how the people of God in the Old Testament viewed law. Psalm 19, for example, describes the law as "sweeter ... than honey and drippings of the honeycomb" (v. 10).

This is why Israelite parents, before they spoke of the law, touched a child's tongue to honey. They wanted the child to associate goodness and desirability with knowing and obeying the law. Perhaps we need to alter our perception of law to imitate our Jewish brethren.

Each time we pray the Our Father, we pray, "Thy will be done, on earth as it is in heaven" (Mt 6:10). How is God's will obeyed in heaven? Perfectly. So our prayer is that we would obey him perfectly. We cannot pick and choose which commandments we will obey; rather, we seek to know his will and do it with our whole heart.

Jesus challenges his disciples that it is not enough to call him Lord and yet refuse to obey him: "Not every one who says to me, 'Lord, Lord,' shall enter the kingdom of heaven, but he who does the will of my Father who is in heaven" (Mt 7:21-27). This passage is an important reminder that everything we do must be yielded to the lordship of Jesus Christ. It is not enough to profess faith in him if we are unwilling to yield our lives to him.

In many areas of our life together Scott and I wrestled with what the lordship of Christ meant. In terms of money, we tithed off the top even when paychecks were small. In terms of time, we honored the Lord's Day by not studying (which we considered to be our work as students) but by resting and offering hospitality to fellow seminarians.

In terms of talents, we found ways of being involved in ministry, even in the midst of hectic graduate study schedules, because we wanted to serve Christ. And in terms of our bodies, we tried to make decisions about food and exercise that kept our bodies fit to serve God. However, we had never specifically considered how our fertility needed to be yielded to the lordship of Christ, too.

When it came to our fertility, our attitude was like that of most Americans: "God, you can have our time, talents, and treasure, but we will manage our fertility. We will have children when it suits our plan." I do not remember even praying about whether or not we should be open to children. We thought we were making a prudent decision involving stewardship principles by contracepting!

Then we were challenged at a new level by 1 Corinthians 6:18-20:

Shun immorality. Every other sin which a man commits is outside the body; but the immoral man sins against his own body. Do you not know that your body is a temple of the Holy Spirit within you, which you have from God? You are not your own; you were bought with a price. So glorify God in your body.

We knew we had to glorify God in our bodies, but did that include our fertility? *Yes*, even our fertility!

In comparison to eternity, how long would our lives be? Our lives are relatively fleeting. How many years of our lives will we be married? And of those years, how many opportunities will we have to conceive a child? And of those opportunities, how many times will we be blessed? And of those blessings, how many will we bring into this world? Our fertility is more fragile than we thought.

Scott and I wanted to yield our hearts fully to Christ. We knew we could trust God to plan our family his way; however, we needed more light shed before we could make the changes that would impact our lives forever. Children were a part of our overall plan, but should *every* act of marriage between us be open to life?

The sacrifices involved seemed enormous. Yet the examples of Mary ("Let it be to me according to your word," Lk 1:38) and Jesus ("Not as I will, but as thou wilt," Mt 26:39), as well as other holy men and women, demonstrated that a yielded will pleases God.

I once shared these ideas as a guest on a Protestant radio show. One caller identified herself as a Protestant very active in pro-life work. She told about a life-changing event.

One day when she was picketing a Planned Parenthood abortuary, she was gripped by a new idea: Her contraceptive use supported the very organization she opposed, since she was using the products Planned Parenthood supported. She realized that to be anti-abortion was not enough; she had to become pro-life. She decided right then and there that she would go home and throw out the contraceptives for good.

After a couple from Littleton, Colorado, had their first baby, they heard a challenging message of truth about openness to life. They did not respond to that message in the same way. Dana reveals their conflict.

The most difficult thing for me was not wanting to hear the message about openness to life. Initially my husband and I did not both agree with the Church's teaching. For me it was absurd, especially when it came from a celibate priest. Personally, I didn't believe him, that it was from God.

The second thing was that my husband accepted it completely and was very firm about it and would not give in. He took it very seriously and was not compromising. Our good Lord put such deep love in my heart for my husband that I had to accept that teaching against my own will. We were expecting our second child, but still we had to work toward unity on this issue.

Then I heard about NFP when I was desperately not wanting to be pregnant every year, because by then we'd had two more children (in the three years after receiving the message). The Lord had obviously a different plan for us because, after taking the first class of NFP, we were expecting another baby, which I am calling "my conversion baby." Now we are completely open to life. We've had another baby after that one was born. We just found out we are expecting our sixth child and are very happy about it.

Though it was not an easy transition to bring their lives into conformity with God's will, this couple honored the Lord as they worked toward unity, and now they have the joy of a large family. They have discovered what Kathy from Cuyahoga Falls, Ohio, observed: "It has been a bond in our marriage that has gotten us through difficult times. It has made us more trusting in God's providence, that God is ultimately in control."

Like many of these couples, Scott and I saw more and more the role contraceptives played in a culture of death, in direct opposition to the culture of life we needed—and wanted—to embrace.

II.
THE CULTURE OF LIFE
Versus
THE CULTURE OF DEATH

CHAPTER THREE

CHERISH THE CHILD

Consider these modern-day proverbs *not* found in the Bible:

"Blessed are the man and woman who have only two children, because they will be able to afford their college education."

"Blessed are the man and woman who have at least four years' spacing between their children, because they will never be stuck double-diapering."

"Blessed is the couple who doesn't have children for at least two or three years, because they will get to know each other."

"Blessed is the couple who has planned every pregnancy, perfectly spaced, for they know the mind of God."

These "proverbs" are the kind of worldly wisdom we hear all the time, though they are without foundation in the Word of God. They do not reflect godly wisdom. In fact, there are no Scripture passages that describe children in negative terms of any kind. According to God, *children are only and always a blessing.*

We are in the midst of a cultural war: the culture of life versus the culture of death. Pope John Paul II urges us to restore the true meaning of human sexuality so that we can build a culture of love and life. He notes the warnings in *Humanae Vitae* of the consequences of rejecting the true meaning of the act of marriage. His words echo Moses' challenge to God's people toward the end of his life:

> I call heaven and earth to witness against you this day, that I have set before you life and death, blessing and curse; therefore choose life, that you and your descendants may live, loving the Lord your God, obeying his voice, and cleaving to him; for that means life to you and length of days, that you may dwell in the land which the Lord swore to your fathers.
>
> DEUTERONOMY 30:19-20

The people of God still have a choice to make: Choose life!

The Value of the Child in Our Society

Today many couples approach the timing of openness to life the same way they would figure out the possibility of acquiring a valuable object such as a house or a car. They weigh pros and cons, as if they were filling out a debit-credit sheet. If there is a net gain, it is time to conceive; if not, they wait.

This approach is fundamentally flawed. The value of a child cannot be quantified. Children are not objects to be obtained; they are gifts to be received, souls placed in our care.

A word of warning: Some people may have been discouraged from ever having children, without really knowing it, through an exercise used in many high schools to discourage teen pregnancy. Some schools use an egg (some use a sack of flour) to represent a baby. Students are paired up and told that for a given amount of time they are to care for the baby (that is, the egg or sack of flour) as a *couple*. They must take time to feed and care for the *baby*, take turns watching the *baby*, and when they both go out, they must get a sitter for the *baby*.

What was the point of this lesson? It taught some of the drudgery of caring for a child so the students would want to avoid pregnancy. It showed the responsibilities without any of the rewards. There was no love or commitment between partners (who were obviously not spouses), no shared family joy, no extended family celebration, and no smiles or coos from the baby rewarding sacrificial care. This program taught students that they should avoid pregnancy as they should avoid infectious diseases, instead of teaching them to welcome new life as they would receive a gift of a million dollars.

The exercise encourages fears about the changes that having a baby necessitates without addressing the grace available through the sacrament of matrimony. Yet St. John tells us, "There is no fear in love, but perfect love casts out fear" (1 Jn 4:18). This is the kind of love God wants us to have in our marriages, a love that embraces rather than fears a child.

Some people have gone so far as to found groups and websites to provide clubs for *child-free* adults who reject what they call *child-centric* living. One such organization, No Kidding, encourages people to choose never to have children and expresses anger at initiatives by the government to help people care for their children. A feature story in the *Lincoln Journal-Star* quoted several of its members.

"'Childless' means lacking. We're 'free from,'" explains Katie Andrews, 31, a middle-school teacher who is married and has no children. "Free from a burden, a responsibility. We're free from the drain on our time and money and resources. We're not 'less' anything."

"Age is part of it. Second is our own freedom to do whatever we want, whenever we want. We're both professional people, and we're committed to our careers," says Lori Krans, 39, who lives in Corona del Mar, California. She and her fifty-two-year-old husband made the choice not to have children for a range of reasons.... Krans, who is Catholic, says she and her then-fiance discussed the issue of childlessness during premarital counseling classes at their church, and no one tried to change their minds about it.[1]

Such thinking is shortsighted at best and dangerous at worst, not only for individuals but also for our society. How tragic that no one in the Pre-Cana class attempted to challenge this couple with the truth.

In his *Letter to Families*, Pope John Paul II says:

A truly sovereign and spiritually vigorous nation is always made up of strong families who are aware of their vocation and mission in history .... To relegate it to a subordinate or secondary role, excluding it from its rightful position in society, would be to inflict grave harm on the authentic growth of society as a whole.[2]

When truth in the fullness of its goodness and beauty is not being pursued, but rather scientific and technological progress for its own sake, utilitarianism can result. Culture is reduced to

a civilization of "things" and not of "persons," a civilization in which persons are used in the same way as things are used. In the context of a civilization of use, woman can become an object of man, children a hindrance to parents, the family an institution obstructing the freedom of its members.[3]

This mentality that embraces sterility and promotes childlessness eventually weakens our whole society.

Aware of the conflict in the United States in regard to life, Pope John Paul II preached in the Washington Mall during his first visit to the United States:

> Human life is precious because it is the gift of a God whose love is infinite; and when God gives life, it is forever. Life is also precious because it is the expression and the fruit of love. This is why life should spring up within the setting of marriage, and why marriage and the parents' love for one another should be marked by generosity in self-giving. The great danger for family life, in the midst of any society whose idols are pleasure, comfort, and independence, lies in the fact that people close their hearts and become selfish.[4]

If we are not careful, our desire to provide well for our families can do more harm than good. We may inadvertently encourage selfishness rather than a spirit of generosity.

The Value of the Child in Scripture

Children are only and always a blessing. No Scripture or Church document declares a *down side* of openness to life. They contain no words of "wisdom" about the child as a burden or an expense or a barrier to the parents' careers or education. Yet many people today, including Christians, do not view children as the unmitigated blessings they are.

Children are not possessions, the next thing to acquire after a car, a house, and a dog. They are not a bonus earned but a gift freely given. Children are not the next item on the agenda once a couple is well established and can afford children. They are not the next venture, once a couple has managed the discipline and care of a dog and feel ready for more of a challenge.

Children are not something a couple deserves just because they are, in fact, better than others having children these days. They are not something to which people are entitled if they are good people or wealthy people.

Children do not have value because we give it to them. They have value for their own sake because they are created by God in his image. Children are pure gift.

Children are gifts *on loan* from God, requiring our stewardship over their hearts, minds, and souls. They are fundamentally *his*, not ours. This perspective may help us to keep a loose enough grip on them so that whenever God wants to bring them home to be with him we can relinquish our *right* to keep them and entrust them to God (though nothing will ever make that easy).

How should we receive a gift? With *joy:* "We accepted openness to life together," says Caroline from Allendale, Illinois, "and we would welcome other children, if it is God's will. We have four glorious kids so far!" Suzanne reiterates: "New life is more precious than material goods or earthly success."

With *gratitude:* "How liberating Church teaching (truth!) is," exults a mother from Phoenix, Arizona, "and how deeply God loves human beings, souls, children! Children are *blessings*, and fruitfulness is a *gift* of God!"

With *humility:* "I feel very honored in being used by God to help create souls for his kingdom," reflects a mother from San Antonio, Texas.

With *great love:* "We had a one-month-old to celebrate our first anniversary with!" revels a mom from Altoona, Pennsylvania.

Shouldn't we seek the blessings of God rather than resist or refuse them?

The child is still a gift, even though there might be very difficult circumstances. One mother relates the difficulty of "becoming pregnant before marriage and then having that child born with a birth defect. We learned to overcome shame with intense cherishing."

Some couples delay openness to life because of fears: How will the child change my schedule, my lifestyle, my budget, my body? If a couple does not differentiate between the burdens that can accompany a child and the child as a burden, their fears may unnecessarily delay or even prevent them from the risk of love's beautiful fruit, a child. The concerns they address may lead them to hesitate in accepting the gift of new life (more about this in chapter 9).

On one of her early trips to the United States, Mother Teresa of Calcutta picked up a little child and was overheard saying, "Why are they so afraid of you?" Or to put it in the words of the comic strip *Cathy*, "My generation has to decide whether to have a child or to be one."

Our culture seems to have lost its understanding of the worth of a child. Just go to parks in large cities and see how many more dogs are being walked than children pushed in strollers. Something is wrong with this picture.

What is the worth of a child? The psalmist captures God's view of children as cherished gifts.

Lo, sons are a heritage from the Lord, the fruit of the womb a reward. Like arrows in the hands of a warrior are the sons of one's youth. Happy is the man who has his quiver full of them! He shall not be put to shame when he speaks with his enemies in the gate.

PSALM 127:3-5

We are in a spiritual battle, and our children are our arrows: How many arrows do you want in your quiver when *you* go into battle? When a man we knew with eleven children was asked if his quiver were full, he responded with a smile, "I always heard a quiver held a dozen."

The image of a child as an arrow illustrates the importance of not simply having children but also training them in the faith. For an archer to make a useful arrow that can hit the target, he sharpens the end and carefully sets the feathers. Likewise, children need to be sharpened with discipline and trained in the faith; then they will go forth into the world accomplishing the work God has for them to do.

The psalmist reminds the people of God to count their blessings: "Your wife will be like a fruitful vine within your house; your children will be like olive shoots around your table. Lo, thus shall the man be blessed who fears the Lord" (Ps 128:3-4). That's not exactly how our culture views children!

Can you imagine a TV cameraman coming to the Martins' home, all twelve of them seated around the table? The reporter says, "Look at this poor man. How does he feed them? They'll never afford to go to college." Yet the psalmist says *this* man is rich! His bumper sticker should read, "I'm rich *because* I have all these kids!"

A large family shows great blessing from the Lord. At the same time, since each child is of infinite worth, even one child in a family is a great blessing. A small family is not a family of limited importance. Abraham and Sarah had just one child, Isaac; and Isaac and Rebekah had just one pair of twins, Esau and Jacob. Yet both of these families were critical in the development of salvation history. And certainly no one doubts the significance of the Holy Family, though there was only one Child in their home.

The Value of the Child for Us

"Children are really the supreme gift of marriage," proclaims Vatican II, "and contribute very substantially to the welfare of their parents."[5] *They* contribute to *our* welfare!

We know *we* contribute to the welfare of our child, right? When we brought the baby home from the hospital, we didn't say, "Your room is the second door on the left, food's in the fridge, holler if you need help." Instead, we gave and we gave—morning, noon, and night. Compared to the rearing of other baby creatures, the child-rearing process is a slow one; human babies are dependent on parents for a long time.

Our contribution to their well-being is obvious. But what an insight to realize how substantially our child contributes to *our* well being. Children give us opportunities to become holy, living a sacrificial life for God and for them.

When we married, we realized we were more selfish than we had previously thought. But as time passed, we learned how to live together; partially we grew less selfish, and partially we learned how to live in harmony while continuing to be selfish. For instance, we did not ask each other to get up in the middle of the night for a snack or forgo sleep so that the other could be served breakfast.

Then we had a baby, and we learned all over again how much selfishness we still had. We discovered many new things. Food does not have to be hot to be enjoyed. The middle of the night can be a precious time to pray, even if we thought we needed to be in bed at that hour. We can be grateful for six hours of sleep, even if it comes in three-hour installments. And we can sing to our baby instead of in the choir this year.

A mother from Bryan, Texas, offered this insight:

Each of my children has taught me more and more about myself and what is really important now. Life-giving love means the new life my children have given to me—they have enabled me to grow in ways that would never have been possible had John and I not simply said, "Thy will be done," and left it in God's hands.

We learn so much by parenting. Anne affirmed this reality: "I matured by taking care of my children. With the birth of the first and each child, my being was flooded with insight—I knew God's mission for me."

Each child is a unique blend of both parents and the gifts God has given him or her. What a joy it is to see each child develop, both individually and as a part of the whole family, the gifts and talents the Lord has given him or her. When I was working on this book, I played a CD that my daughter recorded of her own music. Not only was my heart lifted in worship and thanks, but I realized that this specific music, *her* music, would never have existed apart from her. And *she* would never have existed apart from God's generosity to us and our love for each other.

There are many opportunities to die to ourselves, all for the love of Jesus and this precious little one. And as we bend over to pick up our cross, our Lord teaches us, again, that dying—being a living sacrifice—is what we live for. We *want* to serve him with our time, our talents, our money, and our bodies, *all* of which occurs when we serve him by parenting his little ones.

A child is not an intruder to the blissful married couple's relationship. On the contrary, he or she is the very expression of their delight in and love for each other. "A child does not come from outside as something added on to the mutual love of the spouses," notes the *Catechism*, "but springs from the very heart of that mutual giving, as its fruit and fulfillment."[6]

One of the beautiful things about having a little one is that you fall in love all over again. You gaze into those tiny eyes for the first time and meet face to face the one you have held under your heart for so long. Then you glance at your spouse and see resemblances, and you fall more in love with both of them. When I saw my fifth child, Joseph, for the first time, I said what my heart had felt with every delivery: "You are the one I have loved all these months!"

All our children reflect some aspect of both Scott and me. With the advent of each child, we fell ever more deeply in love.

When we bring children into the world, the sense within the family of love and respect deepens in several ways. First, the husband who participates in the process of labor and delivery has a respect and appreciation for his wife's heroism. He has watched her lay down her life for their child—*his* child—and it is overwhelming. A new relation exists that had never before been possible: He has made her a mother; she has made him a father.

Second, both parents experience a new appreciation for what their parents did in bearing them. So many things can now be understood in the light of this birth. They sense anew the deep love their parents had for them from their earliest beginning. And they appreciate the wisdom they will gain through future conversations and interactions with their parents.

Finally, the gratitude of the grandparents is almost unspeakable. They knew (as the young couple did not) what it would take to bring this child into the world. Their child now has a child. With gratitude to God and admiration for their child and their child's spouse, they receive this little one into their hearts in the unique relationship of grandparent to grandchild. The intercommunion of the entire family bond is strengthened. They realize anew what Pope John Paul II affirms: "The family is in fact a community of generations."[7]

As the months go by we cherish this child, fruit of our love, and both of us discover how much love we receive from our young one. Instead of consuming our love and leaving us dry with nothing left over for our spouse, we find our love for each other deeper than ever. And there seems to be only one thing for all of us to do with our growing love: share it with another child! Then siblings become part of the civilization of love in our family.

When we were expecting our second child, I said to my father, "I know it will work out, but I don't understand how. I love Michael with all my heart; how will I love this child with all my heart, too?"

Dad replied, "Honey, you're thinking about love as if it's something you have to divide. Love isn't divided among those we care about; love multiplies. All of you will love this child, and this child will bring love to you all."

Sometimes people who experience the blessing of children close their hearts to more, but that can change. The last verse in the Old Testament is a prophecy about God's desire in the New Covenant: "And he will turn the hearts of fathers to their children and the hearts of children to their fathers" (Mal 4:6)

One father, a physician from South Dakota, experienced this change of heart recently. "Thank you for helping me to be open to the gift of life again. My last two children are my change of heart. They didn't change my heart. I changed my heart, and they are the gifts that I received."

Children complicate life in all the right ways. Once we adjust to one child, we become more independent as spouses. Then a new child reminds us of the healthy interdependence we must have in marriage. We have to rethink the family priorities. We have to serve each other more. And everyone benefits.

When it comes to openness to life, we have to resist the temptation to think "Been there, done that" with regards to children. It's always new. We have never had this child; we have never been this age; we have never experienced the interaction of our spouse or our other children with this child. And all the other children are older than with the last delivery, so more help is on hand than ever before.

Yes, we face difficulties with pregnancy and delivery and recovery. We wrestle with the personal challenges of varicose veins, nausea, recovery from delivery, and weight gain. We shoulder the physical challenges of extra laundry and cleanup. We struggle with the energy challenges of maintaining the family's schedule of activities while functioning with sleep deprivation. However burdensome all of these challenges may be, they pale in comparison with the privilege of bearing a child. Never forget: *The child is not a burden!*

Many people who have made major contributions to our lives—theologians, artists, musicians, doctors, inventors, others—were the later children of larger families. By limiting our family's size, we are not inviting people into this world who could be significant contributors in all kinds of ways.

Can we trust God to work through us to produce children who will make a difference in our world? According to one account (which may be apocryphal), when Mother Teresa of Calcutta was asked why God hadn't sent someone to cure AIDS yet, she replied, "I asked God and he said, 'I did, but he was aborted.'"

When I offered this thought at a conference, a woman angrily approached me. "You're bringing the same mentality as society: A child is worth having if he or she contributes to society."

I never intended such a utilitarian attitude, but I appreciated her correction and offer it here: Every child is only and always a blessing, regardless of what contribution he or she can make to society. And the contribution each child makes to our growth in Christ is inestimable, no matter how long (or short) the life, regardless of health or mental abilities. We see this reality in countless saints who led rather obscure lives and died quite young.

Author Beth Matthews relates the story of her son Patrick.

About nine years ago, God sent my family on a strange but fantastic journey. In 1991 our third child, Patrick, was diagnosed with autism. And so our odyssey began. Regardless of the medication, diet, treatment, or teachers, Patrick has improved little....

As I drove on down the highway with Patrick beside me, once again I prayed the prayer of St. Ignatius of Loyola and asked for the grace to cherish every moment with Patrick just the way he is. The tears rolled down my face. I thought, *He may never play ball, or say mommy, but he will always be a special child of God.*

And then it came to me. God had blessed me with an escalator to heaven, just what I had prayed for over ten years before. God knew my weakness. He knew I needed much more than a stairway, so he gave me the hand of my beautiful son and asked me to ride. Sometimes it stops, sometimes it goes in reverse, but it always points toward heaven.[8]

Patrick's condition has provided the whole Matthews family with many opportunities to grow in faith, hope, and love. They now have ten children, with hopes for more.

The Value of a Child to Siblings

Many of the virtues we want to teach our children are taught most naturally in the context of family life, with siblings. For instance, we may try to teach Timmy to share his toys, but he does not understand how difficult it is (or how necessary) until his brother Tommy tries to take his toys away.

That one experience provides many lessons: the meaning of sharing and stewardship (Jesus gives to Timmy so Timmy can share with others); the wrong of stealing (Tommy can't just take Timmy's toys); and the need to be forgiving and kind (Timmy can forgive Tommy and then choose to share). The teachable moments multiply with each sibling.

We want our children to embrace sacrificial love, to serve younger children through thoughtfulness and kindness, to share their time and attention as well as their possessions, to see needs around them and offer to meet them without being asked—and so much more. What better place to learn these things than in the context of family life? The more life we have in our families, the more opportunities we give our children for this kind of personal and spiritual growth.

With all the concerns about teenage pregnancy, many crisis pregnancy counselors have noticed something rather puzzling: Sometimes mothers and their daughters do not seem very upset at the news. Perhaps other needs are being met, though obviously in the wrong way. The mother is getting a baby to care for without a pregnancy or delivery; the daughter is getting a baby to enjoy without having to be fully responsible for the baby.

One of these counselors, a forty-five-year-old mother in Lincoln, Nebraska, expecting her ninth child, had observed this scenario numerous times. She posed one of the most profound pro-life questions I have ever heard: *Is it possible that teens are having babies because their parents won't?*

Think about it. Perhaps teens are really longing for siblings. If their parents were having babies, the teens would enjoy the little ones while they witnessed firsthand the challenges involved in having a baby. They would understand babies in the context of a marriage and they would want to remain pure sexually until they were in that kind of a committed relationship. The baby would be a witness of the ongoing generous love of the teen's mother and father, something that every child, no matter how old, longs to see.

On the day of David's delivery, our three oldest children came to the hospital to see the baby and me. After holding David, my big fifteen-year-old, Gabriel, came to my side and gently took my hand. Quietly he whispered, "How can I ever find the words to thank you, Mom?" We both choked up; his gratitude was overwhelming. Children are pure gift, the big ones as well as the tiny ones, to us and to each other.

In the movie *Yours, Mine, and Ours,* two scenarios occur simultaneously: A teenage daughter is pressured by her boyfriend to have sex to prove her love, while her mother is in labor to deliver the first child of their blended family, the nineteenth child of the family. As the stepfather races through the house to get his laboring wife to the car, the teenage daughter asks him what she should do.

The stepfather replies, "It isn't going to bed with a man that proves you're in love with him. It's getting up with him in the morning and facing the drab, miserable, wonderful, everyday world with him that counts." This brief conversation puts the daughter's dilemma in perspective. She turns to the boyfriend as the laboring mom gets in the car and says, "Grow up!" Precisely.

When You Have to Wait for the Gift

Some couples are suffering because, even though they have been open to the gift of a child, asking God for this blessing, they have not yet conceived. They do not know if they ever will. And their suffering may be intensified by people who imply that they are choosing to be childless, practicing contraception, or even rejecting children altogether.

They often are faced with the dilemma: Should they reveal the pain of their struggles with fertility? Or should they remain silent even as they know they are being judged falsely?

Sometimes people wonder whether it is selfish to ask God for a baby. It is not. When a couple is in the right kind of relationship—a sacramental marriage—it is a right desire to share life with a child.

Consider Psalm 37:4-5: "Take delight in the Lord, and he will give you the desires of your heart. Commit your way to the Lord; trust in him, and he will act."

Our focus must always be on the Lord, rather than our desires; as we delight in the Lord, he gives us our desires by conforming our will to his. By committing our way to him, we are praying, "Here is my desire, but I desire your will most; Jesus, I trust in you."

Consider for a moment the Old Testament account of the reward God gave Hannah, the prophet Samuel's mother (see 1 Sm 1). She not only had a natural desire for a child—mocked as she was by her husband's very fruitful second wife—but she also had a supernatural desire to further the kingdom of God. She knew that Israel was suffering under poor leadership, and she was willing to give up her child, should the Lord bless her, for the sake of Israel.

God took her at her word. After many years of prayers, with tears, she heard the Lord speak through the priest Eli that she would have a son. When that son, Samuel, was three years old, she weaned him and then-brought him to live with Eli for the rest of his life. (It's hard to fathom the sacrifice involved here!)

Listen to the account of Eli's blessing, following the couple's annual visit with Samuel.

> Then Eli would bless Elkanah and his wife, and say, "The Lord give you children by this woman for the loan which she lent to the Lord"; so then they would return to their home. And the Lord visited Hannah, and she conceived and bore three sons and two daughters. And the boy Samuel grew in the presence of the Lord.
>
> 1 SAMUEL 2:20-21

Her reward was five more children! Do we think of children in the same way—as rewards?

More will be said on this matter in a later chapter, but for now please know this: Our part is to be open to life; God's part is to open the womb. It is *not* as simple as the claim that those who are good get children, and those who aren't, don't (see Gn 20:18; 29:31; 30:22).

Our heart's openness is a precious gift to God. So perhaps one reason, among others, that a child is delayed is to provide us an opportunity to offer reparation for all those who treat the gift of a child as if he or she is so much garbage. Or perhaps God is preparing our hearts and home to receive through adoption a child whose parents cannot or will not raise him or her. Whatever the case may be, we should persist in prayer and know that God hears and is answering, though perhaps not in a way or within the time frame that we request. (For more thoughts on infertility, please see chapter 11.)

CHAPTER FOUR

CONTRACEPTION = REJECT THE CHILD

Today our society has rejected the call to create a culture of life where men, women, and children who have been created by God are respected for their own sake, rather than viewed as means to an end. As Christians, we have an ethic that acknowledges the inherent value in every human being's life for no other reason than that each person is made in the image and likeness of God. Yet our culture has exchanged this ethic for a so-called "quality of life" ethic that bases a person's right to life on a subjective value judgment of that person's worth to society.

We need to recognize the roots of the cultural war between life and death that rages all around us. It is not too late for us to restore a culture of life.

The Bible and Contraception

Contraception is the deliberate act of thwarting the life-giving nature of the act of marriage. People tend to assume that since most forms of contraception have been developed only recently, the Bible must be silent on this issue. Yet the rejection of fruitfulness is not new. Though methods such as *coitus interruptus* may not be very successful, they were employed in Bible times.

The Catholic Church has interpreted Genesis 38:8-10 as the judgment of God on a deliberate act of contraception. Look at the passage in context:

Then Judah said to Onan, "Go in to your brother's wife, and perform the duty of a brother-in-law to her, and raise up offspring for your brother." But Onan knew that the offspring would not be his; so when he went in to his brother's wife he spilled the semen on the ground, lest he should give offspring to his brother. And what he did was displeasing in the sight of the Lord, and he slew him also.

In other words, the only instance of contraceptive use recorded in Scripture shows that the person received the death penalty for it. Though some people try to attach the penalty to the man's failure to obey the ancient Israelite law known as the Leverite law, neither the textual evidence nor Church tradition support that claim. A note of explanation is needed.

The Leverite law of Israel is incomprehensible to most modern Americans. When a man died without any son, his closest male kin was expected to marry the widowed sister-in-law, and her first son would count as the dead brother's child.

> If brothers dwell together, and one of them dies and has no son, the wife of the dead shall not be married outside the family to a stranger; her husband's brother shall go in to her, and take her as his wife, and perform the duty of a husband's brother to her. And the first son whom she bears shall succeed to the name of his brother who is dead, that his name may not be blotted out of Israel.
>
> And if the man does not wish to take his brother's wife, then his brother's wife shall go up to the gate to the elders, and say, "My husband's brother refuses to perpetuate his brother's name in Israel; he will not perform the duty of a husband's brother to me." Then the elders of his city shall call him, and speak to him: and if he persists, saying, "I do not wish to take her," then his brother's wife shall go up to him in the presence of the elders, and pull his sandal off his foot, and spit in his face; and she shall answer and say, "So shall it be done to the man who does not build up his brother's house." And the name of his house shall be called in Israel, The house of him that had his sandal pulled off.
>
> DEUTERONOMY 25:5-10

The penalty for refusing to perform the Leverite was no greater than public humiliation. For this reason, the Catholic Church has always understood the death penalty given to Onan as applying to the act of contraception. In fact, when Catholics went to Confession for contraceptive use earlier in this century, they would confess the sin of "onanism."[1]

In his book *The Bible and Birth Control,* Charles Provan presents a compelling case for the unifying thread of all sexual offenses deemed worthy of the death penalty in the Old Testament—they are intended to be sterile acts. These include the following:

1. male homosexual intercourse (Lv 20:13).
2. male bestiality (Lv 20:15).
3. female bestiality (Lv 20:16).
4. intercourse with a menstrual woman (Lv 20:18).
5. withdrawal, "wasting seed" (Gn 38:8-10).[2]

Certainly temporary sterility is the goal of all forms of contraception.

In the New Testament we find three references condemning *pharmakeia,* a Greek word from which we get "pharmaceuticals" or drugs. *Pharmakeia* in general was the mix of various potions for secret purposes,[3] including potions to prevent or stop a pregnancy. The typical translation of this term as "sorcery" is inadequate. When *pharmakeia* is condemned in Galatians 5:19-26 and Revelations 9:21 and 21:8, the context is sexual immorality or sexual immorality and murder.[4] It is therefore reasonable to apply these passages to the condemnation of drugs used for contraception and abortion.

What Does Natural Law Reveal About Contraception?

God our Father has taught us what he wants us to do through the Church, especially through Sacred Scripture. He has even stamped into our very being principles of natural law that reveal his design for marital love. The Church's teaching on natural law is a rich part of Catholic Tradition that we understand and appreciate in the light of the Church's role as guardian of truth. Natural law helps us to see that the truth about openness to life is truth for the whole world, not just for Catholics.

Many people misunderstand "natural law" to refer to the laws of nature or physics, such as gravity or magnetism. Or they may think it addresses natural processes: Should you shave a beard or let it grow, should you wear deodorant, and so on.

Actually, natural law is something different altogether. It is the law that explains the primary purposes for the existence of things. Since all people are governed by the natural law, the Church speaks the truth for the good of all mankind when it teaches about natural law.[5]

Let's apply, for example, the concept of natural law to food. Why do people eat? There are many valid reasons for eating: We enjoy food, we celebrate with food, we enjoy fellowship more when we eat, we grow through eating (perhaps a happier thought for children than for adults).

Nevertheless, we can celebrate without food. We can enjoy fellowship without food. We can grow even during times of fasting. So why do we eat as opposed to some other activity? The primary purpose, or end, of eating is *nourishment.* Even when we eat food we do not enjoy, we still receive nutrition.

There can be good reasons why we might forgo the good of food by abstaining from eating; this would not mean we were acting contrary to the natural law for food. However, we would all recognize as a disorder the practices of eating and then vomiting (bulimia) or practically starving (anorexia nervosa). We would also agree that the use of vomitoria (tall jars in the corners of a dining room where the ancient Romans would intentionally vomit so that they could eat more during sumptuous feasts) was unnatural and wrong. To enjoy the pleasure of food while thwarting the consequences of gluttonous actions goes against natural law.

Likewise, there are many reasons a married couple renews their love with the marital act: a feeling of closeness, intimate communication, pleasure, and an experience of union. But there is a primary purpose for the act of marriage that cannot otherwise be fulfilled apart from the act of marriage: the creation of another human being.

This is why *Humanae Vitae* reminds us that "the Church, calling men back to the observance of the norms of the natural law, as interpreted by its constant doctrine, teaches that each and every marriage act must remain open to the transmission of life."[6] If we feast on the love of each other and seek to vomit the contents of our love, we are thwarting the natural law, and our act is disordered.

Even Sigmund Freud, whose psychological theories have shaped so much of modern thought about human nature, echoes in his discussion of sexual perversions the principles of natural law with regard to the act of marriage:

Moreover, it is a characteristic common to all the perversions that in them reproduction as an aim is put aside. This is actually the criterion by which we judge whether a sexual activity is perverse—if it departs from reproduction in its aims and pursues the attainment of gratification independently.[7]

Today, sexual gratification apart from reproduction is considered the norm in many marriages.

We can distinguish the meanings of the act of marriage, but we cannot separate them. Though a prostitute may ply her trade only for money or pleasure, she is still united to the man. St. Paul says, "Do you not know that he who joins himself to a prostitute becomes one body with her? For, as it is written, 'The two shall become one flesh'" (1 Cor 6:16).

Though a couple may engage in intercourse for union and pleasure, they may still conceive, no matter what their birth control measure. Though a woman may be inseminated so that she can have a baby apart from a man, yet that child still has a father—she has not created the child alone. *Humanae Vitae* testifies to the "inseparable connection between the unitive significance and the procreative significance which are both inherent to the marriage act."[8]

By using contraception, we mock what we claim we intend to honor. With our lips we say, "I am totally yours and you are totally mine, until death parts us." Yet with our bodies we say, "I refuse that part of you and I will not give that part of me that could create new life through our love." John Paul II writes:

> When couples, by means of recourse to contraception, separate these two meanings that God the Creator has inscribed in the being of man and woman and in the dynamism of their sexual communion, they act as "arbiters" of the divine plan and they "manipulate" and degrade human sexuality—and with it themselves and their married partner— by altering its value of "total" self-giving. Thus the innate language that expresses the total reciprocal self-giving of husband and wife is overlaid, through contraception, by an objectively contradictory language, namely, that of not giving oneself totally to the other. This leads not only to a positive refusal to be open to life, but also to a falsification

of the inner truth of conjugal love, which is called upon to give itself in personal totality.[9]

Actions speak louder than words, and with contracepting sex, our actions make a lie of our words. "Contraception, directly opposed to the transmission of life, betrays and falsifies the self-sacrificing love proper to marriage, 'altering its value of total self-giving'[10] and contradicting God's design of love, in which it has been granted to married couples to participate."[11]

Contraception degrades human sexuality because it reduces a couple to two individuals seeking pleasure. It represents a rejection of the man's life-giving seed and the woman's life-nurturing womb, choosing to be neuter rather than being the male and female they were created to be. This rejection runs counter to natural law.

Pope John Paul II reminds us, "The person can never be considered a means to an end; above all never a means of 'pleasure.' The person is and must be nothing other than the end of every act. Only then does the action correspond to the true dignity of the person."[12]

So much misinformation is given about contraception that people have not been allowed an opportunity to see the truth, beauty, and goodness of the Church's teaching on openness to life. Dr. William White is one physician who takes time to explain this to his patients, many of whom are not Catholic.

I follow the Church's teachings in my practice, not only because it is God's law, but because I think that anything else would be bad medicine. I try to explain these things to my patients not as a theologian, but as a physician. It is (perhaps) surprising how many seem to respond eagerly to this message, even those who are not Catholic or have no religious predisposition. Even seemingly arcane "theological" concepts like the meaning of the marital act as total personal self-giving and the consequent falsity of contraception are intuitively clear to people who have never been exposed to these ideas before. My job is made easier, I think, because I have nature on my side. "The truth is written in the heart."

Dr. White's patients thus have an opportunity to respond to truth they may never have heard before.

Steve Habisohn, founder and director of the GIFT Foundation, has wisely observed that "contraception is only validated outside of marriage because it is validated inside of marriage."[13] Increasingly, marital and premarital contraceptive intercourse has demonstrated the same degrading characteristics that characterize another sterile choice: homosexuality. These characteristics include promiscuity, lust, unfaithfulness, fruitlessness, disease, sensuality, pornography, and even death.

For those who thought that the Pill would be the great panacea to improve marriages, the facts reveal a very different story. Michael McManus, in his article "Pope Paul VI: Right On Contraception," reports that "since the Pill began to be sold in 1960, divorces tripled, out-of-wedlock births jumped from 224,000 to 1.2 million, abortions doubled, and cohabitation soared tenfold from 430,000 to 4.2 million."[14] Today there is more teen promiscuity, more adultery, more sexually transmitted disease, and more infertility than ever before in our culture. And the consequences of out-of-wedlock unions include, in the words of Pope John Paul II, "orphans of living parents."[15]

The fruits of the culture of death demonstrate that those who break God's law are broken by it. The Church's teaching is clear:

> The Church has always taught the intrinsic evil of contraception, that is, of every marital act intentionally rendered unfruitful. This teaching is to be held as definitive and irreformable. Contraception is gravely opposed to marital chastity; it is contrary to the good of the transmission of life (the procreative aspect of matrimony), and to the reciprocal self-giving of the spouses (the unitive aspect of matrimony); it harms true love and denies the sovereign role of God in the transmission of human life.[16]

Such strong language leaves no room for doubt about the moral status of contraception.

This is the truth of God: he fashioned us, called us into the vocation of marriage, and gave us the power to imitate him as life-giving lovers. Through the Church, he admonishes us not to sin against him and his design for holiness in our lives by deliberately thwarting the life-giving meaning of the marital act, for, as Vatican II insists:

> True practice of conjugal love, and the whole meaning of the family life which results from it, have this aim: that the couple be ready with stout hearts to cooperate with the love of the Creator and the Savior, who through them will enlarge and enrich his own family day by day.[17]

We are called to cooperate with God and our spouse so that, through us, he may bring more life-giving lovers into the world to love and serve him.

The Catholic Church has stood alone in declaring these truths to the world. I appreciate the Church's unswerving stand for the sanctity of marriage. Unfortunately, some Catholics have the misimpression that perhaps the Church has not been clear in her opposition to contraception. They think it is up to them to figure out what is true for them, or what their consciences can live with, in order to know what their practices ought to be. But dissent is not a possibility in this issue; there is no such thing as a "cafeteria Catholic," someone who selects what part of Church teaching agrees with his or her own inclinations and dismisses whatever seems disagreeable.

Contraception and Human Dignity

God, who created us, has established our worth as an immeasurable gift. "Every man and every woman," writes Pope John Paul II, "fully realizes himself or herself through the sincere gift of self. For spouses, the moment of conjugal union constitutes a very particular expression of this."[18] Marital love images the self-donation of the Family of divine Persons as we give ourselves to each other. But contraception contravenes human dignity and limits human freedom by presuming that a husband and wife cannot or will not be able to control themselves or make responsible decisions.

Respect for the person entails respect for the power of the act of marriage: the potential to create new human persons. Though people may not want to communicate disrespect toward their spouse, the imposition of contraception does just that. One mother I know was offended when her husband wanted to resume contraceptive use after they had experienced several years of openness to life. Now that she was sensitive to the indignity of it, she felt, in part, rejected.

When Scott and I threw out contraception and experienced the act of marriage, we felt greater respect for each other and for the power of our sexuality than ever before. I never felt so deeply loved and accepted by him nor so loving and accepting of him. We became keenly aware of the power of each act in a whole new way—a new life could result from *that* act of marriage. Even though we initially switched to Natural Family Planning, every act was physically and emotionally open to new life.

The Abortion-Contraception Connection

Fertility is presented in Scripture as a gift to be valued as precious rather than as a disease to be avoided at all costs. Through our fertility, we experience the life-giving power of love. Christopher West, a student of Pope John Paul II's theology of the body, asks pointedly: "If you pervert the sex instinct, which is meant to be the life instinct, what do you have? A death instinct!"[19]

Though some people claim that contraceptive use is a protection against the temptation of abortion, the fact is that the temptation to abortion is strengthened by contraception. "But despite their differences of nature and moral gravity," Pope John Paul II observes, "contraception and abortion are often closely connected, as fruits of the same tree."[20]

Two women, one from Dallas and the other from Los Angeles, share what happened when their contraception "failed":

From Dallas: When I was twenty, I got involved with a "good" Catholic and became pregnant. When I told the father that I would not have an abortion, he turned completely against me and said I was ruining our lives. (He is now a pro athlete with millions upon millions of dollars.) Knowing my parents would give the same advice, I finally agreed to have an abortion.

Immediately afterward I felt a huge sense of loss and knew I had committed murder. Ironically, it was my anger at this "good" Catholic for not following his Church teachings that eventually led me to seek the Catholic Church. I knew a priest would not tell me what I did was responsible. I sought peace and reconciliation in the Catholic Church and in the process found an eternal home.

From Los Angeles: I had an abortion at age fifteen. It was devastating to me only as I grew older and converted to Christianity and then Catholicism. I was crushed that I was not raised with any concept open to life, even though my father was a cradle Catholic. (He died when I was seventeen.) I didn't tell my husband until we had been married for eleven years.

All this to say that as I became a Christian, as I grew in trusting God, and as I converted to Catholicism, I more and more grieved my past decision and the way I was raised. It is something I struggle with daily. I trust in God's mercy and love, and my family and friends have been wonderful to me. God has infinite mercy and love, and I feel it most of the time, but it never makes the truth of what I did go away.

I will always live with the knowledge that I killed my firstborn child. The Church's teaching had never been taught to me, and when it was, I fully accepted it. It has totally changed how I think about human beings and their value.

Both women have now found healing in the Church. Another woman who had an abortion at eighteen wrote, "The guilt brought me to God and the Church."

Abortion also takes its toll on the fathers who pay for their girlfriends' abortions. One man's testimony includes the fact that he paid for his then-fiancée's abortion. As is often the case, the abortion contributed to their breakup.

Now that he is married, both he and his wife bear the pain attached to his earlier decision. They write: "The reality of abortion has helped us to see that the Church's teaching on human life is more than just a religious conviction. It is a matter of life and death indeed—a supernatural life and a supernatural death."

Abortion can be heartrending even to people not directly involved. A young mother from Round Rock, Texas, wrote: "My friend's sister aborted her baby the same day I first heard my daughter's heartbeat. It broke my heart to know as I rejoiced in the sound of my baby's heart, another mother was silencing her baby's heart."

Many Christians do not realize the extent to which they have been influenced by the current culture of death. My parents' experience provides just one example.

On January 22, 1973, through a decision in the case of *Roe v. Wade*, the U.S. Supreme Court legalized abortion for all nine months in all fifty states. Nine months later, my father announced from the pulpit of his Presbyterian church that he and my mother were expecting a baby. Everyone, we thought, was thrilled; our youngest sibling was already eight.

Outside the church doors, however, my mom ran into a good friend, who said, "Patty, you know you don't have to go through with this." She intuited that at forty-one years of age, my mother probably had not planned this event.

My mother was stunned. She had struggled with being pregnant at this stage of her life, but she had never considered having an abortion. Though my mother is a quiet, gentle soul, she spoke her mind forcefully.

"If I wasn't a Christian woman," she said, "I'd slap you to the ground. Do you know what you just asked me? You asked me to consider killing my baby!" And with that, my mom walked away—and their friendship was never the same.

How could such a conversation happen, especially between two Christian women? It happened, first, because our society lost its moorings. It did not understand that to reject the culture of life is to embrace the culture of death.

Second, it happened because Christians who do not understand why the Church has always opposed contraception and abortion as an attack on human dignity, marriage, and society will reflect worldly wisdom rather than godly wisdom, since the reasons have to be believed in order to be lived. Increasingly, Christian society is becoming indistinguishable from our non-Christian society's culture of death. That direction will not change until Christians decide to restore the culture of life.

Some contraceptives are abortive. All IUDs and some forms of the Pill that are progestin-only do not suppress ovulation; they work by rendering the uterus incapable of sustaining life that has been conceived. One mother wrote, "I learned that an IUD is an abortifacient. I wonder now how many babies I may have aborted while I used it. It grieves me to think that even one was. Yet, I don't know!"

When it was first used, the Pill always suppressed ovulation as well as altered the lining of the uterus so that new life would not thrive. However, there were many serious side effects, including "myocardial infarction, stroke, thrombophlebitis, and pulmonary embolus and death."[21] Physicians discovered that these risks were lower if the dosage of the hormone in the Pill was lowered. Once the pharmaceutical companies altered the levels of hormones, creating low-dose Pills, there was a new consequence: abortions began to occur.

Is ovulation always suppressed? No. Ovulation occurs in two to ten percent of cycles of women taking the Pill. If sixty million women worldwide are on the low-dose Pill, there would be 1.2 to six million ovulations per cycle. This is known as breakthrough ovulation, and it is even more frequent with the progestin-only Pill.[22]

Many women did not know about the abortive action of these contraceptives. One mother wrote: "When I read about its effect, I wept and had to take time to heal over what may have happened. I thank God for his mercy and forgiveness."

Many women also did not read the fine print of possible side effects. I was one of those who did not want to bother reading something so complicated. I just asked my gynecologist whether the Pill was safe, and he assured me it was. Yet there are side effects:

Headaches, migraines, mental depression (even to the point of suicide and/or suicidal tendencies), a decrease or loss of sexual drive, abdominal cramps, bloating, weight gain or loss, and water retention; nausea and vomiting (in about ten percent of users); symptoms of PMS, vaginitis and vaginal infections; changes in vision (temporary or permanent blindness, and an intolerance to contact lenses); gall bladder disease and either temporary or permanent infertility, even after discontinuing the Pill, in users with previous menstrual irregularities or who began the drug before full maturity. Several of the symptoms, such as migraine headaches, contraindicate the use of the Pill because of life endangering complications.[23]

A newlywed from Joliet, Illinois, learned about such side effects first-hand. She reports: "The Pill made me very sick, and finally after about six months it became obvious to me that my health was in danger."

Other Dangers of Contraception

Dr. Chris Kahlenborn has recently published *Breast Cancer: Its Link to Abortion and the Birth Control Pill*, in which he states and documents (with over five hundred references) that there is a definite link between some forms of cancer and both abortion and the Pill.[24] He cites studies that document increases in breast cancer, cervical cancer, liver tumors, invasive cervical cancer, and skin cancer. The results are more devastating if the women were young when they began taking the Pill, and if they took the Pill for a long time.

In terms of human dignity, what self-respecting husband can take a serious look at the possible side effects of the Pill and then ask his wife to begin (or continue) to take it? This is not an expression of love but of expediency. This is not a wise course of action but a foolish one. Until recently, many men may have claimed ignorance as to the side effects, and women may not have understood the risks. However, they can no longer afford to ignore the evidence.

Any time a spouse takes medication, both spouses should be aware of risks and side effects. St. Paul says that men are to love their wives as they love their own bodies (see Eph 5:28). Are they doing that when they permit their wives (or even require them for the sake of convenience) to take such risks to avoid the blessing of a child?

Aren't pills prescribed when someone is sick? Fertility is not a disease! If fertility is not a disease, why are we prescribing medicine? In cancer treatment, the side effects of chemotherapy can be devastating, but it can be worth the risk. There are many side effects to the Pill—are they worth it?

We know that children should not take steroids because the hormones could interfere with healthy growth, but should teens be on the hormones contained within contraceptives? Would a good father or mother expose a daughter to the health risks involved, rather than teach her chastity?

Perhaps the teen has pressured her parents to allow her to use contraception. Yet it is the parents' responsibility to get the facts. Perhaps the teen is getting contraception through her school or a local clinic without her parents even knowing the danger in which she is placing herself.

Lust in Marriage: The Effect of Pornography

In a General Audience in 1980, Pope John Paul II quoted Matthew 5:27-28: "Jesus' words are, 'You have heard that it was said, 'You shall not commit adultery.' But I say to you that everyone who looks at a woman lustfully has already committed adultery in his heart." Then he made a shocking application to marriage: "Man commits adultery 'in the heart' also with regard to his own wife, if he treats her only as an object to satisfy instinct."[25] Neither husband nor wife is to use the other as an object to satisfy sexual desire.

Human dignity is attacked when a spouse commits the sin of lust against his wife. A wife from West Covina, California, reveals her pain:

> My husband has usually "had sex" with me—unfulfilling to me, even though he was seemingly satisfied. He did "make love" with me and to me *once*—and that was after he had made a decision to rid our home of all pornographic material, and he did throw it all away. He confessed and pledged this to me; I felt his complete commitment to me. But he still battles his "addiction" to pornography.
>
> I yearn for a time when we can allow God to enter into our bedroom, and we can both express our love for each other in a manner fulfilling to both of us and pleasing to our God. My memory of the one time I felt he made love to me has left me in tears many times after a truly "sexual" (physical) encounter. I pray for an end to pornography and a rebirth of respect for wives (women). NFP is helping us.

We must denounce such degrading material and call people to repentance if they have been involved in pornography.

After speaking on this topic in Long Beach, California, I was stopped by a woman. She confessed, "My husband orders X-rated films for us so that we can learn how to have good sex. Since we are married, isn't that OK?"

I replied, "No, it cannot be helpful to your relationship. Becoming aroused through viewing others and then relieving yourselves through the act of marriage is both an act of quasi-adultery and a degradation of your spouse by using each other rather than giving yourselves to each other. You should destroy the tapes. Don't just throw them away, because that's how many teens acquire pornographic material. And refuse ever to participate in these acts again."

This woman thanked me for being so honest and confirmed my caution. She *had* felt the infidelity and degradation of which I had spoken. In contrast, purity of desire, intention, and respect are necessary for us to give ourselves sincerely and to receive the gift of the other person.

Christopher West addresses this very point:

As much as lust blinds man and woman to their own truth and distorts their sexual desires, so much does this new life in the Holy Spirit empower man and woman to love one another as they were called to in the beginning. Through the sacraments we can know and experience the transforming power of Christ's love. This is good news. This is great news.[26]

Has the Catholic Church Spoken Authoritatively About Contraception?

When Scott and I first examined the issue of openness to life, we did not recognize the Catholic Church as an authority in our lives. As Protestants, we did not care about papal encyclicals or conciliar statements, though we *were* impressed that the Catholic Church was willing to take such an unpopular stand. Whether or not the Church spoke definitively about contraception did not matter to us then. Now, however, we understand what a critical question this is, for if the Church has indeed spoken with authority on this issue, then dissent on this issue equals opposition to the truth.

In response to open challenges about the Church's consistent teaching on openness to life, the encyclical of Pope Pius XI entitled *Casti Connubii* (1930) declared that "any use whatsoever of matrimony exercised in such a way that the act is deliberately frustrated in its natural power to generate life is an offense against the law of God and of nature, and those who indulge in such are branded with the guilt of grave sin."[27]

This is a clear condemnation. "Any use whatsoever" leaves no room for possible exceptions. Since it is "an offense against the law of God and nature," it applies to all people, not just Catholics. There is no place here for an appeal to conscience. And "grave sin" is none other than serious or mortal sin. It is objectively evil.

Pope John Paul II has consistently upheld the Church's firm stance on openness to life: "The Church's teaching on contraception does not belong to the category of matter open to free discussion among theologians. Teaching the contrary amounts to leading the moral consciences of spouses into error."[28] In 1979 he addressed a French Natural Family Planning group, saying, "There must be no deception regarding the doctrine of the Church such as it has been clearly set forth by the Magisterium, the Council, and my predecessors: I am thinking especially of Paul VI's encyclical *Humanae Vitae*."[29]

Humanae Vitae warned about some of the societal consequences of rejecting the truth it presented: a general lowering of morality, increase of sexual abuse of women, government coercion of people to use contraceptives, and people treating their bodies like machines. There is ample evidence to support the conclusion that, thirty-odd years later, all these consequences are occurring. This is the fruit of a world that has rejected the culture of life and embraced the culture of death.

Through the consistent teaching of the Church for two millennia, the Lord calls all people to welcome life and to do what they can to further the culture of life. Satan, on the other hand, cannot produce life; he is sterile. He can only pervert what already exists.

Genesis 3 makes it clear that there will always be enmity between the godly seed and Satan and his seed. The Evil One can only present a counterfeit, tempting people to reject what is true, beautiful, and good in their elusive search for what will satisfy their deepest longings. And it seems that one of his most useful tools is an appeal to conscience.

What About Conscience?

The Church has clearly taught against contraception. Is the subject still on the table for discussion? No.

Yet people are not living this truth. Why not? They often appeal to their consciences. Since contraception does not seem wrong to them (they may or may not know the reasons why the Church teaches what she does), they say they will let their consciences be their guide. They have a sense that they can pick and choose what they will believe, as if they are making selections from a smorgasbord.

What is our conscience? It is the inner sanctuary of our soul from which we choose good and resist evil in our thoughts, words, and deeds, based on our understanding of right and wrong.[30] It is our moral muscle; we must develop and use it, or else it atrophies. We must follow our consciences, but we must also *form* our consciences according to truth.

The law of God is written on every human heart; the conscience bears witness to it (see Rom 2:15). Obedience to that law is necessary not only to avoid God's anger against sin but also for the sake of conscience (see Rom 13:5). In addition, we have an acquired sense of right and wrong formed by our family, teachers, and friends. But we have to go further; we have to train our consciences by reading, studying, and praying the truth so that our sense of right and wrong is firmly grounded in objective truth.

Though some Catholics may claim that they can use contraception in good conscience, many non-Catholics know Catholics cannot do that. Why not? Is it possible that some Catholics claim ignorance when they know they are acting on an improperly formed conscience? Pope John Paul II concludes that married couples "cannot, however, look on the law as merely an ideal to be achieved in the future: They must consider it as a command of Christ the Lord to overcome difficulties with constancy."[31]

A responsible student who does not want to go into debt to pay for college cannot justify stealing the money to pay tuition. The ends do not justify the means. In the same way, we cannot say that contraceptive use will be temporary in order that openness to life can happen eventually.

We have to ask ourselves, Is the action moral? If not, we cannot do it no matter how we feel about it; if so, we have the option of deciding whether or not to do it. We want to be able to say with St. Paul, "So I always take pains to have a clear conscience toward God and toward men" (Acts 24:16).

We must value a clear conscience by living our convictions. If we ignore our consciences, we will eventually sear them so much that they will cease to be the moral compass we need. St. Paul warns, "By rejecting conscience, certain persons have made shipwreck of their faith" (1 Tm 1:19). The consequences of such a rejection are very great. "To the pure all things are pure, but to the corrupt and unbelieving nothing is pure; their very minds and consciences are corrupted. They profess to know God, but they deny him by their deeds; they are detestable, disobedient, unfit for any good deed" (Ti 1:15-16).

Contraception Is Contra-Life, Contra-Woman, and Contra-Love[32]

Contraception Is Contra-Life

That is what the word means: *contra* means "against"; *ceptus* refers to "conception," or the beginning of life. God made humankind, male and female, in his image. Satan cannot create as God does, so he seeks to mar or even destroy God's image. God is the life-giving Lover, the Spirit of life. Satan is the life-hating destroyer, the spirit of antilife.

The largest promoter of contraception in the United States is Planned Parenthood, sometimes referred to by its critics as "Banned Parenthood" or "Planned Barrenhood." At one time it was on record as an organization promoting contraception *so that* abortions would not occur. Many people thought the temptation to abortion would be minimized by allowing contraception, especially among teens. However, contraception introduced the idea of antilife so that, in fact, it has led to an abortion mentality. Now Planned Parenthood is the single largest abortion provider in our country, funded in large measure by us, the taxpayers.

Pope John Paul II expressed his concern to all of the families in the world:

So-called "safe sex," which is touted by the "civilization of technology," is actually, in view of the overall requirements of the person, radically *not safe*, indeed it is extremely dangerous. It endangers both the person and the family. And what is this danger? It is the *loss of the truth about one's own self and about the family,* together with the risk of a loss of *freedom* and consequently of a loss of love itself.[33]

Contraception Is Not a Solution

Catholic author Mark Shea provides further insights into the destructive nature of contraception:

Its purpose is to introduce an escape clause into the prospect of full commitment. It is autonomy (from the other), power (over our child-free future) and a demand that our right to pleasure remain unencumbered by any "extraneous" business about love and fruitfulness. Its purpose is to separate man and woman, parents and children, God's will and our will. Its goal is to strip-mine the gold of pleasure from the sacramental union of love and fruitfulness, enthrone autonomy and pleasure, and declare love and fruitfulness "optional" rather than that which revelation declares it to be: the very heart of reality.[34]

For all these reasons, we need to catch a vision for life-giving love. How can a child be thought of as a *failure* of contraception? Pregnancy is about something going right, not something going wrong!

Contraception Is Contra-Woman

Every woman is a sacred vessel of life. Whether she is empty or full, like a Communion cup, she is specially set apart by God to bear life. But contraception represents a fundamental rejection of her life-nurturing womb.

In stark contrast to the feminist movement, which touts women's reproductive rights, it is the Church that has addressed the dignity of a woman through her gift of self. When men and women understand the life-threatening and fertility-ending risks of contraception and abortion, they cannot, in good conscience, subject a woman's body to either and call it an expression of love.

One mother wrote, "I wish someone had told me that contraception is morally wrong; that it brings death into a marriage; that it robs the spouses of life and truth—truth about who they are as creatures of God called to make a 'sincere gift of self.'"

Another mother from Pennsylvania told about her journey:

I have learned something I would not have learned another way. I was married to a Muslim, and we used withdrawal our *entire* marriage. I allowed it because it wasn't artificial or abortifacient. (I didn't think it was as effective as it was.) We divorced after three years because he wouldn't have Catholic children.

Sex meant nothing to me. If sex within marriage is not open to life, you can get it anywhere. It was greatly devalued to me. After I divorced, I began sleeping with other men. I hated that it meant nothing to me, and desperately wondered how I could see it as sacred again.

I read many books on love, marriage, and the act of marriage. (The best was *Love and Responsibility* by Karol Wojtyla—Pope John Paul II!) I was married in the Church to a Catholic this past April. My husband is very open to life and however many children God gives us. (Yes, he does have a little fear of supporting them.) As a matter of fact, I became pregnant on our honeymoon! I have found sex with my husband to be guilt-free and more pleasurable than I've ever experienced.

I am not proud of my actions after my divorce at all. I just wish desperately to share my experience if it will help even one person. The biggest difference between sex inside and outside marriage is the openness to life. I think much trust and intimacy revolve around that "vulnerability."

This kind of vulnerability is what the Church refers to as "a sincere gift of self."

Contraception Is Contra-Love

God fashioned us in love. He calls us into the vocation of marriage and gives us the power to imitate him as life-giving lovers. He blesses the generous love of husband and wife with the gift of a child, the embodiment of marital love.

This beautiful vision of marriage was part of what drew Tina and Ken to the Catholic Church.

Our whole attitude toward the meaning of marriage has changed. We now feel and know that God wants all marriages to be a work of grace.

The privilege of being the means God uses to bring an eternal human soul into his kingdom is extremely wonderful, awe-inspiring, and holy. Marriage has taken on a whole new dimension and meaning. We are eternally grateful.

A good example often leads others to truth. A physician from Franklin Park, Illinois, made the following observations relating the wonderful examples both he and his wife had witnessed in their homes before they wed.

My wife and I were both raised in large Catholic families. Our parents never used contraception, and for some reason, we were spared the common experience of significant rebellion against their values. Perhaps the reason was that they held them by conviction. My parents (a founding mother and "father" of La Leche League) were also strong supporters of breastfeeding, with the natural spacing that results, and I guess in our family the joys of a large family (almost) always outweighed the burdens.

Contraception seemed to me not tempting, forbidden fruit, but ridiculous and disgusting. To this day I have never been able to understand how people categorize contraception as a sin of weakness or passion. It seems one of the most coolly calculated acts I can imagine, requiring restraint, patience, and discipline—the very antithesis of passion.

Nancy from Haslett, Michigan, echoes these sentiments.

I think being free of a contraceptive mentality has enabled us to have a pure, natural, and unspoiled acceptance of our sexuality. I never realized how beautiful the Church's teaching on sexuality was until I internalized the appreciation of myself as a cocreator with the Lord. The great dignity and nobility of renewing the marriage covenant in love is something I wish to stress with my children.

What a joy it is to pass these wonderful truths on to our children!
In sum, contraception is against nature, Scripture, Tradition, virtue, and

common sense. We have to be more than antiabortion; *we have to be pro-life.* As St. Paul advised St. Timothy: "For everything created by God is good, and nothing is to be rejected if it is received with thanksgiving; for then it is consecrated by the word of God and prayer" (1 Tm 4:4-5).

CHAPTER FIVE

HOLY COMMUNION AND INTIMATE UNION

Jesus describes himself as the Bridegroom who invites the Church, his bride, to receive him in intimate union through Holy Communion (see Rv 19:6-9). In imitation of Jesus, a groom invites his beloved bride to receive him in intimate union through marriage. These two sacraments of Holy Communion and intimate union, the Eucharist and holy matrimony, enrich our understanding of each one through the other.

Holy Communion Through the Gift of Self

Jesus is the Bridegroom who lays down his life for his bride, the Church (see Eph 5:25). He gives himself for her: "And for their sake I consecrate myself, that they also may be consecrated in truth" (Jn 17:19). He gives himself to her.

Everything he does, he does for her. In return, the Church as his bride freely gives everything she is and everything she does back to him. This exchange of persons is the New Covenant.

In the Mass, Jesus invites his people to respond to his self-offering: "Behold, I stand at the door and knock; if any one hears my voice and opens the door, I will come in to him and eat with him, and he with me" (Rv 3:20). In other words, Jesus desires intimate communion with us. He not only wants to come into our hearts; he also wants to come onto our tongues and into our bodies. That's how completely he wants to give himself.

A similar gift of self takes place in holy matrimony. We give our very selves as gifts to our spouses, and our spouses receive us as gifts. In the process we become channels of sacramental grace to each other.

In imitation of Jesus, we consecrate ourselves to God for our spouses.

Our act of life-giving love in the context of marriage restores us to naked-ness without shame. We can be vulnerable with each other. As that vulner-ability is reciprocated, our communion deepens over time. This is why we can tell our children (as my parents repeatedly tell us) that intimacy gets better and better as we grow in marital love, because we know each other more intimately, give ourselves more fully, and receive our spouse more completely than ever before.

Intimate Union of Two Persons

In the Eucharist, Jesus offers himself to his bride, the Church, under the appearances of bread and wine. The Church is physically united to Jesus as we receive the gift of himself, his own flesh and blood. We have become one body with Christ in a nuptial union as he enters us, the bride, with his divine life.

Likewise, husband and wife are united in a one-flesh union as the wife receives her husband's life-giving seed. Consider Jesus' commentary on Genesis 2:24:

He answered, "Have you not read that he who made them from the beginning made them male and female, and said, 'For this reason a man shall leave his father and his mother and be joined to his wife, and the two shall become one flesh'? So they are no longer two but one flesh. What therefore God has joined together, let not man put asunder."

MATTHEW 19:4-6

In the context of the one-flesh union of husband and wife, St. Paul says, "This mystery is a profound one, and I am saying that it refers to Christ and the church" (Eph 5:32). This marital union becomes a picture to the world of the union of Christ and his bride, the Church. Our sacramental mar-riage is a testimony to the relationship between Christ and the Church. And our physical act of oneness reflects our growing union of heart and mind in Christ.

Did you ever wonder why weddings take place in the context of the

Mass? (As a convert, I did.) Of course, it's a tradition. But why is it a tradition? The *Catechism* explains:

> It is therefore fitting that the spouses should seal their consent to give themselves to each other through the offering of their own lives by uniting it to the offering of Christ for his Church made present in the Eucharistic sacrifice, and by receiving the Eucharist so that, communicating in the same Body and the same Blood of Christ, they may form but "one body" in Christ.[1]

The Mass is the *most* appropriate context for a wedding because the Eucharist is Christ's nuptial gift to the Church.

A husband and wife's nuptial gift—the act of marriage—becomes a more meaningful expression of our love as our love matures. We know each other better with each passing year. We don't "have sex"; we give ourselves to each other. And the more life we share—experiences, challenges, joys, and sufferings—the more we know each other and love each other. We live out the biblical notion that to *know* someone is to enter into the act of marriage.

Our aging bodies are precious reminders of the faithfulness of God through the years and our fidelity to each other. We can be naked and not ashamed. And the love handles, stretch marks, and delivery scars only further endear us to each other. As Scott says, "Kimberly, your body says you have loved me enough to bear my children."

Scott makes the following comparison: Sex isn't "good" in the way that Campbell's soup is "m-m-m good." Sex isn't great in the way that Frosted Flakes are "grrrrrreat!" Sex is *holy*. Just as a chalice is not something you grab to pour a soft drink, so every woman's body is a sacred vessel, set apart for special use.

A wife and mother, Anne, pondered this teaching and then shared her reflection:

> The Holy Spirit led me to see that married love, open to life, had as its model Christ dying on the cross, willing to give his life and his love to souls. I came to understand in my teens that life and love could never be separated, just as Christ's love for souls could never be separated

from his life he willed to give to souls. A priest once passed on [the thought that] a woman's uterus [is] like a chalice, a sacred vessel for holding life and life-giving blood. Just as a chalice is consecrated before its high use, a woman is "raised high" in the sacrament of matrimony to a divine and human mission with a sense of dignity in a coarse world.

Our contemplation of these beautiful insights will increase our sense of wonder and awe at God's design for both the Eucharist and marriage.

Creation of a New Family Bond

The Father sent the Son so that we could become his children.

But when the time had fully come, God sent forth his Son, born of woman, born under the law, to redeem those who were under the law, so that we might receive adoption as sons. And because you are sons, God has sent the Spirit of his Son into our hearts, crying, "Abba! Father!" So through God you are no longer a slave but a son, and if a son then an heir.

GALATIANS 4:4-7

In short, St. Paul told the Roman Christians, we have been given "the spirit of sonship" (Rom 8:15).

Jesus taught his disciples to pray the family prayer, beginning, "Our Father who art in heaven" (Mt 6:9). His Father is now our Father, the Father of the bride. His mother, Mary, is now our mother, for we are her offspring since we are "those who keep the commandments of God and bear testimony to Jesus" (Rv 12:17).

We are now brothers and sisters. We use the language of family to explain our new relationships in Christ. We refer to priests as our fathers, nuns as our sisters, and monks and friars as our brothers.

We gather at Mass as the family of God around our Father's table. The sacrifice of the Mass is our covenant meal. Peace within the family is so important that if, at Mass, we remember that a brother or sister has something against us, we are to leave our gift at the altar and immediately seek reconciliation (see Mt 5:23-24).

I have always felt close to Jesus' Father because my father has been such a beautiful reflection of him to me. But I never thought about my mother's reflecting Jesus' mother until I became a Catholic. Now I see how blessed I am to have a mother who reflects the gentleness, quiet spirit, and meekness of Mary. At first it was awkward to call Mary "Mother"; but the more I do, based on the reality of my pledge to Christ, my brother, the more I see her motherhood embracing me as her daughter.

Protestants are welcome at Mass and can come forward for a blessing, but they are excluded from receiving the Eucharist. Why? They have to wait until their relationship is restored in the Church. Though they might not have left the Church, they still reject the authority God has given to the Church; until they acknowledge and submit to these authorities as their fathers, they remain brethren separated from the family table.

It's similar to the situation of a couple who want to be included in a family reunion years after their parents have disowned the extended family. It's not the fault of the couple themselves that they are estranged. But family restoration has to precede family celebration.

Another helpful analogy is engagement. Though a couple is truly committed to each other, enough to be engaged, they have yet to submit themselves to each other through taking vows. Until they wed, they cannot consummate the wedding.

Likewise, there are people outside the Catholic Church who are genuinely committed to the Lord. However, until they pledge themselves to the Lord's bride, the Church, they cannot consume the Lord in Holy Communion. Reception of the spouse in the act of marriage or reception of the Lord in the Eucharist is so intimate a communion that it must be protected under oath.

The parallels between the Eucharist and marriage should be clear in this regard. Before marriage, we already have a family relationship; we are brother and sister in the Lord. However, that relationship is elevated to a new level in the sacrament of marriage.

On August 18, 1979, the Scott Hahn family was established. We had decided beforehand to call each other's parents "Mom" and "Dad," since a wedding means that we are truly a part of each other's families for good.

(We understood and were committed to the indissolubility of marriage before we wed.)

Three weeks later, when we were visiting Scott's parents, I had an awkward situation. I had showered before I checked to see whether there was a towel for me. Scott was gone. So I cracked the door and called out, "Mom?"

No answer. I tried it again a little louder. After several tries, Mom Hahn came to the bottom of the stairs and asked, "Are you calling me?"

She hadn't recognized my voice as one of her children when she heard someone calling, "Mom." But she came right up and handed me a towel.

Today, we could never imagine calling each other's parents anything other than "Mom and Dad." It took practice. But now the supernatural bond of family relationships through the sacrament of matrimony feels natural.

Cohabitation does not create a family bond; marriage does. As my mother says, "You shouldn't do married things until you are married." Why? We *need* the sacrament of marriage to *live* married life. We have to wait to receive each other in the act of marriage until we are in a marriage.

One summer Scott was doing inner-city ministry in Pittsburgh. He was trying to teach young teens that they needed to wait to have sex until marriage. One boy raised his hand and disputed, "Don't you mean it's wrong to have babies outside of marriage?"

Scott rejoined, "Of course it's wrong to have babies outside of marriage. But you're also not supposed to do what makes babies outside of marriage."

"But," debated the fourteen-year-old, "sex is fun. It's like playing basketball." The crowd laughed, and Scott realized how much work he had ahead of him for the summer.

Sex is not a necessity, no matter what the ad agencies might want you to think. You can die without food; you can die without water; you can die without sleep. You can even die without love. But no one has ever died without sex!

John Kippley tells a story about a priest who hesitated to share the Church's teaching against premarital intercourse. A husband asked whether it would have been OK for the priest to have celebrated Mass the night before he was ordained. The priest quickly said, "No."

The young man responded, "It's the same with marriage. You couldn't celebrate Mass until you received your sacrament; we couldn't celebrate marriage without our sacrament. Of course, we all desired to perform those special acts proper for a priest or a married couple, but we had to wait until the proper time."[2]

Waiting to consummate the relationship until after the vows demonstrates true love and respect for the other person. And doing things in *right order,* as my mother says, strengthens both of the families from which the couple comes, adding to the spiritual capital that we in turn will offer our children.

The Total Gift of Self Means Sacrifice

Love leads to life; life leads to sacrifice.

Jesus does in the flesh what he has always done in his divinity: He loves with complete self-donation. Of course, the difficulty with loving with complete self-donation as a human being is that it requires the ultimate sacrifice of life in death. When Jesus took on human flesh in the Incarnation, his self-offering involved his life, death, and resurrection as the supreme gift of his love for us. It is this self-offering that he took into the Holy of Holies in heaven when he ascended to the Father (see Heb 9:11-14). And it is this same gift—Jesus' Body, Blood, Soul, and Divinity—that we receive in the Eucharist.

My understanding of Christ's self-donation on the cross is different from the understanding I had as a Protestant. As I grew up, Holy Week each year was a time of reflection on Christ's agony on the cross. I pictured God the Father hurling all his wrath for sin onto Jesus as he hung upon the cross. I thought Jesus' cry of abandonment was the consequence of experiencing God's wrath on him and God's rejection of him.

Jesus *did* take our sin on himself as the ultimate Lamb of God, sin that incurred the wrath of God. But I realize now that when Jesus hung on the cross, in total self-donating love for us and in loving obedience to the Father, never did the Father love him more. Jesus did in his humanity what he had always done in his divinity. And the Father was pleased; God saw that it was very good.

Jesus as the second Adam did what the first Adam refused to do: He yielded his will to the Father's will in the garden, knowing it would mean suffering and death. He laid down his life for his bride, the Church. Now he enjoins us to imitate him in laying down our lives for one another.

When we attend Mass as a married couple, we see our sacrifices in the light of the depths of Christ's sacrificial love—in the words of consecration as well as in the crucifix behind the altar. At Mass, we consecrate ourselves to God and to each other anew. We leave with the grace of the sacrament of the Eucharist to live the sacrament of matrimony faithfully.

The *Catechism* describes it this way:

> Christ dwells with them, gives them the strength to take up their crosses and so follow him, to rise again after they have fallen, to forgive one another, to bear one another's burdens, to "be subject to one another out of reverence for Christ," and to love one another with supernatural, tender, and fruitful love.[3]

Our married lives are a testimony to faithfulness and fruitfulness when we follow Christ's example and when Christ indwells us.

Marriage involves a similar kind of sacrifice. In preparation for the wedding, of course, there is much joy. Engagement is that wonderful in-between time. All of the "ifs" have become "whens," and you feel peace. At the same time you don't face the responsibilities of housework or paying bills yet.

Then comes the wedding, and after that, the realities of married life. That is why my mother wisely cautioned each of us to prepare more for our marriages than for our weddings. The wedding was over in a day; we needed to be prepared for a lifetime of sacrificial service to our beloved.

Marriage is not, as some have claimed, the "easy" vocation. No vocation is easy. Consider the challenge of our vows: in plenty and in want; in joy and in sorrow; in sickness and in health; as long as we both shall live. We need the grace of the sacrament to be able to make good on promises of this magnitude. We also need grace to deal with all the little things that bother us more than we realize they will: hair left in the sink, the toilet seat left up, the toothpaste left open, the trash cans left unemptied.

As much as our culture chafes at the suggestion that wives should be submissive to their husbands, it ignores completely what is by far the more difficult command given to husbands:

Husbands, love your wives, as Christ loved the church and gave himself up for her, that he might sanctify her, having cleansed her by the washing of water with the word, that he might present the church to himself in splendor, without spot or wrinkle or any such thing, that she might be holy and without blemish. Even so husbands should love their wives as their own bodies. He who loves his wife loves himself. For no man ever hates his own flesh, but nourishes and cherishes it, as Christ does the church, because we are members of his body.

Ephesians 5:25-30

Husbands are called to a monumental task: to lay down their lives for their wives in imitation of Christ's sacrifice for his bride. All of us are called to love the way Jesus did—he said so (see Jn 13:34). But husbands uniquely image Jesus as Bridegroom. And how did Jesus love? Sacrificially.

Because of our concupiscence, to imitate Christ is to give until it hurts. We are sure we would give sacrificially in some major crisis, such as the injury of a loved one or the defense of the faith from obvious attack. But often the Lord asks us to make little sacrifices to show our love, sometimes in such small ways that our spouses do not even notice the offering.

One time two seminarians visited us for a weekend. I was talking to them when a child with a full diaper walked through, the aroma assaulting us all at the same time. Laughing, one seminarian thought out loud, "I know I'm *not* called to marriage."

I couldn't help quipping back, "Don't choose one vocation to avoid the difficulties of the other!"

We are united to Christ, and therefore we have been crucified with him. Our lives have to reflect this reality. St. Paul writes: "I have been crucified with Christ; it is no longer I who live, but Christ who lives in me; and the life I now live in the flesh I live by faith in the Son of God, who loved me and gave himself for me" (Gal 2:20).

Scott became a Catholic before I did. After he had first become a Catholic, the sight of a crucifix upset me. It represented our differences so pointedly. Then I was hospitalized in a Catholic hospital for a major kidney infection following a painful tubal pregnancy, complete with full C-section cut. I was suffering and I was sad.

As I looked at the cross hanging on the wall of my hospital room—and it wasn't an empty cross but a crucifix—I realized two things. I stared at the crucifix, and for the first time I considered my sufferings in the light of Christ's. It was a reminder that Christ's sufferings were greater than mine would ever be.

At the same time, his suffering made mine meaningful. It made sense out of all of the inconveniences, difficulties, and pain I was going through, *if* I offered them to God in union with Christ's self-offering.

St. Paul reflected on his sufferings and resolved, "Now I rejoice in my sufferings for your sake, and in my flesh I complete what is lacking in Christ's afflictions for the sake of his body, that is, the church" (Col 1:24). Did you catch that odd phrase? "What is *lacking* in Christ's afflictions."

How could Christ's sufferings in any way be inadequate? Christ's sufferings are not inadequate. But we are so much a part of his Body that Jesus permits us, in our offering of suffering united to his, to participate in salvation.

Childbirth: An Offering

For me, the call to lay down my life for my friend has been in sharpest focus with the deliveries of each of my children. The intensity of the joy and the intensity of the suffering are difficult to capture in words; each time I face new struggles and I learn new things. After I understood the principle of redemptive suffering, these self-offerings were powerful spiritual experiences at a new level, and every delivery brought me closer to Christ.

With the delivery of my firstborn, Michael, we learned to wait, and wait, and wait. We took every suggestion people gave us to go into labor; double-dip ice cream cones was my favorite. Still, he was too content to be moved.

Two weeks overdue, I finally went into labor. After thirty hours, five of them on pitocin, nothing much had happened. Scott was awakened from a nap with the news that I was headed toward surgery. I delivered a big (nine pounds, seven ounces!), beautiful, healthy boy; we were overwhelmed with gratitude.

I had two doctors. The morning after delivery, my older doctor assured me that C-sections did not mean we could not have a big family. My younger doctor, his partner, assured me no self-respecting doctor would let me have more than three children. (I told the older doctor what the younger one had said, and he said he'd take care of the difference of opinion.) Nevertheless, I had hopes for a VBAC (vaginal birth after cesarean) with the next child.

In Gabriel's delivery, I went into labor just after the due date and progressed slowly but surely. Because of the possibility of uterine rupture, I could not have pain medication. After twenty-four hours, my doctor said he thought I had the same size baby as my first and requested an operating room for a C-section. I was heartbroken.

One of the hardest things about the delivery was lying on the table in the hallway outside of the surgical room like a hunk of meat rather than a woman about to give birth to her second child. Technicians had been called in on a Saturday morning and they were upset. *They* were upset!

As they prepped me, they didn't even speak to me. They just complained to each other. When my doctor, at my request, asked the nurse to leave one of my arms free so that I could bond with my baby by touching him, the assisting doctor challenged my doctor, saying, "C-sections don't bond with their babies." He did not even speak to me as a person, a mother; it was just a surgical procedure.

I delivered a beautiful boy who quieted the moment he heard my voice. I reached out and stroked his cheek, calling him by name, professing my love. Later, when I saw the doctor, I was at peace with the idea that future deliveries would be C-sections.

Then the doctor told me that he had been wrong: Gabe *was* small enough (eight pounds) that I could have delivered him vaginally, and that maybe I could try again next time! I was frustrated, to say the least, but determined to try again.

When I was pregnant with Hannah, I searched for nearly four months to find a doctor who would give me a chance at a normal delivery. Two weeks after I found him, I hemorrhaged at church, just as the service was ending. I lay down on a pew, trying not to frighten our boys with my tears, while Scott tried to reach the doctor. As Providence would have it, he was less than a minute away—in the church basement! (Neither of us knew the other was at that church.)

The ride to the hospital was so difficult. Is the baby alive or dead? Should we bury a baby of twenty weeks' gestation? Questions were interspersed with ejaculatory prayers, begging God for this child's life. Once we went to the hospital, the nurses would not give us any hope. "An ultrasound will tell us more," is all they would say.

While I was on the phone, talking to my parents through my tears, they wheeled the portable ultrasound machine into my room. When the image appeared on the screen, I gasped. There was our baby, alive and well! We could hardly contain our joy!

Our doctor identified the problem as *placenta previa*—a condition in which the baby implants on the cervix rather than the uterine wall. C-section was our only option, since labor would cause the placenta to detach and the baby to die within ten minutes. Once again, I had to yield my will.

This time, however, I had almost four months to prepare myself for the delivery. Several times there were scares when I bled again or I went into early labor. Since labor had to be avoided at all costs, we scheduled the C-section three weeks before our due date.

This was my first alert delivery. (Previously, I had been in so much pain from intense labor that I was unaware of my surroundings; I just prayed that the anesthesia would take quickly.) Because of the early delivery, there were extra pediatric nurses, technicians, doctors—about twelve people in all. But Scott had to wait out in the hallway until I was prepped.

The nurse didn't get the IV in properly until her third attempt. The anesthesiologist didn't get the epidural right on the first two tries. Tension was building. "Who's in charge of the anesthesia?" I demanded.

A woman behind me responded. "I am, but I am training this intern."

"This is my third delivery," I snapped. "I have given my body to science all I intend to. You're going to do it or we are not having this baby today!"

She agreed to do it. That time the epidural went in correctly.

They strapped down both of my arms while they shaved my stomach and cleansed the area for cutting. I was totally naked for about ten minutes. I lay on my back in a cold delivery room, naked, surrounded by people I didn't know (except for the doctor), and wondering if the anesthesia would actually work. (Sometimes epidurals can be patchy, though I've not experienced that.)

No music was playing. No one was talking to me or explaining why the delivery was delayed (twins were unexpectedly being delivered next door). And Scott still had not been permitted to come in.

I began to cry. Since both arms were strapped down, I couldn't keep tears from flowing into my ears. The intern asked me, "Are you crying because you're happy?"

I just shook my head *no!* I did not want to talk to him.

Finally, they let Scott in. He knew all the right things to say. He has an entire C-section comedy routine, including comments such as, "Don't I leave you in stitches? I'm such a cut up! When I say my wife has guts, believe me; I've seen them!" He adds more lines with every delivery.

Scott dried my tears and asked whether one of my arms could be unstrapped so I could touch the baby after delivery. He helped me refocus on the momentous event of the birth of this precious child, for whom we had waited so long. He cheered me with the jokes and prayed with me. He thanked me for all I was enduring so that this child could have life. It was wonderful. And I delivered our beautiful daughter.

The whole event gave me a small glimpse into *Christ's* sacrifice: naked, laid out in cruciform, feeling humiliated, in pain and fear. I was laying down my life; I was shedding my blood. Yet I had no one mocking me, intentionally wounding, as they did to Jesus.

Jeremiah's delivery was my first Catholic delivery. I *still* wanted a normal delivery. I negotiated with God: "I'll offer up every contraction if I can just have a normal delivery." In my heart, I heard him say, "I'll give you plenty of suffering to offer up with your C-section." End of discussion.

From the enema on, I attached each difficulty to a prayer intention. Offering suffering is not a bargaining chip to lessen pain; *that* was a surprise. Just because I offered something up did not mean it did not hurt. Yet it was a powerful way to channel pain into prayer.

Everything went well at the delivery, with no surprises. Scott was at my side and announced the news: another beautiful boy. So many prayers were answered.

Following Jeremiah's delivery I had intense pain for about an hour. I had taken all the morphine I could have by IV, but it didn't seem to touch the suffering. Though I had eaten nothing, I threw up from the pain. I called the nurse, apologizing for the mess, and requested something else for pain relief.

After calling the doctor, she returned with a large needle and said that it should help. I felt like a beached whale about to be harpooned.

At that moment I didn't think of Jesus; I thought of Mary. I did not want this pain wasted, but I was in too much pain to formulate a complete thought. I could not even say Mary's name, but I thought it, over and over. It was as if I was offering my suffering for her to turn it into a meaningful prayer. *She* would take it to Jesus. That was a new experience.

The night before Joseph's delivery we had a wonderful family dinner at a restaurant. Everyone was in high spirits; the next day was "D-day." (Knowing the delivery date is the one and only benefit of C-sections.)

Later, Scott found me weeping. He asked me what was wrong. I told him, "I feel like I'm lying across railroad tracks and I can't get off. The train is coming, I'm really scared, and everyone around me is happy because they aren't thinking about the delivery, just the baby. I just have to cry it out. I'll be OK."

Given a little more time, I was reconciled to the next day's events and prepared to face them, with God's help. As my friend Terri remarked later, "You were with Christ in Gethsemane, suffering through the whole ordeal ahead of time." Some places of suffering only God can touch.

After a routine C-section, Scott announced it was another beautiful boy. It's hard to put into words what a reward a baby is after you go through so much to bring him into this world. Following Joseph's delivery, they added pitocin to my IV to help my uterus clamp down in order to limit blood loss. That area had just been sutured, so it was very painful.

For the next two and a half hours, I prayed *one* decade of the rosary— that's all. I slowly breathed out one word for as long as I could before saying the next. I learned that it's not how many prayers we say so much as how well they are said.

Before David's delivery they discovered that I had a hepatitis B infection. So, for the safety of the baby, they gave me an antibiotic by IV beforehand. It caused pain I had not experienced previously. This time a slow decade of the rosary preceded the whole process of delivery. I could tell immediately when the IV was empty.

I am thankful that the C-section turned out to be the best yet. Before the surgery, the nurses and anesthesiologist introduced themselves and said how excited they were for us. Gentle music played in the background, warmed blankets covered me so that I shivered less and was never completely naked, and various staff kept checking with me to see whether I was OK.

I'm so grateful for all the ways this staff helped minimize what is difficult. And, as always, Scott kept the focus on God's good gift we were about to receive: another beautiful boy, David!

Suffering Yields Joy

One woman has experienced something I hope I never will. Since she had lost a baby at delivery one year previously, throughout the next pregnancy she faced a great fear: Would she deliver a healthy baby this time? Once at the hospital, the doctor attached an internal monitor to the baby and, to his dismay, noticed the baby's heart rate completely drop off with the contraction. The baby's umbilical cord was being compressed, and only an emergency C-section could deliver the baby alive.

But there was a *major* problem: No anesthesiologist was available at that moment. The doctor spoke quickly to the husband: "You have to trust me. If we do not deliver this baby, he'll be dead in less than ten minutes. We have to operate *now.*" Then he told the incredulous husband to lie across his wife's chest to hold her down, so that he could cut her *without anesthesia.*

Incredible as it may sound in this day and age, that is exactly what happened. The baby was safely delivere, and within minutes an anesthesiologist arrived and gave the woman gas. I cannot fathom how excruciatingly painful that had to be. (I'll never complain about having a C-section with anesthesia to her!)

How difficult the decision must have been for them to allow it. But both the baby and the mother lived, and the couple believes they made the right decision. What a sacrifice!

I do not share these details about deliveries because I want to strike fear in your hearts and discourage you from having babies. Far from it. I want you to know that if God has brought me and millions of other women through the dangers, difficulties, indignities, and dying to self that are inherent in the process of creating and delivering a baby, he can do the same for you.

On one level, a very human level, I never want to go through anything like this again. But for the honor and privilege of bearing another soul for Christ and for the joy of our family, I would do it *all* again in a heartbeat.

Love leads to life, and life leads to sacrifice. We do not seek suffering, but we know it is worth all the suffering for the joy that is set before us, just as it was for Christ, who for the joy set before him (our salvation) endured the cross, despising the shame (see Heb 12:2). As one friend said to me recently, "If you want to follow Jesus, you better look good on wood."

Give Thanks for the Gift

In the Old Testament there were many kinds of sacrifices: grain offerings, thank offerings, sin offerings, animal sacrifices, and others. One sacrifice in particular prefigured the one perpetual sacrifice of the New Covenant: the *todah* sacrifice. Rabbis taught that this was the only kind of sacrifice that would continue after the Messiah came.

The *todah* was an ancient Jewish sacrifice of thanksgiving for a particular and personal reason. Many of the psalms are *todah* psalms, following a familiar pattern. First, someone recounts a great difficulty he faced, perhaps illness, attacks by enemies, or war—usually life-threatening circumstances. Next he tells how he cried out to God and was delivered. Then he concludes with an expression of thanks (see Psalm 63, for one example).

The man who offered the *todah* sacrifice would do four things. First, he invited his family and friends to join him in thanksgiving. Second, he brought a lamb to be sacrificed at the temple as an offering for his salvation from great difficulty or even death. Third, he consecrated bread in his home with those who had gathered while the lamb was being sacrificed in the temple. (This was the only consecrated bread laypeople could eat.) Fourth, he offered a cup of wine in thanksgiving for God's saving act. Does this sound familiar: bread, wine, giving thanks?

The sacrifice of the Mass is in fact called the Eucharist based on the Greek word *eucharisteo*, which means "thanksgiving" or "sacrifice of praise." We go to Mass to offer thanksgiving to God as our *todah* offering for Christ's sacrifice on the cross.

Together we proclaim God's mighty deeds for our salvation: God Almighty took on human flesh, laid it down on the cross, took it up again through the resurrection, and then ascended to the Father in heaven. In heaven he is our High Priest, who offers himself as the perpetual, once-for-all sacrifice. *This* is our Eucharist made present in the Mass: Jesus himself![4]

Thanksgiving is an important part of marriage as well. That is why my father read Colossians 3:17 at our wedding: "And whatever you do, in word or deed, do everything in the name of the Lord Jesus, giving thanks to God the Father through him." He admonished us to fill our hearts regularly with thanksgiving to God for our spouse. Nothing quiets a critical spirit within us more quickly than setting our thoughts and prayers on our spouse; the more specific our thanks, the better.

Thanksgiving for Christ's work in us and in our spouse inspires our thanks for our spouse. St. Paul writes, "Rejoice always, pray constantly, give thanks in all circumstances; for this is the will of God in Christ Jesus for you" (1 Thes 5:16-18). When are we to give thanks? When we feel like it? When everything is going our way?

No. We are to give thanks in *all* circumstances. Why? Because it is God's will.

Sometimes thanksgiving is a real sacrifice. I didn't understand the psalmist's references to offering a sacrifice of praise, nor did I understand why Mary had the title "Our Lady of Sorrows," until our third miscarriage.

Only days before we had celebrated the good news about a new baby with our children and rejoiced at Mass as a family. Our hearts were so full of joy that it was easy to praise God.

Then I lost the baby. With heavy hearts we told the children, and then, again, went off to Mass. The Scripture text came to mind about offering a sacrifice of praise, so I prayed, "It *is* a sacrifice, but Lord, I *will* praise you! I just want you to know that I will always have this sorrow in my heart for the three babies I have never held in this life."

The Lord spoke to my heart: "And do you think that my mother will ever get over her sorrow when she saw me wounded and mocked, and then held my lifeless body, the body that she gave me, in her arms? Do you see why she is 'Our Lady of Sorrows'?"

Now I understood. Our Lady of Sorrows became a comfort to me. And I knew that I could rejoice in the midst of my suffering, holding at the same time heartfelt gratitude and sorrowful anguish. Once again, Christ's self-offering was my model for life.

Possible by the Power of the Holy Spirit

The Holy Spirit overshadowed Mary so that she conceived Jesus (see Lk 1:35). When she said, "Behold, I am the handmaid of the Lord; let it be to me according to your word" (Lk 1:38), she was saying to Jesus, in effect, "This is my body, this is my blood, given for you."

Mary's *yes* was her self-offering. Her *yes* meant more than providing a place for Jesus to reside within her; she gave him human nature. Her self-offering made his possible: only as fully divine *and* fully human could the God-Man redeem us.

In the Mass, the Holy Spirit overshadows (in the *epiklesis*) our offering of bread and wine and transubstantiates our gifts into Christ's Body and Blood. Then the Holy Spirit unites us to Christ as we receive him in the Eucharist. Finally, the Holy Spirit empowers us through the Eucharist to imitate Christ through our self-offering, especially in the sacrament of marriage.

The Spirit hovered over creation as later he overshadowed Mary (see Gn 1:2). When the Father made Adam, he breathed into him the breath of life, his Spirit (see Gn 2:7). Adam, when first he saw Eve, exclaimed, "This at last is bone of my bones and flesh of my flesh; she shall be called Woman, because she was taken out of Man" (Gn 2:23). Not only does Adam recognize the gift of this woman for him, but he expresses his desire to give himself to her.

The Song of Solomon, according to Pope John Paul II, is a commentary on this verse—how lovers desire each other's flesh. In the act of marriage, the two partners in their self-offering say to each other, "This is my body, this is my blood, given for you."

This self-offering is deepened when a new life is conceived. In imitation of Christ, every woman who delivers a baby is laying down her life for a friend. As I lay on the delivery table, I thought, "This is my body broken for you; this is my blood shed for you." Later, when we talked about it with the children, they could see the interconnection between love, life, and sacrifice. I had laid down my life for my son or daughter just as Jesus freely laid down his life for his sons and daughters.

Speaking of married couples, the *Catechism* declares: "The Holy Spirit is the seal of their covenant, the ever-available source of their love and the strength to renew their fidelity."[5] The Holy Spirit enables spouses to live the sacrament of marriage so that they grow in holiness.

The Holy Spirit strengthens our faithfulness and renews our love. He helps us put our trials in perspective. The closer we draw to Christ, the more he produces virtue in us, for "the fruit of the Spirit is love, joy, peace, patience, kindness, goodness, faithfulness, gentleness, self-control; against such there is no law" (Gal 5:22-23).

If we lack something, we can ask for it. "Let us then with confidence draw near to the throne of grace, that we may receive mercy and find grace to help in time of need" (Heb 4:16). The Holy Spirit will give us what we need *when* we need it; we do not need the patience for three children when we only have two.

Let's be honest. None of us has what it takes to be completely virtuous as the parent of even one child. However, we can expect to produce more of all the fruit of the Spirit as we grow in Christ so that we can parent in the Spirit rather than in the flesh however many children the Lord gives us.

The Gift of Self is Fruitful

The Eucharist is Jesus, the source of sacramental grace. The *Catechism* affirms that "Communion with the flesh of the risen Christ, a flesh 'given life and giving life through the Holy Spirit,' preserves, increases, and renews the life of grace received at Baptism."[6] When we receive Jesus, we become more like him. He loves us as we are, but he loves us too much to leave us this way. We bear the fruitfulness of his divine life as long as we abide in him, as St. John teaches (see Jn 15).

Though we have to attend Mass only weekly, in fulfillment of the admonition in Hebrews 10:25 not to neglect to meet together, we are able to attend Mass daily in most areas of the United States. In doing so, we not only receive the grace of the Eucharist; we, in turn, become channels of grace to others, especially to our spouses and children.

As it is in the Eucharist, the gift of self is fruitful in marriage as well. We are called to imitate God as life-giving lovers. We embrace each other and all that that means. *This* is responsible sexuality:

In particular, responsible fatherhood and motherhood directly concern the moment in which a man and a woman uniting themselves "in one flesh," can become parents. ... This is a moment of special value both for this interpersonal relationship and for their service to life: they can become parents—father and mother—by communicating life to a new human being....

In every case conjugal union involves the responsibility of the man and of the woman, a potential responsibility which becomes actual when the circumstances dictate. This is true especially for the man. Although he too is involved in the beginning of the generative process, he is left biologically distant from it; it is within the woman that the process develops. How can the man fail to assume responsibility?[7]

Through our love and generosity, souls that would not otherwise exist will be created. The souls of children still to be conceived aren't in heaven waiting for bodies. The Church teaches that God creates a soul when he enables us to create a body.[8]

The Church has spoken clearly. Our bodies are temples of the Holy Spirit. How can we put anything into our bodies that could desacralize our sexuality and possibly kill our children? Since contraception literally means *against life*, could this be God's idea? No. Only Satan impedes or destroys the fruit of marital love.

The act of marriage with contraception is practically a different act from what the couple intends. First, the focus is on what you receive more than what you give; it reduces sex to an end in itself. Second, it is a rejection of the life-giving power of the act of marriage. It promotes sterility rather than embracing fertility as God's good gift, and thereby desecrates what God has declared to be holy.

Third, it turns the most profound truth the couple wants to say—"I am totally yours and you are totally mine"—into a lie, because the woman refuses the life-giving seed of the man and the man refuses the life-receiving, nurturing womb of the woman. Finally, it is a refusal to sacrifice for the other. Like Adam and Eve, the couple decides what is good (infertility) and what is evil (pregnancy). Where is God in this decision?

Dr. Bob McDonald, psychologist and deacon, spoke on some of the side effects of the contraceptive mentality of parents on their children. These children were in counseling, struggling with depression and grief. These were their concerns:

Parents don't really like children.

I'm blessed to be alive; it's good that I was conceived at a convenient time.

Luxuries are preferred to children; trinkets and toys are more important.

I ought to have other brothers and sisters. Where are they? They should be here.[9]

There is a generational force to the parents' decision not to be open to life. Not just individuals but whole bloodlines will never develop.

In contrast, the Lord appeals to us through his gift on the cross of divine life for his bride: What is our vision of marriage? Does it reflect this total self-donating love he has for us that is life-giving and sacrificial? If it once was, but now we have lost the vision, he can reinspire us. We cannot allow the spiritual poison of contraception and sterilization to damage our marriage and our family.

Once we admit to ourselves that contraception is serious sin, we need to go to Confession right away. If we ignored opportunities to learn Church teaching, if we chose not to form our conscience, we need to go to Confession and ask the priest to assist us in repenting appropriately. If we did not know that it was serious sin, we may not have mortal sin on our souls; however, contraception is still an objectively grave error that causes great damage regardless of intention or knowledge.

Whether or not it was sin committed with vincible ignorance, the truth must be embraced. A mother from Monroeville, Pennsylvania, shared the result of their change from contraception: "It had a positive, life-giving, mutually-respecting-each-other impact. We are gifts to each other, not mere playthings to be used at each other's whim." God can undo the damage and restore spiritual health. That's the greatness of grace!

Prepare Properly to Receive the Gift

A family once voiced their opinions about the Mass they had just attended. The mother couldn't believe the poor quality of the choir. The father thought the homily rambling and long. The son said the altar boys were clumsy. Then the little girl spoke: "Not a bad show for a buck."

We may laugh at this scenario, but all too often people approach Mass as if it is a performance to attend rather than the greatest feast in which we can participate.

We need to make a point of getting to Confession regularly so we are ready to receive the Lord worthily. It's like bathing before the marital embrace. When we approach the church for Mass, we leave a critical spirit at the door. We have come to receive the Lord and to be received by him.

Since my father is a Protestant pastor, I asked him once whether it drove him crazy to hear a lousy sermon when he visited other churches. He replied, "No. I just ask, 'Jesus, what do you have for me today?' There's always something he wants me to learn."

I appreciate Dad's example when frustrations about the homily or singing distract me. I do not want to miss this opportunity to draw closer to our Lord. I want to receive all that he has for me.

Sometimes we may have legitimate concerns about the rubrics of a particular Mass. We need to address those concerns to the appropriate authority. However, we are not the liturgical police, and we should not be critical of the priest or our bishop in front of our children except for the rare occasion when the children could be led into sin or error, should we remain silent.

We can offer up the suffering we have when people do not participate, leave early, or complain. We can encourage change. However, the Mass is never *dead* as long as Jesus is there.

Just as we must prepare our spirits to receive the gift of the Eucharist, we must also prepare for the marital gift of ourselves to each other. We must receive our spouse with humility and leave criticism out. We are both unworthy of such unconditional love, and yet, by the mercy of God, we can give and receive it in marriage.

This means choosing to speak and act in a way that communicates respect for our spouse. It means focusing on our spouse's strengths rather than weaknesses. In short, it means proclaiming wordlessly what St. Paul describes as the task of love: "Love bears all things, believes all things, hopes all things, endures all things" (1 Cor 13:7).

Love also forgives and asks forgiveness. The three hardest words in the English language are "I am sorry," and the four hardest are "I am sorry, dear." Repentance and forgiveness are never easy, but being in right relationship is essential for a thriving marriage.

We must make intentional preparations to receive the gift of the other person in intimacy. Spontaneity is not all it is cracked up to be. We must ask ourselves how we are *making love* throughout the day: How have we loved each other? How have we helped each other?

We prepare for the act of marriage through what I call *foretalk*—conversation about the day, concerns about the children, touching base on upcoming events—and *forework*—doing acts of service for each other such as cleaning out the garage, setting up the garden, playing with the children, or washing the car. Then we are ready to give and to receive the other in the marital embrace.

Trust in Divine Providence Is Necessary

In the Lord's Prayer we ask, "Give us this day our daily bread" (Mt 6:11). We are not just asking God for the bread that sustains our bodies; we are asking for the Bread of Life. In the Eucharist we recognize that Jesus has withheld nothing from us. His gift calls us to submit our lives to him in a fresh, new way. We respond, "Jesus, you have given all to me; I give all of me back to you."

From the cross, Jesus uttered these words: "Father, into thy hands I commit my spirit" (Lk 23:46). He calls us to do the same: to entrust our lives, our marriages, and our families to the providence of God. God has a mission for us. All he requires is that we, like Jesus, place our trust in him.

In a similar way, trust in Divine Providence is also necessary for marriage. God designed us; God planned marriage. His purpose in making rules is not to spoil all the fun. He wants us to succeed in marriage, and that means we have to do it his way. God as self-donating lover has called us to reflect him in our marriages and in our families as life-giving lovers and life-loving givers.

We have the freedom to set all kinds of goals for our marriages and families. Yet at the same time we must pray, "Thy will be done." We do not know the future, but we know the One who knows the future. And he can be trusted.

We Need a Heavenly Perspective

In his book *The Lamb's Supper*, my husband, Scott, demonstrates how the Book of Revelation reveals the heavenly liturgy. The first part of Revelation is the Liturgy of the Word, and the second part is the Liturgy of the Eucharist, culminating in the Lamb's Supper. Heaven descends; through the words and actions of the priest, the Spirit transforms our offering of bread and wine into Jesus' self-offering. At the Lamb's Supper we are surrounded by saints and angels.

No matter how discombobulated we feel, going to Mass should change our perspective. For example, we may wonder, for heaven's sake, why are we doing what we are doing with all these children? Mass gives us an opportunity to focus on thanksgiving rather than complaining, to pray about our concerns rather than gossip, to see other people or situations around us in the light of God's love and grace for them. At Mass, we acquire a heavenly perspective, and we leave more heavenly-minded so that we can be more earthly good.

We need a heavenly perspective on our marriage as well. If we ask God to give us one, he will. It will look something like this: the closer we are to God, the closer we are to each other. If we picture a triangle, with spouses at the sides and God at the top, then we see that the closer we get to God, the less distance there is between us.[10]

Somehow our marriage is a picture to the world about the relationship between Christ and the Church. Some days that image is in sharper focus than others. How can we strengthen our marriage so that we are good witnesses, so that our marriage more accurately portrays the nuptial relationship between Christ and his bride?

Keep Christ between you—it lessens friction. Want to set your spouse straight? Act rather than react: offer prayers, affection, and sacrifices. Just as we need to choose Jesus every day, we need to choose our spouse every day. This is an act of our will.

Frequent Reception Allows Grace to Flow

When Scott wanted to establish weekly Communion at our Presbyterian church, an elder questioned whether it might become less meaningful if it were more frequent. Scott said that Communion could be compared with the act of marriage: would a husband love his wife less if he made love to her more frequently?

The key is this: Repetition does not make Communion boring, because you are receiving a Person. When a child asks me why Mass is so long, I reply, "Because our love is so short." The Eucharist is always Jesus, but receiving him can become more meaningful if we prepare more carefully physically, mentally, and spiritually beforehand. And when the bond with Christ seems weak or dry, reception of the Eucharist strengthens our love.

The act of marriage is, among other things, a cure for concupiscence, as long as there is no lust. In writing about married couples who abstain from sexual relations, St. Paul cautions, "Do not refuse one another except perhaps by agreement for a season, that you may devote yourselves to prayer; but then come together again, lest Satan tempt you through lack of self-control" (1 Cor 7:5).

Sometimes mothers feel utterly exhausted; we don't feel like a *hot dish,* especially if we have had a baby recently. We may need our spouse to accept our sacrifices throughout the day as our love-offering and not expect to make love. At other times, we need to prepare to give ourselves physically to our spouse regardless of our tiredness. If the goal is to be available for the act of marriage only when we feel completely rested, it could be years before we are ready!

Communication is key to harmony in this vital area of the marriage relationship, especially after the first child has turned life upside down. The husband has never had to share his wife's time or attention so much with another person; the wife has never given herself so constantly all day and much of the night as well. Additionally, both spouses are coping with the flux of her hormones and many new experiences (such as a baby with colic, recovery from the major surgery of a C-section, or threats of breast infections).

Assume that both of you really want to love each other. Talk and pray, and you will find what works best for you.

Sometimes a husband can "make love" to his wife with a back rub or a foot massage rather than intercourse. Maybe the wife can plan a nap so that she can give herself to her husband. (Or the husband could offer to care for the children so that she could get an after-dinner nap.)

Maybe you could set up a schedule (weekends only for the next three months) or a time limit (don't ask after ten in the evening). Or you could change the time of day to make love during baby's naptime, if the dad works close to home—a quick call to a cell phone could be just what you need. *You* can make it work. And it is important that you make it work so that Satan does not get a foothold.

Marriage is the primary family relationship. Be sure not to show greater love to your children than your spouse, even when you give greater amounts of time and energy to the children. As a mom, you can have so many hugs and kisses in a day from the children that you don't have the same needs for physical affection from your husband that you used to have. However, you will love your children best when you love your spouse first.

When the doctor diagnosed *placenta previa* in my pregnancy with Hannah, we were told there was a great risk that bleeding would occur again. After I consulted with the doctor, I returned home with strict instructions. "Scott, there's good news and there's bad news. The good news is that the baby looks good and healthy. The bad news is that we have to abstain until six weeks postpartum, which is six months from now."

My visiting brother-in-law laughed; Scott and I just looked at each other. How could we do that? Once you're married, who wants to go back to acting like you're engaged? Thank God we had practiced the virtue of self-control before marriage, and in our marriage through Natural Family Planning.

We found ways to show our love and affection for each other. Scott helped me with leg massages to limit my varicose veins; he gave me back rubs to help with my aches from bed rest during periodic bleeding; and we took walks when we could. God was gracious to us. We made it through the experience closer to each other, more in love, and with a new baby girl in our arms.

Fear can limit us from really giving ourselves to our spouse frequently. So we have to face our fears head-on. One woman was offended at the suggestion that Satan could damage a marriage when one spouse withheld relations from the other. She said that once a month for intimacy should be enough for her husband.

I asked her, "Are you willing to ask him?" She looked embarrassed. The point is that we are not to withhold ourselves from each other.

Sometimes we need to commit to love each other physically because we need to experience unity in the midst of difficulties; it may be the very time to draw together rather than apart. When Scott became a Catholic and I did not want to be a Catholic, we were in a period of great conflict. We needed some tangible expression of our unity in the midst of our disunity.

So we made a commitment to make love regularly. If we were furious with each other, not feeling like the other had listened, we had to resolve things enough to be able to express love genuinely and physically. We had to be kind and respectful in our conversation, though we felt our differences so acutely. We kept communication open so that neither of us felt misused by the other person. God used the act of marriage, open to life, to carry us through conflict that could have ended badly.

How could we be so vulnerable to each other in the midst of such confusion and conflict? Here are the facts we reviewed.

First: We are married.

Second: The act of marriage is a covenant renewal.

Third: We know the act of marriage is to be open to life (one of the few Christian principles on which we agreed).

Therefore, each of us said to the other, "I choose to love you physically as an expression of my genuine love for you and my commitment to you." We acted on what was clear about the will of God, believing that in his time, he would help us with what seemed so unclear.

Here is a word of caution: We need to balance our marital duty to give ourselves to each other physically with sensitivity and respect. We are not to withhold ourselves to frustrate or harm our spouse; neither are we to compel our spouse to have relations. *Humanae Vitae* notes: "It is in fact justly observed that a conjugal act imposed upon one's partner without regard for his or her conditions and lawful desires is not a true act of love, and therefore denies an exigency of right moral order in the relationships between husband and wife."[11] Love is given and received as a gift.

Remember Your First Love

In the Book of Revelation, Jesus addressed the church in Ephesus. This particular church had had a rich beginning with St. John and Mary in the congregation, and St. Paul and then St. Timothy as pastors.

> I know your works, your toil and your patient endurance, and how you cannot bear evil men but have tested those who call themselves apostles but are not, and found them to be false; I know you are enduring patiently and bearing up for my name's sake, and you have not grown weary. But I have this against you, that you have abandoned the love you had at first. Remember then from what you have fallen, repent and do the works you did at first. If not, I will come to you and remove your lampstand from its place, unless you repent.
>
> REVELATION 2:2-5

The people had lots of good works, but that was not enough; they had forgotten their first love. Jesus has to be first.

They must not have repented, either, because the church in Ephesus eventually disappeared. This is a sobering thought: We must not forget our first love, Jesus. Faithfulness to Christ leads to spiritual fruitfulness; unfaithfulness leads to spiritual death.

In a similar way, we must remember our first love in marriage as well. Solomon wrote a beautiful description of how a husband should view his wife, no matter how long they have been married:

> Drink water from your own cistern, flowing water from your own well. Should your springs be scattered abroad, streams of water in the streets? Let them be for yourself alone, and not for strangers with you. Let your fountain be blessed, and rejoice in the wife of your youth, a lovely hind, a graceful doe. Let her affection fill you at all times with delight, be infatuated always with her love.
>
> PROVERBS 5:15-19

We must set our hearts on Jesus as our beloved, and on our spouse as our beloved.

Remember that God's desire is faithful marriages that lead to the fruit of godly offspring. The *Catechism* reminds us: "This human communion is confirmed, purified, and completed by communion in Jesus Christ, given through the sacrament of Matrimony. It is deepened by lives of the common faith and by the Eucharist received together."[12] We need to come to Jesus *together* for strength to live by grace.

I hope that meditation on these rich parallels between the Eucharist and matrimony will deepen our love both for Jesus and for our spouse. May our participation in one sacrament enrich our participation in the other. Our first love, Jesus, calls us to imitate his faithful and fruitful intimacy with his bride in our own marriages. For "the family is indeed ... the 'sanctuary of life.'"[13]

III.
HOW CAN WE LIVE
THIS BEAUTIFUL DESIGN?
THE EMBRACE
OF THE BODY OF CHRIST

Chapter Six

Embrace the Truth

Now that we have seen the beauty of God's design for marital love, how do we share it in a compelling way? To withhold the truth in the name of "tolerance" is not love, but to bludgeon people with the truth is not love, either. Our goal must be to share this vision of life-giving love so that others will grow in Christ.

The Mercy of God

A Scripture that has challenged me in marriage, and especially during pregnancy, comes from St. Paul:

> I appeal to you therefore, brethren, by the mercies of God, to present your bodies as a living sacrifice, holy and acceptable to God, which is your spiritual worship. Do not be conformed to this world but be transformed by the renewal of your mind, that you may prove what is the will of God, what is good and acceptable and perfect.
>
> Romans 12:1-2

Why does this passage mean so much to me? First, because St. Paul appeals to us "by the mercies of God." It is not enough for us to feel inspired by various books and encyclicals, though the inspiration is helpful. It is not enough to have our hearts stirred toward obedience by great homilies or speeches, or even by the lives of holy men and women who are living the beautiful design God has for marriage. Inspiration alone might give us some energy to attempt living marital love faithful to Christ, but we might be tempted to do so in our own strength.

The bad news is that we do not have the resources in and of ourselves to love our spouse or our children the way we should. The good news is that God has not asked us to do anything in our own strength; he has all the strength we need. By his mercy, he empowers us to live authentic marital love.

How does the Lord strengthen us by his grace?

First, he renews us through the sacraments: Confession on a regular basis; frequent reception of the Eucharist; reception of each other through the act of marriage without contraception.

Second, he sustains us through difficulties and sufferings.

Third, he reinforces our firm resolve to yield our hearts continually to the truth of God. This is not a one-time decision; there may be many important decisions to turn from sin and turn toward God. We must make an ongoing, daily self-offering to God, acknowledging our need for his strength to be faithful.

Our Bodies Are Living Sacrifices

Once we yield our hearts to God, we need to yield our bodies to him as well. By offering our bodies as a "living sacrifice," we experience the physical side of being spiritual. I used to think this kind of sacrifice meant dragging my body out of bed fifteen minutes early for prayer. Now, that may be a sacrifice, but the kind of sacrificing St. Paul advocates is much more all-encompassing.

How can we present our bodies as a living sacrifice? Within the vocation of marriage we are living sacrifices through pregnancy, delivery, and care for our children. We voluntarily say yes to loving God and each other by being open to life.

But that's where the voluntary part ends. Almost immediately following conception all kinds of involuntary opportunities for sacrifices begin. We don't become a mother or father at the birth of our child but rather at his or her conception.

God, in his mercy, does not tell us everything our yes will mean. Most likely, Mary did not understand everything her yes would mean. She had much to ponder; however, she still gave God permission to work in and through her life as he saw fit. Like Mary, we don't have to know everything our yes will mean; we just have to yield ourselves, trusting God.

Our yes is voluntary; it is a good act of our will. In a sense, however, we are still in control. So the kind of involuntary service pressed on us by circumstances beyond our control is sweeter yet, for we have to yield to God's better plan as an act of trust. Sometimes our will coincides with God's will, but often it does not.

When I first thought about pregnancy, I thought a lot about the baby without thinking about the difficulties. I did not plan on throwing up, walking off charlie horses, getting up in the middle of the night to go to the bathroom, or tossing and turning as I wrestled with five pillows to support my belly properly for comfortable sleep. And yet these and many other difficulties were involuntary sacrifices that are involved in being a living sacrifice. They were part of God's invitation to mature in my dependence on him and my interdependence with Scott.

I've grappled with nausea. (There's nothing quite like battling nausea all day only to make dinner for the family, for months on end.) I've struggled with weight gain and then weight loss. I've suffered loss of sleep due to problems with nocturnal bladder control, bruises from running an enlarging stomach into doorways (I forget I'm thinner straight through a doorway than sideways by about the seventh month), and a myriad of other physical inconveniences. All this reminds me for nine months that I am not inhabiting my body alone.

My body is a living roadmap with many signs to direct others to the sacrifices involved in having babies. During pregnancy I acquired stretch marks and varicose veins that continue to be reminders of the offering of my body. So far I've had seven cesarean sections (six deliveries and one tubal pregnancy) and four D & C's (to stop hemorrhaging after deliveries or miscarriages). I've been cut up and down; I've been cut sideways. (My scar now looks like an anchor!) Scott says these are wounds borne for Christ, so I'll probably have them on my resurrection body!

The number of C-sections I have had has not yet precluded more babies, since the doctor has been able to excise scar tissue. (The record for C-sections is fourteen in Texas!) However, there is still so much scar tissue from the surgeries that it is unlikely babies conceived in the future will find healthy tissue for implantation. More miscarriages may be in our future.

The physical challenges of children do not end with delivery. Nursing has its own trials, as wonderful as it is: engorgement (I now know why the cows come on their own to be milked at the end of the day); dripping, especially in public (men's cotton hankies are worth their weight in gold); and being the only one on call day or night for feedings.

Getting my body back in shape, especially the more children I have, has been tough. When the hormonal signal is sent that I'm pregnant, my stomach muscles give up the ghost! Then there's the attempt to get enough consecutive hours of sleep to be able to recuperate from childbirth and major surgery so that I can function as a wife and mom with kindness.

Is this overwhelming to read? I don't share this to discourage you. Instead, I want to demonstrate how, through the marital act, we *choose* to be a living sacrifice.

Do you know what the problem is with *living* sacrifices? We keep crawling off the altar! If we were dead, we would just lie there. But in our human, weakness, we fluctuate between truly wanting to entrust ourselves completely to God and taking back our lives to manage them on our own. When we try to do things in our own strength, we usually fall flat. Then our loving Father has to pick us up and put us back on the altar so that we can, by his mercies, be the living sacrifices he has called us to be.

Sacrificial Living Is Spiritual Worship

We all know that we go to Mass to worship the Lord. However, our worship does not end there. The Mass concludes with these words: "Go in peace to love and serve the Lord and one another." To this we respond, "Thanks be to God." What do we mean by these words?

We are asking God for the grace to continue our worship as living sacrifices as we go out into the world. We have just received the Lord; we are living tabernacles of his presence. Now we are to live the life of the Crucified One, dying to ourselves and serving God and others. Spiritual worship is loving God with everything, including our bodies, including our fertility.

Transformed Thoughts, Formed Conscience

How can we face all these challenges? How can we do so in such a way that we become holier as a consequence? The *Catechism* says, "In the formation of conscience the Word of God is the light for our path (Ps 119:105); we must assimilate it in faith and prayer and put it into practice."[1] We need to read and study the Scriptures so that we make informed choices.

Romans 12:2 holds the key: It's all in the way we think. St. Paul commands us not to think the world's way but God's way, to transform our thoughts by renewing our minds in truth. "The education of conscience," says the *Catechism,* "is indispensable for human beings who are subjected to negative influences and tempted by sin to prefer their own judgment and to reject authoritative teachings."[2]

. We need clarity on how the world thinks and how God thinks about each facet of marriage and family life so that we know who is influencing us. How should we view men? women? marriage? children?

Once we understand how God views these things, we train our hearts to act on our convictions. Forming our consciences, our moral muscles, means that we submit our hearts and our minds to the truths of the Church and of Sacred Scripture. We must engage our will and our intellect to examine why the Church teaches what she does so that we will respond in faith. *Without* understanding, altruism can degenerate into bitterness and despair; *with* understanding, unselfishness can generate physical and spiritual fruitfulness and hope.

Let me give you a practical example. Before my fourth delivery, a nurse suggested, "You should get your tubes tied while the doctor's in there."

I quickly replied, "Don't touch those tubes. I would love to come back here and have another baby, even if it means another C-section."

As they wheeled me toward the operating room, I could hear the nurse tell other nurses, "She's had four sections and she's gonna come back for another one!" They were incredulous, not because they had not seen a woman with five sections, but because I was anticipating its happening again, even though I knew the cost. By the mercy of God, I had trained my heart to follow truth, and I could witness to the life-giving power of love even in the midst of suffering.

Later, I lay in my hospital bed, pondering, *God, how can you ever give me enough grace to face this again? I'm still a human being with a low threshold for pain.* (Typically, I'm on morphine for two to three days after delivery, although lately I have had less so that I can nurse sooner.)

Then I consciously made myself review what is true.

"O God, you have given me this beautiful son, Jeremiah, and he has a soul that will exist for all eternity. Thank you that out of my body you produced this child. Thank you for this expression of my husband's love for me and mine for him. Thank you for the incredible gift this little boy is to each of his siblings. Thank you for the prayer intentions for my suffering I have offered in union with Christ's sacrifice on the cross."

This kind of prayerful review helped me realign my will with God's will for the future.

After I came home from the hospital, our daughter said, "I like him, Mom, but I want a sister." I shuddered.

I turned away quickly because I did not want her to see my body cringe at the suggestion of another delivery. After all, there was only one way she would get a sister, and there was no guarantee the next one would be a girl. (In fact, the next one *was* a boy, and the *next* one was a boy!) My reaction to Hannah's remark showed me that my heart still needed to renew my thoughts.

As I repeated what was true, asking God for mercy to think his thoughts after him, I found that within two weeks I was spontaneously thinking, with joy, about another baby yet to come. It did take two weeks to train my heart, but thank God, it took only two weeks for my heart to be open to God's blessing of another child. I praised God because he had broken through the pain. The memory of the pain was real, but the greater reality was much more compelling.

Not only does the wife's mind need renewal, but the husband's mind as well. I will be forever grateful for my husband's perspective. My body has gone through many changes; I do not look the way I looked when we first got married. But Scott affirms my womanly beauty.

In contrast to Scott's response, some men dishonor their wives by imposing the world's perspective on womanly beauty rather than honoring their wife's body, through which they have just received the incredible gift of a son or daughter. Men need to challenge other men to think about their wife's body the way God does.

The goal is not to look as if we never had a baby—after all, we did! A womanly figure is not the same as a prepubescent teen's figure, thank God. We do want to be physically fit so that we can serve God well. But diet and exercise must be in moderation given our state in life. We are not to conform the way we see our bodies to the way the world says we should look. We are to transform our thinking about ourselves according to truth.

Prove the Will of God

We prove the will of God through living truth, once we have understood the difference between worldly "wisdom" and godly wisdom. There's a radical difference between time-bound fads and timeless truths. The world presents dangers to the civilization of love: selfishness rather than giving oneself for others; individualism at the expense of the community; and passion without responsibility. As Pope John Paul II warns, the world gives human weaknesses "a certain 'veneer' of respectability with the help of seduction and the blessing of public opinion."[3]

The *world* says, "You've got to put yourself first. You're number one. Never forget, it's all about you."

But *God* says, "You have to put me first, others second, and yourself third."

The *world* says, "What will best serve you, your finances, your career, your education?"

While *God* says, "What will best serve me?"

The *world* says, "Children are an economic liability. You should set up a kind of debit/credit sheet to justify having a baby. Children interfere with your education and your career. They ruin your body and probably kill brain cells just in caring for them."

In contrast, *God* says, "Children are the supreme gift of marriage because they reveal the life-giving power of love. They are an undeserved, unmerited gift."

The *world* says, "If you have miscarried, you don't need to go through that again. Don't risk pain; avoid it at all cost. Don't risk loss. It's purposeless."

"On the contrary," declares the *Lord,* "I redeem all things. I can redeem

the suffering of miscarriage. I can redeem the pain and suffering of pregnancy and delivery. All of life, the joys and the sufferings, offered to me are
filled with purpose, though you may not know the purposes until after this
life. My suffering makes your suffering meaningful."

The *world* says, "Do not lose your identity. Control your life. You don't
need men. Or if you want a man, go ahead and get married, but be a
'DINK' (Dual Income, No Kids). If you want one or two kids (a boy for him
and a girl for you) to make your All-American family, fine, but make sure
you get sterilized afterward, so that you control your future."

Yet *God* says, "If you want to find your life, you must lose it for my sake
[see Mt 16:25]. You have to die to yourself in order to live life abundantly.
Admit it: The bad news is, you aren't in control of anything; but the great
news is, I am. You don't know the future, but I do. You can trust me with it."

The *world* says, "Look how much you agree with the Catholic Church.
They're asking a bit too much to tell you to go against your conscience.
They're coming into your bedroom and demanding rights. You need to be
true to yourself. After all, you're still a good Catholic according to Fr. So-
and-So."

And *God* says, "It isn't a question of where you agree with the Church but
rather whether or not you will obey the Lord speaking through his
Church."

Healers of the Body: Doctors

Doctors have a sacred trust to heal rather than harm their patients. A growing number of physicians are affirming life by rejecting any involvement in
abortion. However, more physicians need to see the connection between
abortion and many forms of contraception. Even more, they need to
embrace the consistent teaching of the Church for the well-being of their
patients. *Humanae Vitae* offers this exhortation:

> We hold those physicians and medical personnel in the highest esteem
> who, in the exercise of their profession, value above every human
> interest the superior demands of their Christian vocation. Let them
> persevere, therefore, in promoting on every occasion the discovery of

solutions inspired by faith and right reason, let them strive to arouse this conviction and this respect in their associates.[4]

Patients who understand the Church's teaching can encourage physicians to practice medicine in such a way that it reflects these truths.

Some doctors have come to a conviction against contraception slowly. Their patients often inspire them to make a decision that runs directly contrary to the demands of our culture and, in fact, their own medical training. One physician wrote:

Concern for my patients first opened my heart and mind to NFP. I began to see a pattern in which the contraceptive 'help' I was prescribing to my healthy patients was not actually helping them, but potentially causing them harm. Physically, I was stunned by the many adverse reactions to hormonal contraceptives.

Many physicians may not know about the harmful side effects and abortifacient possibilities of contraception. Perhaps we can share this information with them.

When a young woman in her twenties, still a virgin, approached Dr. John Hartman, his answer surprised them both.

She asked me which of all the methods of family planning did I consider the best, not just in terms of effectiveness, but also for her marriage. My answer came after a short pause: NFP. I shared with her why and she shared her gratitude.

Although I was sure she was unaware of the effect she had on me, I mark that incident to this day as a turning point in my NFP conversion. ... For my ears to hear the answer that my lips gave was every bit as convicting to me as my refusal to be a part of medical school abortions. I had said it—now I have to live it!

...as each step along the way called for its own courage or its own decision, each step likewise became a source of joy to me as I contemplated the pleasure it gave me to speak the truth, unfettered, unambiguously, and uncompromised. Such was the effect for me of proclaiming NFP best for her marriage.[5]

It is not easy for doctors to rethink what they were taught in medical school. Yet it is necessary for them to evaluate properly whether or not their training honored God. Catholic doctors and nurses need to be fully Catholic. Some physicians who have taken courageous stands against contraception have faced opposition among their Catholic colleagues. One wife documents her husband's struggle.

My husband happens to be a member of a local Ob/Gyn group that professes to be Catholic, but he is the only one of the five who refuses to prescribe birth control pills. He is frequently persecuted in subtle and not-so-subtle ways, and the situation is compounded by the fact that his partners are staunch supporters of Right to Life, speak for them, and sit on the boards at local and state levels. ...

He has many stories to tell about how women have inspired him with their faith and openness to life often at risk to their own lives, while he inspires them by praying with and for them, and by remaining firm and unyielding in faith issues.

Someone who takes a stand against contraception deserves our support and encouragement, especially since he or she may not get the same treatment from colleagues.

Doctors may unwittingly weaken the physical health of their patients by recommending the Pill. As mentioned earlier, cancer research has identified the Pill as one factor that increases the possibility of many kinds of cancer, including breast cancer. Factors that can *reduce* the risks of breast cancer include: childbearing at an early age, nursing for prolonged periods, and bearing more than one child, according to Dr. Chris Kahlenborn.[6]

If our doctor prescribes contraceptives or sterilizes patients, we can gently share the truth and pray, pray, pray. We should assume the best of our doctor and see him or her as a friend to win more fully to the truth rather than as an enemy to defeat. My Ob/Gyn, Dr. Rogelio Mupas, credits his change of mind and practice to his patients who cared enough about him, and the women he assists, to share the truth with him and pray for him.

Recently, he wrote the following to me: "Our existence, our coming to life, was due to women's unselfish love. They put their lives on the line so children may live. Openness to life with life-giving love will determine the future of humanity."

Healers of the Soul: Priests

In every Catholic wedding, the priest asks for the couple's free consent regarding children: "Will you accept children lovingly from God, and bring them up according to the law of Christ and his Church?"[7] Yet in premarriage counseling and general teaching in the parish, some priests are less than supportive of the Church's teaching about openness to life.

One of my friends gave birth to a fourth child in five years. During the baptism, in front of all the family and friends gathered, the priest said to the couple, "You know, you don't have to do this every year!" It was not meant as a joke; the couple did not know how to respond.

Some priests permit couples to contracept either because they misunderstand the teaching of the Church or they disagree with it. Their seminary training may have been deficient in moral theology, and, once in ministry, they may have been too busy to study much on their own. Or they may understand the issue but dissent from the Church's position on it. This is an untenable position.

The teaching of the Church is clear. As we have noted, in 1930 the papal encyclical *Casti Connubii* was issued to address a variety of concerns raised by the allowance of some contraceptives for serious reasons by the Anglican Church. It declared:

> But no reason, however grave, may be put forward by which anything intrinsically against nature may become conformable to nature and morally good. Since, therefore, the conjugal act is destined primarily by nature for the begetting of children, those who in exercising it deliberately frustrate its natural power and purpose sin against nature and commit a deed which is shameful and intrinsically vicious.[8]

There is no ambiguity on this point.

Whether the priest's lack of clear teaching stems from misunderstanding or dissent, we can offer this book and copies of relevant Church documents so that he is better informed. We should always assume the best and pray hard ahead of time. And we need to double-check our attitude so that we communicate genuine love and respect.

Sometimes a priest is concerned about offending people who are married, since he is not. This is where the priest, in light of his spiritual fatherhood, must focus more on fathering his people than befriending them.

Any good father identifies poison to his children and then removes it; he would never give his children a choice to consume it. Any good priest has to identify contraception as the poison that it is and urge his spiritual children to have nothing to do with it. Just as a father must discipline his children regardless of whether his children will like him, so the priest must teach the truth regardless of the response of his parishioners. (We like to be liked by our children, but true friendship with them is possible only if we take our parenting seriously.)

Some couples do not understand the role of the priest as their spiritual father who is bound by God not to withhold the truth from his people. They communicate rather clearly that in their opinion the priest should not address an issue that does not personally affect him. Of course, faithful marital love *does* affect the priest, because our holiness or sin affects the whole body of Christ.

The teaching of the Church requires priests to speak forthrightly about this issue. *Casti Connubii* specifically addresses priests on this issue:

We admonish, therefore, priests who hear confessions and others who have the care of souls, in virtue of Our supreme authority and in Our solicitude for the salvation of souls, not to allow the faithful entrusted to them to err regarding this most grave law of God; much more, that they keep themselves immune from such false opinions, in no way conniving in them. If any confessor or pastor of souls, which may God forbid, lead the faithful entrusted to him into these errors or should at least confirm them by approval or by guilty silence, let him be mindful of the fact that he must render a strict account to God, the Supreme Judge, for the betrayal of his sacred trust.[9]

This teaching is not a matter of personal opinion but of objective truth.

Silence is not an option, for someone may mistake silence as consent and make decisions dangerous to their soul and their marriage on that basis. "The confessor is bound to admonish penitents regarding objectively grave transgressions of God's law and to ensure that they truly desire absolution and God's pardon with the resolution to re-examine and correct their behavior."[10]

Sometimes a couple approach a priest to marry them in the Church, though they do not really want to live a Catholic marriage. One or both people may be in the midst of a crisis of faith in general. They need to come to faith internally first; only then can they respond with obedience from the heart regarding contraception. At the appropriate time a priest should "remind them in a positive way of the invitation to the sanctity of love, and of the importance of their duties in the area of procreation and the education of children."[11]

We need priests to speak the truth in love. One newlywed couple from Milwaukee, Wisconsin, wrote: "Along with making NFP required in premarital counseling, we need even more priests who are strong enough to teach God's truth about premarital sex."

Faithful priests share the truth, sensitively albeit thoroughly, with those who may not want to hear. Here is the testimony of one couple.

We lived in communist Czechoslovakia, where the Church's teaching was not as freely spread as in the U.S. ("Big" families were history.) After fleeing to West Germany, for the first time in my life I read the Bible. That was my preparation to accept in my heart many changes in our life, even though the price was high. We didn't have a Slovak-speaking priest living near who could guide us or explain [to] us the unclear chapters and verses of the Bible, so we made an appointment with one who lived far from us. We prepared many questions.

He told us about the Church's teaching on openness to life. It was shocking for us to hear it because we were about two months from moving to the USA and we did not know one person there; we did not have a job, car, apartment, or house; we did not speak English; and we heard that we could not use contraception. At that time it was obvious that there are just two ways, and we have to choose one. That helped us to reevaluate our life.

This couple is deeply appreciative that the West German priest did not withhold the truth about openness to life from them, even though it was difficult. Once they understood the truth, they were able to embrace it.

Another mother related the consequence of seeking out the priest who dared to preach on contraception:

Suddenly, I understood that contraception was a physical wall between my husband and myself. Using contraception stifled and broke down our communication; it denied us our dignity. I finally caught a glimpse of what marriage could be when practiced in the light of God's grace. After years of struggling with self-esteem, I realized my place as a woman of God, clothed in his dignity. My husband also saw the light. So after twenty years of marriage, we are practicing NFP. The results are that we are more intimate than ever and our communication has opened up tremendously. I no longer resent him or feel that I am being used. I also won't feel ashamed to talk to our teenage daughter about such matters.

A faithful priest spoke the truth in love, and a family was restored.

Reject the Lie of Abortion

The first method of birth control condemned in *Humanae Vitae* is abortion.

[T]he direct interruption of the generative process already begun and, above all, directly willed and procured abortion, even if for therapeutic reasons, are to be absolutely excluded as licit means of regulating birth.[12]

Not only is this a tragic and sinful choice of unmarried women but also of currently married women. One out of every five women getting an abortion this year will be a married woman, utterly rejecting the fruit of her committed love.[13] A wife and mom from West Covina, California, expressed her sorrow.

I used to feel [abortion] was dictated by situation, whether or not it was appropriate. Now I know it is simply wrong—a quick fix to cover up, which infects our souls. We would have healed faster from losing our child [through adoption] than dealing with the guilt and depression [of abortion].

Often marriages do not survive the assault on the fruit of their love.

One bumper sticker succinctly summarizes the point: "Two victims in every abortion—one dead, one wounded." In fact, each abortion produces a number of casualties, including fathers and grandparents who are not permitted to grieve in the family, either because abortion is acceptable societal practice or because the shame is too great. As one grandmother said, "How can I grieve when they don't?"

As we have noted, some forms of birth control are abortive. The IUD does not inhibit ovulation or prevent sperm from reaching the fertile egg; rather, it renders the uterine lining unable to support life in most instances.

The Pill also acts as an abortifacient some of the time. Besides suppressing ovulation and altering mucus in order to hinder sperm migration, "the progestin component of the combination pill and the progestin-only minipill cause the inner lining of the uterus to become thin and shriveled, unable to support implantation of the embryo (newly fertilized egg)."[14]

Two types of progestins, Norplant® and Depo-Provera®, can be abortive. Neither inhibits ovulation completely; consequently, the altered endometrium prevents implantation so that a fertilized egg, the developing human being, dies. Side effects for both methods include: hair loss, acne, weight gain, headaches, decreased libido, and irregular bleeding (on average as much as a hundred days out of the first year for Norplant users).[15] Other possible side effects for Depo-Provera include increased risks in breast cancer, uterine cancer, osteoporosis, arthritis, and severe fetal abnormalities if a woman gets pregnant while taking "the shot."[16]

Reject the Lie of Sterilization

The next form of contraception addressed in *Humanae Vitae* is sterilization. Equally to be excluded, as the teaching authority of the Church has frequently declared, is direct sterilization, whether perpetual or temporary, whether of the man or of the woman.[17] Permanent forms of sterilization would be tubal ligations and vasectomies. Temporary forms of sterilization would include various forms of the Pill.

What about those who see sterilization as contributing in some way to the whole person? For instance, isn't it good for a couple to enjoy intercourse without the fear of a life-threatening pregnancy?

> Neither can one invoke the principle of totality in this case, the principle which would justify interference with organs for the greater good of the person. Sterility induced as such does not contribute to the person's integral good, properly understood, "keeping things and values in proper perspective." Rather does it damage a person's ethical good, since it deprives subsequent freely-chosen sexual acts of an essential element.[18]

When an act is intrinsically evil, a possible good cannot mitigate against the prohibition. This teaching also provides the basis for answering other societal questions regarding sterilization.

Can sterilization be justified in the case of handicapped or retarded people whom the state deems unfit for bearing children? In the post-Vatican II document *Sterilization in Catholic Hospitals,* we read: "Nor can any public authority justify the imposition of sterilization as being necessary for the common good, since it damages the dignity and inviolability of the human person."[19]

On a recent trip to California, I addressed the issue of dissent from the Church on this teaching. I spoke about our obligation not to use contraception or sterilization, especially under the guise of selecting our doctrines like food in a cafeteria. A woman slipped me this note: "I had already scheduled my sterilization for next week. Will cancel. The cafeteria is *closed.*"

What a blessing for this woman to hear the truth and respond before she made a costly physical and spiritual mistake. Others have not been so fortunate. A woman in Florida shared her story:

> Please warn people that sometimes now doctors do sterilizations differently. After we came to a conviction that we were wrong to have had

my tubes tied, we wanted to undo the damage. I contacted my sur-
geon to get the medical file so that we could proceed. When I said why
I needed the information—to reverse my sterilization—the doctor
explained why that was not possible. He had not tied my tubes; he had
removed them. Nothing was there to restore. We were, and still are,
devastated.

It is too late for this couple to reverse their sterilization. How insidious is
this, that without the couple's knowledge, they signed away permission for
tube removal instead of just having her tubes tied!

Other couples also have experienced devastating effects as a consequence of sterilization. Suzanne recounts her heartbreak: "My husband was
sterilized because he did not want any more children, even though I did.
Eventually we were divorced and our marriage was annulled."

Only God knows how often people have signed away their generative
capacity without knowing it. When we arrived at six in the morning for my
scheduled C-section delivery, there were a number of housekeeping things
to do, among them signing permission papers for surgery. Though it was
early in the morning, I thought I should take the time to read the form
before signing. I will be forever thankful I did.

The form was typed with blanks for the physician, procedure, and my
signature. The correct physician was listed, but on the procedure line I was
stunned to read "repeat Caesarian section *and sterilization.*" Sterilization? I
spoke quickly but with measured tones: "I do *not* give permission for sterilization!"

Scott leapt out of his seat. "Sterilization! Let me see that!" He grabbed
the paper and rapidly read what I had read.

The nurse became flustered and profusely apologized. As she retrieved
the form, she said, "There must be a mistake. I'm so sorry. I'll tear this up
in front of you and get a new form." She exited quickly.

We were incredulous. Human errors occur, but this was not a small error.
How many times might other people have signed away the possibility of
bearing another child without even knowing about it? Fifteen minutes later
my blood pressure was still 150/80!

"You're still really upset about that form, aren't you?" the nurse asked.

"You're darn right I am! I might have given permission for my sterilization without knowing it. Then I'd have tried to conceive again, and only later would have discovered the truth. I wouldn't even have been able to demand a free reversal, since I was the one to sign the form." It was a sobering thought, even in the midst of great joy over the baby's arrival.

Reject the Lie of Contraception

The third category of unlawful ways to regulate births addressed by *Humanae Vitae* is artificial contraception. "Similarly excluded is every action which, either in anticipation of the conjugal act, or in its accomplishment, or in the development of its natural consequences, proposes, whether as an end or as a means, to render procreation impossible."[20] This would include all current forms of barrier method contraception, as well as all sexual practices outside the bond of marriage, where the sperm can be fruitful.

Contraception contributes to the deterioration of marriages in a number of ways. Adultery is far more prominent now than in the 1930s. Contraception enables people to risk having an extramarital affair without fearing the consequences of pregnancy, much as youths avoid pregnancy in premarital affairs. And adultery contributes to the increase in divorces.

Contraception can make women feel used, treated more as objects for lawful sexual intercourse than as persons being loved. Hormonal contraception can make women feel the symptoms of either pregnancy, PMS, or both simultaneously, which can make life together difficult for both husband and wife. Barrier methods of contraception are intrusive in the act of making love, and they are messy. They are also not as reliable as hormonal contraceptives, so there can be more tension about the possibility of "failure"—that is, pregnancy. Enter contestants for the blame game.

A number of modern-day theologians who dissent from this teaching have been outspoken, confusing the laity as to how clear and binding Church teaching has been on sterilization, and, for that matter, contraception. Yet Pope John Paul II declares, "The Church's teaching on contraception does not belong to the category of matter open to free discussion among theologians. Teaching the contrary amounts to leading the moral consciences of spouses into error."[21]

Not only theologians but all Catholics need to understand that teaching on openness to life is not subject to approval by the individual, but rather it is an essential teaching to be affirmed and followed.

Restoration Is Possible

Restoration is always possible. If you have been contracepting, stop. Talk over what you have been reading and praying about with your spouse, for, obviously, this issue involves both of you.

Since contraception is serious sin, don't take it lightly. As soon as possible, go to Confession. The priest can help you sort out your degree of culpability. Do not assume it was not serious sin for you, thus missing this opportunity to get things right with God.

Now is the moment of grace to which you need to respond. Nothing you say will shock the priest; he has heard it all before. Not only will you leave the confessional with sins forgiven; you will also have the sacramental grace you need to continue to make the right choices.

A couple from Richfield, Minnesota, offer this testimony:

In the fall of 1976, I quit the use of the Pill in hopes of again having another baby. By February of 1978 I was still not pregnant. This was the first time we had ever experienced any difficulty achieving a pregnancy. We were becoming quite frustrated.

On Monday, February 20, I [sensed] that I needed to confess the use of birth control pills. I was shocked and fearful—I must have confessed it at some point. After all, I was a good Catholic girl and certainly would have confessed it. By Wednesday I had just about convinced myself I had confessed it, and if I hadn't, it wasn't really my fault if the priest had misdirected us.

That night my husband wanted to know if I had ever confessed the fact we had used birth control pills when they weren't medically necessary. I was devastated. There was no use trying to tell myself I had confessed it. The truth was out. I had not!

We decided right then we'd need to go to Confession on Saturday.

The gravity of the sin was forever implanted in my mind. I begged Jesus to please let me live long enough to go to Confession, as I didn't want to die and go to hell.

By Saturday, I was a nervous wreck, but I knew what we were supposed to do regardless. Thanks to the Lord, the priest was very understanding. This was the Saturday after Ash Wednesday. Our Lent that year began in a profound way. [The next week I conceived.]

That Lent was the most wonderful of my life. I spent most of it in tears, promising the Lord I would never use birth control again. I went to daily Mass and became overwhelmingly aware of the fact that if the only sin ever committed was the one we had done through birth control, Jesus would have still had to die on the cross to save us. The more I realized it, the more I promised him I'd always respect life and let him control it.

The answer the Lord had given to us was "repent." If we had achieved a pregnancy when we first tried, we would possibly never had been given the gift of true repentance, or at least we would not have been open to it. I wish everyone could experience just one Lent like we did. It will always be one of the most important gifts I have received from Jesus, the gift of a repenting heart. We also would have missed the gift of his love and forgiveness for us.

What a powerful testimony of the great grace of God.

Deacon Bob McDonald offers the following three admissions to make in repenting of contraception. "First, I recognize I'm engineering my own marital breakdown. Second, I repent of my self-centeredness and poverty of love. And third, I surrender my entire self to God first and to my spouse."[22]

If you have been sterilized for any other than a medically necessary reason, you also need to go to Confession. The current opinion of moral theologians is that you need only make a sincere act of contrition. You are not required to get a reversal; however, many people have experienced great blessing in their marriages by undoing what they have done. In any case, to minimize the ongoing *benefit* of sterilization, you might consider periodic abstinence as a practice. (Much more about this in chapter 12.)

If you have been involved with an abortion (having one, paying for one, or even taking someone to get one), you need to go to Confession right away. This is serious sin. Don't let the Evil One distract you from repentance by telling you that God cannot forgive you. One great resource is Project Rachel, a postabortion reconciliation network throughout most of the dioceses in the United States, as well as in a few other countries.[23]

Diane from Long Beach, California, recalled the difference the Church made in the aftermath of her abortion: "I had an abortion at age seventeen in 1971. I was grateful my Dad made me go to Confession, and I started volunteering at a crisis pregnancy center. Now I love the Church's teaching. I just wish I would have known about it at the time."

At Franciscan University of Steubenville there is a tomb for unborn babies in which five aborted babies are buried. Cardinal John O'Connor was so moved by this memorial that he returned to New York and established one on the grounds of his seminary. Then he asked the Knights of Columbus to take as their mission the establishing of tombs for the unborn throughout our country.

The Knights have now established hundreds of such memorials, not only in our country but in other countries as well. These tombs are special places for mourning aborted babies. Frequently at our youth conferences at Franciscan University, flowers, rosaries, and baby toys are left atop the tomb. It's beautiful and heartbreaking to see. If you have had an abortion, you may want to find this kind of a special place to grieve, for your loss is real and the Lord wants to bring you comfort.

To embrace the truth about the Church's teaching on openness to life means more than rejecting abortion, sterilization, and contraception, though it means no less. *Humanae Vitae* and subsequent documents call us to lift our vision high, to see the wonder and beauty of reflecting the inner life of the Trinity in our homes and through our bodies as living sacrifices. The Lord will give us the grace we need to be faithful and fruitful.

CHAPTER SEVEN

EMBRACE THE TRUTH IN LOVE

What does it take to live the splendor of the teaching of the Church on matrimony? Faith, hope, and love. Scripture offers us insights that will help these virtues flourish in our lives.

"We Walk by Faith, Not by Sight" (2 Cor 5:7)

A woman from Carmel, Indiana, posed this question: "My husband has decided that our daughter will be our only child because he only makes enough money to afford college education for one child. This is breaking my heart. What can I say to him?"

First, he is presuming a number of things: that his job will continue, that he won't get good raises, that his child will live to be college age, that his child will not so resent the fact that she's never had siblings so she could go to college that she's still unwilling to go, and that the child will never be talented enough or bright enough to earn a scholarship to college.

Though the Catholic Church places great importance on the education of children, and a college education would be a wonderful provision for their future, nowhere does she command us to provide for their college education. Instead, this father has ignored the clear teachings of the Church and disregarded his wife's longing for more children, placing his trust for the future in himself rather than in God.

James 4:13-16 states that only God knows the future. We can plan for the future—in fact, it is prudent to do so—but then we must submit our plans to the Lord. "Commit your way to the Lord; trust in him, and he will act" (Ps 37:5).

We do not know the future, but we know the One who knows the future, and in his faithfulness we place our trust. We have to live God's call God's way. Our faith is rooted in the faithfulness of God our Father; this is simple, but it's not simplistic.

St. Paul reassures the believers in Philippi: "My God will supply every need of yours according to his riches in glory in Christ Jesus" (Phil 4:19). He'll supply our *needs,* it says, not necessarily our *wants.*

Our focus needs to be on God's ability rather than on our inability. We may not have the emotional or financial resources for another child until that child arrives. The promise is not that we will have the needed resources in advance; rather, "Let us then with confidence draw near to the throne of grace, that we may receive mercy and find grace to help in time of need" (Heb 4:16).

Jim from Ann Arbor, Michigan, comes from a large family. He said that his parents' philosophy was to have one child more than they could afford. That way they would always need to trust God to provide, and God always did. As one ancient Indian proverb says, "Each child brings his own bread."

Look at the example of Mary. When the angel of the Lord comes to her, she doesn't say, "Behold, I am sufficient to raise the Son of God. I have what it takes." Rather, "Mary said, 'Behold, I am the handmaid of the Lord; let it be done to me according to your word'" (Lk 1:38). Mary does not say she is adequate to the task, but rather, she is available. That is what God asks of us.

God doesn't ask us to bear and raise children all by ourselves. Rather, he asks us, "Are you available? Will *you* say, 'Behold, I am the handmaid (or the manservant) of the Lord; let it be done to me according to Thy word'?"

Sometimes we are painfully aware of our inadequacies when we consider having a baby. St. Paul reminds us, "No temptation has overtaken you that is not common to man. God is faithful and he will not let you be tempted beyond your strength, but with the temptation will also provide a way of escape, that you may be able to endure it" (1 Cor 10:13). God promises he will not allow us to be tempted beyond what we can bear; he will be with us and will assist us.

It is not a matter of believing more in ourselves. We do not muster courage to tackle this mission by our own resources. Rather, we acknowledge that we do not possess what it takes to build our family as a house of God, although God does. We know that as a fruit of the Spirit, faith can grow.

Four women from North Carolina once came to our home for a visit.

Each one had a question bearing on openness to life. Their situations included a newlywed of six months, a woman with three young boys and a husband who was out of work, a woman with infertility who had already adopted one child, and a mother with seven children who had blood pressure problems.

As I left for a holy hour, they jokingly asked me to ask Jesus if any of them should have a baby. I teasingly replied, "I don't need to ask; I already know the answer: Yes, yes, yes, and yes. But I'll ask Jesus anyway." We all laughed, and I left.

When I was gazing at the Blessed Sacrament, I thought, *How presumptuous of me, Lord, to decide beforehand what you would say to these precious women. Do you have a word for me to take back to them?* I had the strongest sense that His answer was, "Keep your eyes fixed on me."

When I returned home, the women asked if I had a word for them. "As a matter of fact," I began, "I think I do. It's not 'yes,' as I said earlier. It's 'Keep your eyes fixed on Jesus. Whatever you do, do it in faith.'"

Jesus' words for me to share were also the words for me to hear. One year later I met up with the four women in Charlotte—and *I* was the only one who was pregnant!

"Character Produces Hope" (Rom 5:4)

Hope is seeing God's vision for building the kingdom, one person at a time. The *Catechism* exhorts us to generosity in our families as one of the ways we contribute to the kingdom. God wants to build his kingdom through us, not so much by influencing crowds of people with a great speech, as by our day-in, day-out obedience to God—as author Eugene Peterson has called it, a "long obedience in the same direction." It is faithfulness in our marriage that yields the rich fruit of godly offspring, as we noted earlier.

Hope is the God-given ability to look at our ragtag collection of little ones and see part of the army of God. It is the sense that God knows what he is doing in calling us to this incredible task of changing the world one diaper at a time. And hope is what God produces in us through trials that are met with endurance.

To realize the hope that God has placed in our hearts, we must rely on his strength to accomplish his will his way: "But they who wait for the Lord shall renew their strength, they shall mount up with wings like eagles, they shall run and not be weary, they shall walk and not faint" (Is 40:31). Even when we feel drained of physical strength, God can give us the strength to soar.

When we feel weak, we should resist the temptation to discouragement, remembering Jesus' words to St. Paul, "My grace is sufficient for you, for my power is made perfect in weakness," and St. Paul's response, "I will all the more gladly boast of my weaknesses, that the power of Christ may rest upon me" (2 Cor 12:9). The question is not whether we are strong enough for God to use us, but rather, *are we weak enough?* His power is perfected in our weakness.

As we grow in grace, we grow in the fruit of the Holy Spirit. The more we grow spiritually, the more love, joy, peace, patience, kindness, goodness, faithfulness, gentleness, and self-control his Spirit produces in our lives (see Gal 5:22-23). Year by year, we *will* grow—we *will* become more like our Lord.

Someone once said to me, "I don't know how you have the patience for six kids." It has developed over time, and it is being developed in me. I did not start out with the patience I have, and I hope God will produce more in me, for their sakes. I believe he will.

God forms our character sometimes through the challenge of being fertile and sometimes through the challenge of infertility. We know couples who had one or two children effortlessly and then experienced tremendous difficulty conceiving again. In addition, some couples have been open to children for years without ever conceiving.

One friend told us at Christmas that she was having her second baby the next August, a boy. I was amazed; how could she know already? She wasn't pregnant yet, but since she got pregnant the first month she tried for the first child, she was quite confident that would happen again.

She planned to get pregnant in January with a strategy they had learned to conceive a boy. I asked her to let me know when the baby came. Fifteen years later, after much heartache, they finally conceived again.

Another friend bought an expensive winter maternity coat, telling me it was worth the expense because she would be sure to have all her babies in winter. However, her next two children were born in spring and summer.

Someone else will have to benefit from that nice coat.

No matter how many children we have, none of us know for sure that we will ever have another baby. Being open to a new life does not automatically result in new life. Our fertility is a fragile gift.

Even our struggle to conceive, offering him the suffering as we wait and hope, is a part of building the kingdom. Nothing is wasted when we offer it to God.

> More than that, we rejoice in our sufferings, knowing that suffering produces endurance, and endurance produces character, and character produces hope, and hope does not disappoint us, because God's love has been poured into our hearts through the Holy Spirit which has been given to us.
>
> ROMANS 5:3-5

If we offer our sufferings to God, we can grow in hope rather than discouragement or despair. In a mystical way we can also strengthen the whole Church.

"The Greatest of These Is Love" (1 Cor 13:13)

God is the life-loving Giver and life-giving Lover who beckons us to follow him. God loves life; he is Being itself. He is the One who has called all creation into being and given it its life. And he loves the creation he has made. In addition, God loves giving life through his creation, empowering married couples to imitate him in giving themselves to each other, and in so doing to create new life. This is a circle of love and life that flows from God through the family to create a civilization of love.

Charity is the key. "Charity is the soul of holiness.... Charity makes renunciation more acceptable, lightens the spiritual struggle, and renders more joyous the gift of self."[1] Charity needs to be the guiding principle for all of our interactions in the family so that we build up the individuals as well as the whole family at the same time.

Prayer in the family, for the family, and by the family strengthens our intergenerational communion of love: from God the Father, through faithful generations, to the present family, with the goal of our return to the Father. The communion of conjugal love leads to the community of love of the family. The communion of persons becomes the communion of saints.

For a family to be a civilization of love, the members need to celebrate life at each stage, being open to new life as well as welcoming older relatives from our extended families into the inner circle of our nuclear families. Pope John Paul II has observed: *"Families today have too little 'human' life.* There is a shortage of people with whom to create and share the common good; and yet that good, by its nature, demands to be created and shared with others."[2] As the fathers of the Second Vatican Council insisted, for a culture to be a civilization of love, it must order its laws "to preserve the holiness and to foster the natural dignity of the married state and its superlative value."[3]

We have been created by Love for love. In giving ourselves to our spouse in total self-donating love, we find ourselves.

> Then Jesus told his disciples, "If any man would come after me, let him deny himself and take up his cross and follow me. For whoever would save his life will lose it, but whoever loses his life for my sake will find it. For what will it profit a man, if he gains the whole world and forfeits his life?"
>
> MATTHEW 16:24-26

Self-denial, embracing the cross, and following Christ are not lofty ideals as much as part of the daily vocation of marriage. All Christians have been called to the life of the cross, not just nuns and priests. As a wife from Greeley, Colorado, says, "Marriage is one of the ways to follow Christ; therefore, we should expect challenges (crosses) and great joy if we live our marriage faithfully."

Recently Pope John Paul II beatified a twentieth-century Italian mother named Gianna Beretta Molla. Blessed Gianna discovered, midpregnancy, that she had a large ovarian cyst. Her doctor recommended an immediate abortion. Since she herself was a physician, she understood that her refusal to abort the baby put her own life at risk. A few days after her baby's birth, after much pain and suffering, she died of septic peritonitis. The pope said this about her:

A woman of exceptional love, an outstanding wife and mother, she gave witness in her daily life to the demanding values of the Gospel. By holding up this woman as an exemplar of Christian perfection, we would like to extol all those high-spirited mothers of families who give themselves completely to their family, who suffer in giving birth, who are prepared for every labor and every kind of sacrifice, so that the best they have can be given to others.[4]

Blessed Gianna sacrificed her life so that her daughter could live. What a testimony to her children!

John Kippley, cofounder with his wife, Sheila, of the Couple to Couple League, encourages people to tell their children and grandchildren: "The Church's teaching is in your best interest—in this life, in this marriage, as well as for the next life."

Jesus gave himself for me, for you. In exchange, we are to give ourselves to him, including our bodies. We are temples for the Holy Spirit to indwell. "Do you not know that your body is a temple of the Holy Spirit within you, which you have from God? You were bought with a price. So glorify God in your body" (1 Cor 6:19, 20).

This is not a suggestion; it is a command. We have been purchased at a dear price, the life of the Son of God. Now we imitate his sacrificial life by laying down our lives for him. As St. John concluded, "We love, because he first loved us" (1 Jn 4:19).

Offer Practical Help

We must not hold back the truth from others because of fear. Jesus' words to believers were these: *"If* you continue in my word, you are truly my disciples, and you will know the truth, and the truth will make you free" (Jn 8:31-32). Our task is not to set people straight but to set people free!

People need to be challenged by our words *and* our actions to be faithful—and we all know which speak louder. Though some people fear that obedience to the Lord on openness to life means bondage, the opposite is true. Let's share the truth with joy!

Jesus told his disciples: "Come to me, all who labor and are heavy laden, and I will give you rest. Take my yoke upon you, and learn from me; for I am gentle and lowly in heart, and you will find rest for your souls. For my yoke is easy, and my burden is light" (Mt 11:28-30).

How can that be? When we live in the way God intends us to live, as sacrificial lovers, obedience is not burdensome. What *is* burdensome is rejecting the truth about God's design for marriage and then trying to have a blessed relationship.

It is not enough for us to know the truth and share it. We must speak the truth with a heart full of love and compassion. Rather than standing over others in judgment because of the poor (and often uninformed) decisions they have made, we are to come alongside them and offer prayer support and practical help.

A couple from Rochester, New York, had a life-changing experience through faithful Catholics involved in their local parish and parish school. "We reevaluated contraceptive use due to my husband's renewed interest in the faith and my increased contact with those who loved and practiced the faith."

Our hope is to encourage a renewed commitment to live the truth. Like Mary, who accompanied our Lord as he carried the cross, we want to accompany our family and friends as they take up the cross the Lord has given them, especially as they are open to life.

Bear One Another's Burdens

It is not enough for us to remind each other of the Church's teaching on openness to life and then merely observe each other from the sidelines, judging whether or not others are being faithful to this teaching. Rather, we have to be involved in the ongoing struggles that faithfulness to Christ's teaching means in each other's lives.

Perhaps that is why our marriage vows are said publicly instead of privately. The people who witness our commitment to each other, including our pledge to be open to children and teach them the faith, need to support us both by holding us accountable and by offering practical help. The Church does not tell us to be open to new life and then leave us there; she beckons us to receive strength and assistance from the whole body of Christ.

As the body of Christ we need to take the teaching on procreation so seriously that we ask ourselves, how can *we* enable young couples to be open to new life? What concrete things can we do to assist others so that *they* witness with their lives to the world the relationship between Christ and his Church?

St. Paul gives this challenge: "Bear one another's burdens, and so fulfill the law of Christ" (Gal 6:2). This too is not a suggestion but a command. Children are not burdens; however, much involved in the care of children can be burdensome, such as extra laundry, lack of sleep, lack of time to clean house, or lack of a break for prayer or fun. It may not take much service to help young couples keep their hearts open to each other and to the Lord. We can be powerful channels of grace to young families who want to live authentic Catholic lives *if we offer practical assistance.*

Mary's Service to Elizabeth

Our Blessed Mother is an example of this kind of ministry. At the same time Mary found out that she was about to conceive Jesus, she learned that her kinswoman Elizabeth was expecting as well. She immediately went to be with Elizabeth; she did not hesitate. She wanted to share in Elizabeth's joy, and she wanted to share her own joy with a kindred spirit.

Instead of focusing on her own needs in pregnancy, Mary wanted to serve (just as Jesus later said he came to serve rather than be served; see Mt 20:28). She may have had nausea or been very tired on her three-day journey by donkey to Ain Karim, Elizabeth's home. Yet she knew that Elizabeth, now six months pregnant, would need her.

Elizabeth was overjoyed to see Mary. Even Elizabeth's unborn child, John the Baptist, leapt in the womb with holy joy at the greeting of the Messiah's mother. Mary loved Elizabeth throughout the last three months of her pregnancy by bringing Jesus to her and by many acts of service.

Ministry to Moms

When families are young and growing, with many demands on Mom, there is often little extra money for help with babysitting or housecleaning. Many times in our early marriage we could not afford both a babysitter and ice cream cones for a date. But we still needed time out alone to be refreshed for the challenges of the next day. Sometimes friends offered free sitting and made our dates possible.

In imitation of Mary, a number of college students at the Franciscan University volunteer three hours per week, free of charge, to young, growing Catholic families in what we call Ministry to Moms. This ministry is a dynamic expression of mutual love and support. The students offer a wide variety of services, tailored for a particular family. In exchange the students may do their laundry while working and are included in a weekly family meal.

Everyone benefits, as is typical with sacrificial love. The students see godly women in action, women who are too busy managing their families and homes to hang out on campus. The students, many of whom have left young siblings at home, have an opportunity to be with little ones. The children in the family get to have a *big sister*. And mothers receive help they need without having to budget for it. This kind of practical help has been an encouragement to all involved.

One young mother in our area, Teri, was having an extremely difficult pregnancy. She had severe vomiting that lasted from four to seven hours each day. Yes, *hours!* Her husband was going to school full time and working long hours, so she had to care for their two-year-old most of the day and several evenings alone. A Franciscan University household of young women (similar to a faith-based sorority) volunteered to come to Teri's home three evenings a week, for three hours, to make dinner for the daughter, play with her, and get her to bed. They did this for more than a month, free of charge.

These women made an enormous difference in helping this young mother stave off depression and make it through the toughest experience of her life. They lived out these verses: "We who are strong ought to bear with the failings of the weak, and not to please ourselves; let each of us please his neighbor for his good, to edify him" (Rom 15:1-2). We need to do more than tell others the truth about the Catholic Church's teaching; we need to be willing to be part of the solution to their dilemmas.

For instance, sometimes emotional support is needed more than financial assistance. Anne from Fairview Park, Ohio, suggests inviting large families for a visit or a meal or offering to host a support group for mothers of large families. Often larger families are excluded from hospitality because of their size; people are intimidated by the thought of hosting a large group.

When we had only three small children, we began to notice a decline in invitations from smaller families. One woman invited only Scott and me, because, as she said, "I don't know how to adjust the recipe to include three children." Had she asked, I could have told her that they ate very little.

Larger families, on the other hand, seemed quite comfortable including us—the more, the merrier. What a blessing to experience larger families in various social settings: backyard barbeques, baptism and First Communion celebrations, and Sunday brunches. Being with other large families helped us envision ourselves as a larger family. We are most grateful.

Older Women Train the Younger Women

St. Paul commands older women to teach the younger women, "what is good, and so train the young women to love their husbands and children, to be sensible, chaste, domestic, kind, and submissive to their husbands, that the word of God may not be discredited" (Ti 2:3-5). Are older women looking for opportunities to do that? Are women in their middle years preparing to do that? And are younger women praying about receiving that ministry from an older woman?

Older women who mentor younger women provide a vital ministry. Whether or not older women offer to mentor or younger women respond to mentoring may make the difference in whether or not the Word of God is discredited. Though many of us do not live geographically close to our mothers, grandmothers, and other older women in our family, we still can and should learn from older women. We need mentors.

Meanwhile, older women who do not live near their daughters or daughters-in-law should still look for opportunities to teach younger women. They have gathered so much lived wisdom that the young need. When we pray about it, the Lord can show us those with whom we can have a type of spiritual mother-daughter or older sister-younger sister relationship, depending on how far apart we are in age.

One of my desires, when I am older and my children are older, is to dedicate one day each week in service to four families, two hours per family. That is not an overwhelming commitment. But I know it could make an enormous difference in a number of lives.

Our society encourages older people who have learned how to live selflessly in raising their families to have a selfish mentality. A current bumper sticker reads, "I'm spending my grandchildren's inheritance." There's nothing wrong with enjoying the fruit of our labors, but shouldn't we remember the proverb: "A good man leaves an inheritance to his children's children, but the sinner's wealth is laid up for the righteous" (Prv 13:22)?

There is no such thing as retirement in Christian service. If you are older, you have graduated from the school of involuntary service to the school of voluntary service. Galatians 6:9-10 gives this admonition: "And let us not grow weary in well-doing, for in due season we shall reap, if we do not lose heart. So then, as we have opportunity, let us do good to all men, and especially to those who are of the household of faith."

Notice that doing good is not limited to relatives; we are to make the "household of faith," fellow Christians, a priority. Are we noticing the needs around us? What are we doing to assist families so that they grow in obedience?

When many of their friends were leaving their families in the New York City area to retire to Florida, one couple felt pressured to follow suit. Yet they explained to their friends that they wanted to stay near their married children. They wanted to support their marriages and family life. The response was ridicule: "Get on with your own lives!"

The grandmother said to me, "Yes, the warmer climate would be nice, but we have relationships with our children, in-laws, and grandchildren we could never have had if we had moved away. We help teach them in their home schools and we share the faith together."

Let me be clear: I am not suggesting that grandmothers should be providing day-care for their grandchildren. (If grandmothers work out that arrangement with their children, that is their choice.) I believe there is an essential difference between grandparenting and parenting. Children need their mothers to mother them, and they need their grandmothers and grandfathers in a different and special kind of relationship.

One grandmother in my area named Margaret bore ten children and now has over fifty grandchildren. She has the gentlest and kindest of ways. For years she has lived with different adult children and helped the families. She has gone from home to home assisting with homeschooling, baking something to leave for dinner, and buying little gifts so that each grandchild knows that she thought of him or her individually.

Her children bought her a home, and almost every day the yard is filled with grandchildren playing. She is so humble (she would probably be mortified to know I used her for an example), but she has blessed me from a distance as I watch a mother and grandmother who is so sacrificial and so beloved. She has taught me much, and I trust she is mentoring her daughters and daughters-in-law well.

In contrast to Margaret, there are older women who are vocal in their rejection of the Catholic Church's position on openness to life. A mother from San Antonio, Texas, writes:

My family is Catholic; however, my mother strongly discourages my brother and me from having "too many children ... too close in age.... It's child abuse because you don't have time to spend with them." This hurts me very much. I think she would even support me if I did use contraception. I feel this viewpoint is far from the Catholic Church but sadly is a majority opinion among many church members.

These differences in convictions can be very difficult to discuss.

Some grandparents are not sure they want the role. Several friends were rebuffed by their mothers when they requested assistance that was *not* daycare. Here are a few actual responses to young mothers.

"I've put in my time," one grandmother vented. Put in time? We "put in time" in school detention, in chores we don't want to do, and in prison. Now is the time to get to enjoy these precious grandchildren.

Another woman thought out loud, "I'm not really into the grandmother thing." Some thoughts are not worth sharing. We do not have to grandmother the same way anyone else does, but these children are to be prized as jewels in our crown.

"I've raised my kids; you raise yours," retorted one woman to her daughter. Of course, grandparenting is not about raising our grandchildren, but we all know testimonies of the impact of godly grandparents on grandchildren. Let's not miss the opportunity.

"I've come to help you with this first baby, but after this, you're on your own," asserted a grandmother who had had eight children of her own.

Are older people in our society forgetting the profound privilege that is theirs if they have been blessed with grandchildren?

We must not let selfishness creep back in after so much has been uprooted through our years of parenting. It is one thing to regret the physical limitations we may have to lift children or care for them; it's another to refuse to mother the mother, our own daughter or daughter-in-law. If we are insecure about our ability to grandparent well, we need to remember who gave us the grace, strength, insight, and wisdom to parent in the first place. The Lord will show us how to pray for them, how to mentor our adult children, and how to grandparent in such a way that we contribute to the civilization of love in our larger family circle.

Go back to the truth about children: They are only and always a blessing. If our children are generous with the Lord and each other so that we get to be grandparents, we need to receive those children as the blessings they are. We must thank the Lord for his kindness to us and ask him what he wants us to do as grandparents. We should never underestimate the power of the prayers and love we offer as grandparents, even if we live far away.

Perhaps we struggle with the fact that we were not model parents ourselves. We must remember that the grace of God covers a multitude of sins. Children are a tremendously forgiving lot. We need to ask for forgiveness and begin our friendship anew. Grandparenting can be like a second chance.

An older couple from Ohio offered several kinds of help.

I baby-sit so they can get a break—no one offered this to me. We encourage dads to "bond" with their babies at delivery and to help with their newborns. We help financially, if we can. We pick out articles for them to read, and most of all, we pray. We keep telling them how awesome it is to have the children.

Another couple from California said something similar about assisting couples who are not their children:

We baby-sit whenever asked. We help in housing, errands, and such whenever we sense a need. We help them financially. We pray for them. We helped one man go to computer school. We helped three ladies with part-time work. We support and encourage them always and love them all dearly. We wish we could do more.

Practical support may even make the difference between life and death, as Mary from the Chicago area discovered:

My friends and I started Care and Counseling in Dawners Crane, Illinois, to offer girls with unplanned pregnancies an alternative to abortion. We found over and over the girls were afraid and felt alone and helpless. We found families who wanted to adopt or helped them keep their babies. It altered my complacency in regard to not speaking up and protecting women in trouble.

Sometimes people want to help families but they do not know what to do. The appendix at the back of this book may help. It contains a list of suggestions for meeting a variety of needs of mothers with young children. It is divided into a number of critical times when a particular kind of help might be best.

Whatever your strategy, check with the mother first to be sure your offering is helpful in her particular situation.

Emotional Support and Friendship

One young mother felt like a failure as she observed a mother of five children in her neighborhood.

When I had my first child I was overwhelmed with how time-consuming parenting was. I had a neighbor who would walk down the street at ten in the morning (I was hardly dressed by then) with five kids in tow looking like a million bucks. One day I stopped her and asked, "How do you do it? One takes my every moment."

Totally without patronizing, she said, "Oh, I was the same way. You'll be fine."

It was so encouraging.

Another older mother put it this way: "One child took all of my time; the rest could take no more."

Sometimes young mothers just need to hear that others faced similar struggles and lived to tell the tale. Other times they need a listening ear, someone who will take their concerns to prayer.

Occasionally, my sister and I have called each other to "set the alarm." That's our code phrase for requesting concentrated prayer that day. We pray for each other, set the timer to go off in an hour, and then pray again when the timer goes off. Then we reset the timer and do it again. Throughout that difficult day we know we have someone who is praying often and very specifically for us.

Couples have real concerns that can be addressed: lack of money; how to manage money on a budget; fears about pregnancy and delivery; fears the baby will alter their relationship; postpartum blues or even depression; concerns about being good parents. We can offer them suggestions, support, sympathy, and prayers.

We can also offer information about organizations ready to offer practical help if the mother is on bed rest. Sidelines, for example, is "a national organization that supports women on bed rest due to pregnancy complications. Each patient is assigned a phone support person (volunteer) who has also been through bed rest."[5]

Sometimes we can forget how much our older children have grown since our last pregnancy. They can be so helpful. Once I was pregnant at the same time as both my sisters. My younger sister (expecting number two) was half joking and half complaining to our other sister (expecting number six) and me (expecting number five), "You guys have so much help!"

"Yes," I rejoined quickly, "but we *grew* it!" Now she is experiencing the joy of her fourth child with lots of homegrown help of her own.

Joanne, mother of nine, suggests, "When someone is pregnant, be very positive and supportive no matter what number child it is." Each child should have baby showers; everyone is worthy of celebration! As another mom put it, "Rejoice with other parents at every new birth. Give gifts and offer prayers."

There is a sense in which our experiences are common ones, no matter how unique they may seem. When I stress out about some aspect of pregnancy or impending delivery, Scott begins a mantra with which I am now very familiar, "Thinner women have done this before. Fatter women ... taller women ... shorter women ... younger women ... older women ... " Somehow it helps me to remember how many millions of women have survived the ordeal.

The Sacredness of Motherhood

Historically, motherhood has been upheld as a noble task. Today, that work is ignored in some circles, as if anyone could be a child's caregiver. Or motherhood is denigrated as a waste of time and talent. Pope John Paul II said of motherhood, *"That work should be acknowledged and deeply appreciated."*[6] He went on to say that motherhood is Mary's highest calling, higher than any of her titles, such as Queen of the Universe, Queen of Apostles, or Queen of Angels.

Mary is a wonderful example for us as mothers. We need to treat our children with the same love and respect that our Blessed Mother showed her Son. One time I had a powerful experience living this truth.

Scott and I were in a hotel the night before giving speeches at a major conference where thousands of people were expected to be in attendance. We had Joseph with us, since he was still nursing. My only opportunity to work on my talk had been after the baby went to bed.

When I finished the talk preparation at about 2:30 A.M., he awoke. I calmed my panicked heart with the thought that a little milk would put him right back to sleep. Scarcely had my head touched the pillow, and he began to cry again. We repeated this scenario about three more times.

Finally, I was really panicked and exasperated. He began to cry again, and I leapt out of bed in anger. In a flash, the Lord spoke to my heart and said, "Pick him up like you would pick up Jesus."

I realized how misplaced my anger was. He was just a little baby in need of his mother, not an inconvenience for a speaker. I picked him up so gently, with great love and gratitude for the gift that he is, thinking about Jesus as a baby.

And guess what happened? He went right back to sleep, and the sleep that I got that night was good enough to do what I needed to do the next day.

Joseph Cardinal Mindszenty wrote this tribute to motherhood:

The Most Important Person on earth is a mother. She cannot claim the honor of having built Notre Dame Cathedral. She need not. She has built something more magnificent than any cathedral—a dwelling for an immortal soul, the tiny perfection of her baby's body. ...

The angels have not been blessed with such a grace. They cannot share in God's creative miracle to bring new saints to heaven. Only a human mother can. Mothers are closer to God the Creator than any other creature; God joins forces with mothers in performing this act of creation....

What on God's good earth is more glorious than this: to be a mother?[7]

What a beautiful description of this noble call.

We must treasure the time we have right now with little ones underfoot. These *are* the good old days we will remember in the future! This time of intensive care for the children will go faster than we think; ask any older person. Then we will watch them go out the door in search of their own adult adventures.

We have a unique relationship with these particular children that only we can have. God is the one who has decided that we are to parent them; he does not make mistakes. Personality and temperament differences notwithstanding, we are right for each other.

We have to be careful not to miss special opportunities to mother these children in our search for meaningful work. For me, there is no work more meaningful or rewarding than being the mother of Michael, Gabriel, Hannah, Jeremiah, Joseph, and David; there is no more important book to write than the living epistles of my children.[8]

To invest ourselves in this calling of motherhood means to die to some of our dreams and to let God resurrect them in another form. Instead of singing in the choir, my mom sang to and with us. Instead of teaching a lot of Bible studies when we were small, my mom taught us.

There are dreams the Lord has asked me to set aside, for a time, so that I can give more of myself to my young ones. And we must remember that the older ones still need us, too. Sometimes their needs for meaningful conversations are even greater as they sort through how to maintain and develop their own faith-transformed thinking despite the pressure to cultural conformity on so many issues.

Fr. Dominic from Ghana once told me that the word in his native language for "mother" is *obaatan,* which means "woman who collects dirt." What a beautiful phrase to summarize so much of what we do: we change dirty diapers; we sweep dirt out of our homes; we clean dirt off clothes; we bathe our children and wash their hands before a meal; we wash out their wounds before we kiss them; and we help clean up the relational mess when reconciliation is necessary between father and child or between siblings.

My favorite Mother's Day card came to my mom from my brother. It said: "Happy Mother's Day. Just want you to know I forgive you for all the times you wiped your spit on my face!" (Don't we all do that!)

Haven't you ever wondered why children always give us, their mothers, the trash, even if they have to reach over Dad to give it to us? It is because we are women who collect dirt. Mothers reflect the work of the Holy Spirit in cleansing and "coming clean" or making a good Confession. We bring order out of chaos. We help our husbands and children get a fresh start on the day. What a joy!

Like Mary, we need time for reflection, to ponder in our hearts the amazing things God teaches us through our motherhood and how he uses us in those whom we mother physically and spiritually. We should take advantage of evenings of recollection, retreats, praying the rosary and daily Mass. Remember St. Therese's thought: it is not great things we do for God as much as small things done with great love.

IV.

DOES GOD'S DESIGN FOR OUR MARRIAGE INCLUDE ONE MORE SOUL?

CHAPTER EIGHT

NATURAL FAMILY PLANNING (NFP)

When Scott and I changed from using contraception to practicing Natural Family Planning, we experienced other changes as well. Each of us had a greater respect for the part the other played in the life-giving power of the act of marriage: Scott's life-giving seed, my life-nurturing womb. We had a greater sense of awe at the beauty of God's design in and through us.

Since every act of marriage was now open to life, we thought much more about the possibility of pregnancy than ever before. We had not previously noticed the pattern God had designed in me. My deepest desire for Scott was when I ovulated, the very time we were abstaining. This reinforced the idea of a month-to-month decision. Did we really want to wait?

Initially, when we told family and friends of our change from birth control to NFP, we were told we were foolish; we were *risking* pregnancy. We were amazed! We realized that all of us, though we were Christians, had bought into the cultural mindset that pregnancy was a *risk*. What a negative thought!

What kinds of images does the word "risk" connote? We *risk* financial loss in the stock market. We *risk* possible disaster that a parachute will not open when we jump out of a plane. We *risk* infection following an accident or surgery.

How could the joy and blessing of a new human being–a soul to exist for all eternity–be thought of in such terms? Rather, we should speak of the *possibility* of pregnancy or the *opportunity* for pregnancy.

Shortly after our decision to switch, I was present for a lecture on forms of contraception as part of my seminary "Marriage and Family" class. The professor included "rhythm" but not Natural Family Planning in his list. I was surprised. He concluded with the joke, "What do you call people who use rhythm? Parents!"

While the class laughed heartily, I tried to think about how I could engage him during the break. With my heart pounding, I approached the professor, asking why he had not mentioned Natural Family Planning. He said he had not heard of anything besides rhythm. I assured him they were not the same thing. Then he asked me to share for ten minutes after the break with the class what I had told him. Nothing like being put on the spot!

I introduced the class to NFP. I clarified that rhythm was based on a set formula for all women regardless of the length of their cycles or the day they ovulated. That was why it had not worked very well.

However, I informed them, now we have much more information about how a woman's body works, how signs such as basal temperature and mucus changes throughout a woman's cycle reflected chemical changes that prepared for or followed ovulation. That information helps people to know when to try for a baby or when to abstain in order to postpone a pregnancy. In this approach, any act of marriage remains open to life.

There was an amazing response from the class. Many people were genuinely interested in something that sounded so positive, natural, and simple. It was the first of many opportunities to articulate a view about the marital embrace different from what evangelicals and, I discovered later, many Catholics had heard.

What Is NFP?

Natural Family Planning is a method of identifying the signs of fertility and infertility in a woman for the purpose of making conception more or less likely. Since a man is typically fertile all the time, the focus is on identifying the woman's time of fertility, thereby discerning the time of mutual fertility for the couple.

Every act of marriage is to be open to life. That does not mean that we have a moral obligation to have every baby we possibly can. Nursing, for instance, is highly recommended, though it can cause many months of amenses. Nor are we limited in our use of the act of marriage to times of potential fruitfulness; for God has built into the overall cycle of a woman times of temporary and, eventually, permanent infertility.

It *does* mean that every act of marriage is not to have its life-generating faculty thwarted. To postpone pregnancy can be a good end, given criteria we will discuss later; however, the end cannot justify any means. The means have to be licit as well as the end. NFP *is* licit because when we use it, every act of marriage continues to be open to life.

NFP is the Lord's provision through the teaching of the Church for the regulation of births *for serious reasons*. As *Humanae Vitae* notes:

> If, then, there are serious motives to space out births, which derive from the physical or psychological conditions of husband and wife, or from external conditions, the Church teaches that it is then licit to take into account the natural rhythms immanent in the generative functions, for the use of marriage in the infecund periods only, and in this way to regulate birth without offending the moral principles which have been recalled earlier.[1]

Note that *Humanae Vitae* respects *both* spouses' conditions, while making it clear that NFP must not be used as a way of refusing to bear life.

During times of mutual fertility and with the agreement of both the man and the woman, a couple abstains from the marital act for the purpose of not getting pregnant. At the same time, they are to follow the example of a couple from Round Rock, Texas: "Sexual intimacy has always been open to life. With every act we ask each other, 'Are you open to life?' even if it's during a time of postponement."

Pope John Paul II teaches:

> It is not possible to practice natural methods as a "licit" variation of the decision to be closed to life, which would be substantially the same as that which inspires the decision to use contraceptives: only if there is a basic openness to fatherhood and motherhood, understood as collaboration with the Creator, does the use of natural means become an integrating part of the responsibility for love and life.[2]

NFP involves abstaining from the act of marriage periodically. However, this kind of abstaining is not what St. Paul condemns as "pretentions of liars.... For everything created by God is good, and nothing is to be rejected if it is received with thanksgiving; for then it is consecrated by the word of God and prayer" (1 Tm 4:1-5).

The act of marriage is good. But a temporary fast (like that from food) can also be good. St. Paul recognizes the validity of abstaining for prayerful reasons (see 1 Cor 7:5), with the caution that a prolonged sexual fast could give an opportunity for temptation by the Evil One.

In recent years, scientists have developed NFP based on information about a woman's fertility cycle.

The two most popular modern methods of Natural Family Planning are the sympto-thermal method and the ovulation method. Both of these methods are based on an awareness of a woman's present signs of fertility or infertility. Thus, they are both a far cry from Calendar Rhythm, which was based only on past cycle history.

The sympto-thermal method makes use of changes in a woman's cervical mucus pattern and changes in her basal temperature pattern, and some women also record physical changes that occur in the cervix. These signs of fertility and infertility are used in a cross-checking way.[3]

The ovulation method, developed by Drs. John and Lyn Billings in Australia, teaches women how to evaluate their cervical mucus for signs of fertility. In 1976, Dr. Hilgers and associates built upon the Billings' work to develop the Creighton Model Natural Family Planning System. "This method, being based on the presence or absence of the cervical mucus discharge, is based on the system of very sensitive *biomarkers*. These include the menstrual flow and other bleeding episodes, dry days and days when mucus is present."[4] Women chart carefully and, with the help of trained professionals, evaluate their reproductive health.

The sympto-thermal method combines several ways of examining the signs of fertility (basal temperature, mucus patterns, and cervix patterns), giving a couple information from several sources on which to base their decisions. However, in developing countries where thermometers might be a luxury item, the ovulation method (mucus pattern analysis only) has been taught very successfully. Both methods rely on careful recording of information gathered. Both methods work well.

When people use NFP correctly and consistently, they acquire useful information either to achieve pregnancy or to postpone one. One couple from Milwaukee, Wisconsin, began marriage using NFP "in order to conceive. An NFP instructor gave me tips on how to insure my chances of conception. I followed the advice and conceived our first child the next month. I married at the age of thirty-six—I had no time to waste."

A couple from Wheat Ridge, Colorado, shared a similar story:

We began trying for a baby (and calling it just that!) on the wedding night. We're both from large families (by today's standards) and wanted to have a large family. [We used NFP] to find out when would be the best times to try for pregnancy—not to avoid it! It has made me very aware of my wife's biology. And my wife says it has helped her to appreciate the unity of husband and wife and God's participation in the marital act. When we were married—both of us for the first time—she was twenty-eight and I was forty. We were both more than ready to start a family.

A couple from Los Angeles, California, agrees: "We only practice NFP to try each month to determine our best time to conceive."

More and more couples experiencing at least temporary infertility are taking NFP classes and discovering what a helpful tool charting can be. In fact, often doctors can offer only limited assistance until the couple has at least six months worth of charts.

When couples use NFP to postpone pregnancy, they experience a 99 percent effective rate.[5] This is slightly more effective than the Pill. The difference between artificial contraception and NFP is not simply artificial versus natural, though that *is* a major difference. One mother from Wyandotte, Michigan, reported:

I knew of no other option than the Pill. Then I ran across a book at the grocery store about NFP. I recognized returning fertility and wanted to find a workable natural method. The Church's teachings and NFP along with the grace of the sacraments have made it possible to grow together in our marriage and our faith.

NFP cannot hurt you in any way. There are no harmful side effects.

What NFP Is Not

When W.C. Fields was on his deathbed he reportedly asked for a Bible. A friend who knew he was not religious asked him why he wanted a Bible then. He responded: "I'm looking for the loopholes, the loopholes."

NFP is *not* the Catholic loophole. It is not contraception Catholic-style. Archbishop Charles Chaput of Denver teaches:

> Contraception is the choice, by any means, to sterilize a given act of intercourse.... Natural Family Planning is *in no way contraceptive.* The choice to *abstain* from a fertile act of intercourse is completely different from the willful choice to *sterilize* a fertile act of intercourse.[6]

Note the key difference between enjoying the marital embrace while specifically thwarting the potentially life-creating consequences, and refraining from that embrace during the time of mutual fertility as a matter of concern and prayer.

NFP is *not* the rhythm method. A mother from Schiller Park, Illinois, discovered the rhythm method first.

> My husband belonged to the Methodist Church. We talked through the contraception issue before we were married; he agreed we would not use any type of contraception. My belief that contraception was wrong began in Catholic grade school when the *Baltimore Catechism* addressed this issue.
>
> I hoped to have six or eight children, and my husband accepted that. We expected to get pregnant right away, and when we didn't (it took four months!), I thought I had a fertility problem. Then we had a baby in December and were pregnant again the following March.
>
> During that pregnancy I looked for information about the "rhythm" method, which was the only NFP I had ever heard of, as my husband was not eager for a baby every year. This was in 1956. I found a book in Sears & Roebuck on calendar rhythm in 1957. This was helpful, and we never had a surprise pregnancy, although there was a lot of abstaining involved. When my fourth baby was born, we discovered La Leche League (1961). Suddenly, God's plan for human

fertility became much clearer. We welcomed the natural spacing that successful breastfeeding afforded us. After our sixth baby, the pastor asked how long we were going to "keep this up." There weren't many pats on the back from the local clergy (and there still aren't). It wasn't until after our seventh child that we found the Couple to Couple League.

It would have been nice to have all the information we eventually garnered given to us in Pre-Cana classes. But perhaps we would have been much more cautious. (With rhythm it's a little easier to "take a chance," and "chances" are great kids!) NFP is a really accurate way to plan a family; it would be easy to use it in a selfish way, especially if one's teacher does not stress that NFP is for serious reasons.

Whether a couple uses the rhythm or NFP method to delay pregnancy, they need a serious reason to do so.

NFP is *not* what Catholics can do so they can be just as selfish as anyone else in our culture. A mother from Ohio wrote, "We have had to communicate a lot as well as discipline ourselves." A mother from Nebraska said, "It made our prayer life together stronger."

"NFP is not easy," admitted a mother from Texas, "especially for newly married couples. When it is a time of postponement, it is very difficult to refrain from being intimate. [But] we knew that NFP is a gift from God and it's our decision if we are postponing." Another mother from Texas concurred: "By having intercourse less frequently, our passions actually heightened."

The self-discipline, interpersonal communication, and mutual respect required to make NFP work is not typical behavior for selfish people. Nevertheless, a couple needs to check their motives periodically to be sure selfishness does not creep in.

What is the difference between utilizing infertile days (with NFP) and rendering individual acts infertile (through contraception)? *Humanae Vitae* addresses this point:

In reality, there are essential differences between the two cases; in the former, the married couple make legitimate use of a natural disposition; in the latter, they impede the development of natural processes.

It is true that, in the one and the other case, the married couple are concordant in the positive will of avoiding children for plausible reasons, seeking the certainty that offspring will not arrive; but it is also true that only in the former case are they able to renounce the use of marriage in the fecund periods when, for just motives, procreation is not desirable, while making use of it during infecund periods to manifest their affection and to safeguard their mutual fidelity. By so doing, they give proof of a truly and integrally honest love.[7]

NFP, used in faith, can strengthen marriages.

NFP is *not* better simply because it is natural rather than artificial. (After all, a thermometer is a piece of technology.) Though there are health benefits for people who switch from contraception to NFP, it is not the artificial nature of contraception that makes it immoral, nor the naturalness of NFP that makes it moral. Pope John Paul II concludes:

When, instead, by means of recourse to periods of infertility, the couple respect the inseparable connection between the unitive and procreative meanings of human sexuality, they are acting as "ministers" of God's plan and they "benefit from" their sexuality according to the original dynamic of "total" self-giving, without manipulation or altercation.[8]

The key difference is that, with NFP, every marital act is open to life.

NFP is *not* the norm for married life, even though a couple can benefit greatly from using it. It is God's provision and the Church's wisdom to provide for very difficult situations. Marci experienced a health benefit:

I've used my NFP charts primarily to keep my eye on my endometriosis. Using the sympto-thermal method, I know when something is not right from temperature patterns. Using NFP, I have been able to prepare for a cyst rupture (seeing an unusually high temperature in the morning tells me something is going to happen that day), and I have known something was wrong when I see strange temperature patterns and mid-cycle spotting. Instead of going on the Pill or some other hormonal treatment for my endo, I can learn how to live with it using

NFP (and of course having some good painkillers on hand when needed).

Thank God that couples have been able to use NFP to help with physical difficulties such as endometriosis management, temporary infertility, and repeat miscarriage. However, a physician from Franklin Park, Illinois, offers this caution:

I do not believe NFP is necessary or desirable for most married people. I do believe everyone should know about it, and about where to learn the method if necessary, but I really don't think everyone needs to know all the details about how to do it, much less practice it. I disagree with those who say every woman should chart her cycles. Such a preoccupation with physiology is abnormal.

An analogy might be a food diary, where someone writes down every morsel consumed. This might be necessary for someone with diabetes, allergies, or severe obesity, but would be considered obsessive-compulsive for someone without a nutritional problem. In sexuality, where the interpersonal relationship is so important, such preoccupation with the physical may even be more harmful. Since NFP, i.e., periodic abstinence for the purpose of avoiding pregnancy, is appropriate only "for grave reasons," that is in cases of dire necessity, it is an unhealthy focus on bodily functions for those who have no such grave necessity.

Some people might think this states the case too strongly, but this doctor highlights the fact that NFP is more a prescription for difficulty than a vitamin for healthy living. Abstinence has a place when we have serious reasons to postpone pregnancy. The key is this: If we don't want to reap, we should not sow. Otherwise, we mock God (see Gal 6:7-8).

The *Virtue* of Planning

My experience is common. I enter a room noticeably pregnant and someone asks, "Was this child planned?" I pause before answering, a thousand thoughts crowding my brain. What is the right answer?

If I say, "No," I might be offered condolences before I can explain my joy. If I say, "By God," I might still be offered pity because God gave me what they presume to be an unwanted baby. If I say, "Yes," I will be offered praise for doing such a good job at planning. All these answers fall far short of the truth.

Whether or not a baby has been planned has become our society's litmus test for whether or not a child is wanted. A young mother, Rita, was approached immediately after Mass. "I was having my third baby in five years and a fellow parishioner asked, 'Is this baby planned? Is it wanted?'

"I was so surprised. I told her, 'They weren't all planned, but *all were wanted!*'"

Another couple in nearly identical circumstances felt cornered after Mass. A couple, similar in age, asked if their third baby was planned. The father mused, "God planned the baby. How about you? Think you'll have a third?"

The other couple smiled in a somewhat condescending manner. "No," replied the father smugly, "we intend to be smarter than you."

Smarter? There is nothing smarter about refusing to be open to life.

We *can* prayerfully examine our lives and, when there is a serious reason to postpone pregnancy, based on our limited knowledge, abstain from sexual relations when we think we will get pregnant. However, every act of marriage is to remain open to life. And if a marital act results in new life, that child is a completely unmerited gift from God.

We love God and entrust our plans to him, including our use of NFP. We place our trust in God, not NFP, believing he is trustworthy to give us children even when we think we cannot handle them, because his view is different from ours.

Does anyone really *plan* a child? No! We plan when we will be open to life or when we will abstain from relations to avoid pregnancy, but *God alone decides to make a baby.*

In fact, we cannot have a baby that God has not planned. One of the difficulties with the phrase "Natural Family Planning" is that it lends credence to the notion that families ought to be planned. Consequently, family members or friends may imply that a couple has to justify *not* using NFP.

Responsible parenting does not equal NFP, but it may include it.

Prudence does not equal postponing pregnancy until we can justify being open to life. Responsible parenting is taking responsibility for our lovemaking.

Pope John Paul II says, "The concept of 'responsible parenthood' contains the disposition not merely to avoid 'a further birth' but also to increase the family in accordance with the criteria of prudence."[9] We open our hearts, minds, and bodies to new life and, if there is difficulty, we discern proper use of NFP. Our goal is generosity with the Lord and each other.

How to Use NFP Well

How do we use NFP well? First, we pray for right motives. We ask God for wisdom with such a beautiful gift as the act of marriage, aware that concupiscence can fog our thinking.

Second, we discuss the concerns on our hearts as well as share our dreams and desires with our spouse. We listen carefully to each other, to hear each other's heart. We call each other on to heroic generosity.

We also must balance legitimate concerns with faith, knowing that simply being open to life or choosing to practice NFP with every act of marriage open to life can both be expressions of faith in God and his plan for our lives. The question is, Do we have serious reasons to postpone pregnancy? The question is not, Can we justify being open to life?

Third, we seek wisdom from people we respect: our pastor or spiritual director, doctor, parents. They cannot tell us what to do, but they can sometimes see our situation with more objectivity than we do. A mother from Ann Arbor, Michigan, wrote:

> I knew very little about NFP or the Church's teaching on it prior to Father's introduction. He gave us guidelines and answered questions. We began married life using NFP, after being directed to use it the first year to avoid pregnancy and to learn to live as husband and wife. Later we used it to space the children two years apart. However, we were always open to life, praying to welcome God's holy will.

We weigh our counselors' insights, knowing that the decision is ours alone to make.

The fathers of Vatican II declared:

The parents themselves and no one else should ultimately make this judgment in the sight of God. But in their manner of acting, spouses should be aware that they cannot proceed arbitrarily, but must always be governed according to a conscience dutifully conformed to the divine law itself, and should be submissive toward the church's teaching office, which authentically interprets that law in the light of the Gospel.[10]

We carefully consider our service to life (including, when necessary, NFP) in the light of present circumstances. Then we act as prudently as possible.

Fourth, if we discern that there is no serious reason to postpone pregnancy, we love each other and see what happens. If we discern that there is a serious reason to delay pregnancy, we learn the best method of NFP and practice it faithfully until the difficulty is resolved. At the same time, every act of marriage remains open to life both physically and emotionally; God must have permission to fulfill a better plan than we have.

Periodically, we review where we are in the process of discernment. Through ongoing transformation of our thinking to reflect God's truth, we will gain new insights that cast new light on our situation. Circumstances change, and we may need to alter our practice accordingly.

Unlike contraception, this process of discernment necessitates cooperation and communication. One couple from Wadsworth, Ohio, said, "We have grown in unity, self-sacrifice, communication, and appreciation of each other's desires and needs."

Not only do couples communicate about the deeper issues of intimacy, but the discussions often open overall communication. Rachel and Matt, from Baltimore, Maryland, said, "We began talking more and more about everything, besides intimacy issues. That's good!" And Theresa from Illinois shared that through the use of NFP, she and her husband "both learned, gradually, that occasional self-discipline in the sexual area led to more occasions to talk and spend time together in other ways."

Paul, a dentist from Akron, Ohio, described the spiritual growth he and his wife experienced following a vasectomy reversal.

We did not use NFP when we got married but began using NFP after I had a reversal. I believe NFP has had a positive effect on our marriage due to the fact that we both allow the will of God, not science, to be done. NFP has been a special kind of blessing for me as a man because at times when I would like to become intimate with my wife and I know that it is not a good time in her cycle, I use this as a small sacrifice in reparation for the sins I have committed over my life in regards to sensuality.

When NFP is practiced in faith, it produces good fruit.

Just because a couple agrees to practice NFP temporarily does not mean it is easy. One husband relates the struggle: "The difficulty comes in using NFP for a long period of time, which has caused emotional struggles. During my wife's fertile cycle and most sexually desirous times, abstinence is required in NFP. This is perceived as rejection on an emotional level." Here again, cooperation and communication are essential.

Other Blessings of NFP

NFP can be a valid expression of self-giving. A wife and mother from Chicago, Illinois, said, "It's strengthened our love, a challenge to grow in faith and trust in God."

NFP can deepen our appreciation of how God has made us, especially how he has made women. A mother from Monterey, California, said, NFP "has kept sex a sacred act and brought us closer together."

NFP can release new joy as the couple honors the principle of openness to life, according to Carl.

We started looking into NFP when breastfeeding of our son was starting to taper. We have only been using NFP for one month. I feel like we are on fire again; my wife says she feels like a teenager again. The passion is awesome. This is the reason: something was held back before; or more precisely, deep down, we knew something was wrong. After we made the commitment to NFP, that feeling was completely erased, replaced with a deep sense of God's blessing. I hope this doesn't sound odd, but our lovemaking now is more like a prayer. That could never have happened before our commitment to life-giving love.

This thought is confirmed by a mother from San Antonio, Texas: "We are more respectful of our physical relationship. We cherish it very much and know our union may bring forth children at any time."

NFP can be a tool with which God develops virtue within us. A mother of twelve from San Diego, California, wrote, "NFP has deeply affected our relationship. My husband is considerate. He is more responsible."

After practicing NFP in early marriage, Maria and her husband, from Milwaukee, Wisconsin, found that the virtues of self-control and prudence were needed to face new challenges. "Through NFP we became more attuned to each other's spiritual and physical needs. It also prepared us for my pregnancy, where, because of sickness and fatigue, there have been times of abstinence."

The self-discipline that NFP requires fosters thoughtfulness and loving consideration of our spouse. Could this be one of the reasons that couples who practice NFP have an extremely low divorce rate, between 1 and 2 percent, as compared to the rest of the population?[11] Being fertile does not mean we are untouchable; rather, we find other ways of loving each other, including tenderness without arousal that could be frustrating.

A mother from Boone, Iowa, summarized her experience:

NFP has brought forth in our marriage the beautiful fruit of trust in each other, intimacy, trust in God, openness to life, and KIDS. These are all great blessings in my relationship with my husband. My openness to and respect for life came from my Presbyterian mother, God bless her. She always accepted, loved, and nurtured us. We older three kids all knew our little sister had been a "surprise," but it didn't affect how Mom and Dad viewed or treated her. If anything, we all loved her more. That was the greatest teaching by example, and that predisposed me to agree wholeheartedly with the Catholic Church teaching.

My larger family experience echoes this mother's experience. My parents' twenty-fourth grandchild was born last year (from five children). There is such a celebration of love and life—a constant encouragement to embrace our spouse, trusting the Lord to provide, and then jubilation with the announcement of each new life.

Is It Possible to Misuse NFP?

Can NFP be misused? Yes, any good gift can be misused. We need to double-check our motives. The *Catechism* cautions couples in relation to licit regulation of births: "It is their duty to make certain that their desire is not motivated by selfishness but is in conformity with the generosity appropriate to responsible parenthood."[12]

No matter how flawed our motives for practicing NFP, our sin will at worst be venial, as opposed to the sin of contraception, which involves objectively grave matter. Why is there a distinction? NFP is abstaining from rather than entering into the act of marriage during the time the couple is mutually fertile; contraception is the deliberate thwarting of the life-giving nature of the act of marriage.

The fact that our misuse of NFP is *only* venial sin should not necessarily comfort us. After all, time is spent in purgatory for venial sins. And venial sins can beat a path to mortal ones. So how do we sort through our motives for legitimate use of NFP?

We need a strategy. First, we must guard our hearts from our weaknesses and sins through prayer. Next, we must develop our consciences according to truth. This includes renewing our hearts so that we are genuinely open to life with each marital act. We will have to struggle to replace our culture's indoctrination with God's truth; it takes effort. And finally, we must bolster our resolve to live with our spouse for God, continually filling our hearts and minds with truth about marital love, and placing our marriage in the trustworthy providence of God.

What Are Serious Reasons?

Sometimes we are so thankful that our relatives or friends have agreed to practice NFP, instead of using contraception, we hesitate to mention the need for *serious* reasons. But we may be withholding important information. As one woman mentioned, "Even though we have always been open to life, I never knew until a few years ago that NFP was only to be used under serious conditions."

There is no neat list for us to consult. *Humanae Vitae* declares:

In relation to physical, economic, psychological and social conditions, responsible parenthood is exercised, either by the deliberate and generous decision to raise a numerous family, or by the decision, made for grave motives and with due respect for the moral law, to avoid for the time being, or even for an indeterminate period, a new birth. Responsible parenthood also and above all implies a more profound relationship to the objective moral order established by God, of which a right conscience is the faithful interpreter. The responsible exercise of parenthood implies, therefore, that husband and wife recognize fully their own duties towards God, towards themselves, towards the family and towards society, in a correct hierarchy of values.[13]

We need to consider carefully what those values are. When Rita shared these values with her non-Catholic spouse, "he accepted it as a trust-in-God issue and a self-control issue for responsible parenthood."

Prayer is critical in the discernment process regarding the seriousness of our reasons to use NFP. Ever respectful of the freedom within the sacredness of the marriage bond, the Church does not dictate the specifics. She entrusts the process to us.

Sometimes we face conflicting considerations. For instance, 1 Timothy 5:8 says, "If anyone does not provide for ... his own family, he ... is worse than an unbeliever." So financial concerns are valid. At the same time, Matthew 6:25-34 tells us not to be anxious; God will take care of us. God does provide. As a couple, how do we balance these two truths?

These are the kinds of concerns a couple needs to address before marriage. What principles about ongoing openness to life will guide future discussions once they have children? The closer they can come to one heart and mind on those principles, especially before marriage, the less conflict they will experience over the issues related to children during marriage. If they anticipate grave reasons at the beginning of marriage, they might consider postponing the wedding.

As best as you can, try to clarify your guiding principles before you marry. Once married, you will discover that both of you may not agree—one spouse may think NFP is necessary right now, while the other does not. Listen to your spouse's heart and be vulnerable to share your own. This is not a power struggle; "love does not insist on its own way" (1 Cor 13:5).

Both openness to life without NFP and use of NFP can be done in faith and should only be done in faith; fear is not a right motivation. We must honor each other through ongoing respectful conversation, prayer with and for each other, a desire for unity, and balancing our conflicting convictions until we understand God's will for our marriage. The Lord who brought us together will show us the way.

Here are three questions to aid discerning use of NFP:

1. Do we have serious and grave reasons for using NFP?
2. Have we prayerfully considered how temporary our use of NFP needs to be?
3. Are we in agreement about using NFP?

Sorting through these criteria is not easy, as Peter and Mary from Illinois recognize:

> Having always thought that we were using NFP properly to space our children, we now have doubts. Is our human judgment, about slowing the pace of births to preserve Mary's health or to do a better job of homeschooling, simple prudence, or is it evidence of a lack of faith? Or should we say, "Our loving God knows best how this contemplated birth will affect these matters, and, even without NFP, he will choose the proper time if and when he wants to send us another blessing?"
>
> We know that just because we "decide" to have another child doesn't mean that God will bless us with one. We also know that as a couple in our mid-thirties, if we throw out the NFP charts and completely open ourselves to God's design and timing, we could be blessed with many more children. Is it not natural to be overwhelmed with that thought, even though we really do trust in God and his love for us?
>
> We do not wish to find ourselves in the shoes of the Gospel's rich man (Lk 18:18-25), sadly walking away from Jesus and his demands. Neither do we wish to view childbearing as a numbers game, as if God "scores" our holiness by some sort of per-child formula.

Though it might be difficult to read about Peter and Mary's struggle, I find it a blessing. They ask poignant and pertinent questions I need to ask myself. They communicate the reality of the challenge before us.

Our fertility is a fragile gift—how are we to be good stewards of it? What are legitimate, serious concerns that warrant the practice of NFP? How will my spouse and I entrust our lives at a deeper level to God, being open to life in the hope that he will use our humble gift of marital love to build his kingdom?

Stewardship of Our Fertility

As married couples, we have a mission: Our love is to issue forth in new life, as an act of Christian stewardship. The fathers of Vatican II taught:

> Parents should regard as their proper mission the task of transmitting human life and educating those to whom it has been transmitted. They should realize that they are thereby cooperators with the love of God the Creator, and are, so to speak, the interpreters of that love. Thus they will fulfill their task with human and Christian responsibility, and with docile reverence toward God, will make decisions by common counsel and effort. Let them thoughtfully take into account both their own welfare and that of their children, those already born and those which the future may bring. For this accounting they need to reckon with both the material and the spiritual conditions of the times as well as of their state in life. Finally they should consult the interests of the family group, of temporal society, and of the Church herself.[14]

We flesh out the love of God through our gift of life.

Not only are we to transmit life, we are to do so *in faith*. Whether or not NFP is temporarily part of this mission, we are to live in faith. Romans 14:23 says that "whatever does not proceed from faith is sin." NFP can be an expression of faith; however, NFP is not required to live a life of faith.

That being the case, does Natural Family Planning mean we are wresting control from God? Does *any* use of NFP exhibit a lack of trust in God?

No. The Lord, through the Church, has given us NFP as a gift so that we can balance, to the best of our abilities, our desire for children with other concerns. We thank God there is a way to honor him in the midst of difficulties. We use NFP in faith as long as there is a serious reason for doing so.

Herein lies the challenge: Couples can embrace openness to life without the assistance of NFP and be making a well-reasoned, responsible choice; and couples can embrace openness to life including NFP as an expression of their trust in God. Both can be responsible and faith-filled choices.

A couple who trusts God to plan their family can be a powerful testimony of the providence of God. They should be praised rather than criticized for living their conviction. A couple who embraces trust in God at this level should not be treated as though they are out of touch with reality or fundamentally irresponsible. They should not be castigated for having the humility to trust God with the spacing and sex of their children. God *can* be trusted with the number, sex, and spacing of our children.

Any couple who chooses to live sacrificially the culture of life among people who are rushing headlong into the culture of death are a living sign of contradiction. Far from a flight into fantasy that smacks of irresponsibility, a couple who entrusts their family size to God demonstrates heroic virtue, admitting that God understands the myriad details of life better than we do. At the same time, as Pope John Paul teaches,

> God the Creator invites the spouses not to be passive operators, but rather "cooperators or almost interpreters" of his plan. In fact, they are called, out of respect for the objective moral order established by God, to an obligatory discernment of the indications of God's will concerning their family.[15]

This is a cooperative effort between the couple and God.

We must pray, be sensitive to each other, and assess the seriousness of our situation so that we might truly trust God and act responsibly. However, Pope John Paul II clarified that "responsible parenthood [is] in no way exclusively directed to limiting, much less excluding children; it means also the willingness to accept a larger family."[16]

The clergy must call married couples to responsible parenthood,

> to emphasize the awareness and generosity of the spouses with regard to their mission of transmitting life, which has in itself a value of eternity, and to call attention to their role as educators. Certainly it is a duty of married couples—who, for that matter, should seek appropriate counsel—to deliberate deeply and in a spirit of faith about the size of their family, and to decide the concrete mode of realizing it, with respect for the moral criteria of conjugal life.[17]

No matter how generous we are with God, we will never outgive him.

NFP and Unmarried Teens

Just a brief caution regarding teaching NFP to unmarried teenagers: Don't do it. NFP is powerful knowledge. In typical teenage fashion, they may assume they will not get pregnant if they are using NFP; however, they do not count on the strength of desire they will experience during ovulation (which is part of God's plan). This is information they do not need, requiring virtue they may not yet possess to refrain from using it.

Should NFP Classes Be Required?

Marriage preparation is prime time for helping couples to make an informed decision about contraception and openness to life. Every couple wants to have a successful marriage; no one gets married hoping it will fail. So this is an opportunity not to be missed.

We should give the most accurate information possible on NFP so that people understand when it can be used (serious reasons), why it can be used (moral principles that differentiate it from contraception), and how it is used (practical teaching on methodology). The Couple to Couple League offers excellent classes taught by couples who are truly convicted about and live the truth. In fact, Mary and John, an NFP teaching couple for twenty years, offer ongoing support: "We have offered our telephone number to all couples we've taught to give them encouragement, spiritual and emotional support in following the Church's challenge, and invitation to celebrate love and life according to his plan."

The leaders of Engaged Encounter in Wichita, Kansas, work with their parish priest to offer a Pre-Cana course. The first class introduces the couples to the scope of the lessons, including communication skills, financial skills, and how to fight fair.

The second class is the one on openness to life and NFP. The teachers conclude the class by telling the couples that if they are currently sleeping together, they need to stop from that night until they wed. The couple needs to go to Confession for it as well, and there are priests there that night to hear their confessions before they leave. They can go home having made things right with each other and God.

Further, the teachers acknowledge that sometimes couples cohabit. Since that is an occasion of sin (and it has the appearance of evil even if they are not sleeping together), the instructors offer a solution: That night there are families represented who are willing to take in one person of each cohabiting couple and offer them a free room until their wedding day. Talk about clear teaching and concrete solutions to real problems!

Information on NFP should be taught in the larger context of the mission of openness to life in marriage. Pope John Paul II writes:

> Closely connected with the formation of conscience is the *work of education,* which helps individuals to be ever more human, leads them ever more fully to the truth, instills in them growing respect for life, and trains them in right interpersonal relationships.... The work of educating in the service of life involves the *training of married couples in responsible procreation.* In its true meaning, responsible procreation requires couples to be obedient to the Lord's call and to act as faithful interpreters of his plan. This happens when the family is generously open to new lives, and when couples maintain an attitude of openness and service to life, even if, for serious reasons and in respect for the moral law, they choose to avoid a new birth for the time being or indefinitely.[18]

Pam, from Vermilion, Ohio, said, "I think couples should be aware of the option of NFP, but they need to be encouraged, exhorted, to only use NFP (to postpone pregnancy) for serious reasons. They need to be encouraged to be open to life right from the start."

Some young couples are getting married with a beautiful understanding of the vocation of marriage. Ryan and Rachael, newly engaged students, summarized the Church's teaching this way: "God's gift of his life-giving love from the cross parallels and sanctifies the life-giving love present within the sacrament of marriage. It is quite simple, really: Live for others, die to self, love like God. That is Christian marriage."

What a blessing for a couple to head into marriage with such a clear understanding of the nature of marriage. Pray for them as they seek to live these truths in a world that mocks such a vision.

If such a class were merely suggested, numerous couples would opt out due to time constraints or disinterest. They might assume that if it is not required, it must not be very important. A mother from North Ridgeville, Ohio, concluded, "I wish I would have understood God's role in the sexual act instead of simply learning the parts of the body and how babies are born. I think that someday it will be important for my children not only to know the Church's teaching, but to understand why we adhere to it."

Sometimes Church authorities have intervened when couples have planned to teach NFP in the context of the Church's teaching on marriage, hard though it is to believe. A woman from Texas reports: "We could not discuss the morality of NFP or the Church's teachings, but instead had to promote its healthy aspect. After my training, I really felt that people were being taught Catholic 'birth control' and the 'serious reasons' were being ignored."

In Illinois, a priest said he would not require NFP for marriage preparation because he would rather have couples living in ignorance than in serious sin. Shocking though it may sound, the Church affirms, in the context of Confession, that the priest should not instruct the penitent about conjugal chastity. The concern is that the penitent, when confronted by a sin he or she didn't intend to confess at that time, might not express contrition for that sin; unconfessed sin cannot be absolved.

> The principle according to which it is preferable to let penitents remain in good faith in cases of error due to subjectively invincible ignorance, is certainly to be considered always valid, even in matters of conjugal chastity. And this applies whenever it is foreseen that the penitent, although oriented towards living within the bounds of a life of faith, would not be prepared to change his own conduct, but rather would begin formally to sin.[19]

However, the priest should choose other contexts in which to instruct parishioners so that their marriages *are* in conformity to truth.

> Nonetheless, in these cases, the confessor must try to bring such penitents ever closer to accepting God's plan in their own lives, even in these demands, by means of prayer, admonition, and exhorting them to form their consciences, and by the teaching of the Church.[20]

One such context could be a required Pre-Cana course, including instruction on NFP.

If the parish priest or, better, the local bishop required the class, couples would find the time to attend. If it were taught well, their interest would be engaged. An NFP teaching couple in the Long Island, New York, diocese reported:

> If all Pre-Cana couples had to attend NFP classes it would be great, but if it is not a full part of Marriage Preparation (diocesan-wide), it isn't effective. Our own experience is with two parishes on Long Island who made NFP classes a mandatory part of their parish Pre-Cana program. As the teaching couple, we expected couples to want to be there. When it was mandatory, we had little cooperation and some downright negativity! This made it an unpleasant experience for those couples who wanted to hear about NFP.

Ingrid, from Pound Ridge, New York, advised, "From what I have read on NFP, I wish it had been a requirement when I got married. It can only do good for the couples."

Teachers of the class should not have an underlying assumption that the couples must use NFP. Rather, they should want the couples to have the information should a serious reason arise. Robin encouraged such a class in this way, because "otherwise they might be suckered in by the contraceptive advertisers who lump NFP in with 'rhythm' and spread misinformation about it."

As a young mother from Round Rock, Texas, pointed out, "So many [couples] aren't even aware [NFP] exists." Monica and Edmund also encourage parishes to have such a required class: "This is a contraceptive culture, and the Church must help couples live the teaching of Christ." "It would be a big step in counteracting the culture of death," concurred a mother from LaCrosse, Wisconsin.

Tina, a convert to the Catholic Church, noticed how many Catholics reflect current cultural attitudes. "I would have openness to life taught in a very orthodox way. Since converting I have been stunned at how many Catholics I have met that speak of children as possessions: 'I only want two kids,' 'Oh, I could never have lots of kids,' and 'She is crazy to have all those kids.' It bothers me very much."

Context for presenting NFP is very important. Anne acknowledged the value of this kind of a class "only if moral and spiritual outlooks are incorporated throughout." She echoes Dan and Jean's concern: "Our experience with other couples is that many use NFP without serious reasons. When NFP is taught, it's taught in a moral vacuum." A mother from Monterey, California, writes that the class should be required, "so that they know that this is available to them and will become aware of the Church's teachings."

Often couples get caught up in the details of their wedding day and do not adequately prepare for marriage. Anne mentioned some of the frustrations she encountered in marriage that could have been lessened by a good Pre-Cana class.

I wish someone had prepared me for the anti-child, anti-woman, anti-sex remarks, coarse and crude and prying, that others (Christians, Catholics, medical personnel, relatives, STRANGERS) would make.

I wish someone had prepared me for husband-wife disagreements or misunderstandings, even when both accept the Church's teachings. My husband came to marriage a bit with the mindset that since he had abstained from sexual relations before marriage and since he and I would not use contraception, he "deserved" or was entitled to sexual relations as often as he wanted.

I also know it took my husband a very long time to realize how tiring pregnancy was for me. It caused resentment and misunderstanding, before he saw that many levels of intimacy as gift were involved. For my part, I wish I had known how much physical closeness was necessary for my husband to be close emotionally.

Couples could avoid future conflicts, or at least lessen friction, if they understood principles involved in communication and cooperation necessary for a healthy marriage, especially in the area of their physical relationship.

Difficult Situations

When one spouse struggles with using NFP, there can be a variety of conflicting emotions. Luanne's husband "outwardly agreed, but inside felt rejected." A mother from Lockport, Louisiana, shared, "I'm really not thrilled with NFP. When my husband and I use NFP for extended periods of time, he has lustful thoughts and desires. This makes NFP particularly difficult and unpleasant for us both!"

Patricia and William thought NFP would help them, but it added stress. One spouse struggled with fear of whether or not NFP would be effective.

> [We began using NFP] after we had five children, four and under. NFP did not have a joyful impact on our relationship. We had a life with a house full of babies, a husband trying to establish a law practice while continuing education in graduate school, and aging parents who needed our help and relied on us for sociability and support.
>
> We had extremely irregular cycles (thirty-five to sixty days). The little time we had for each other seemed to conflict with the restrictions. We have always been a couple who tried to extend ourselves as much as possible and just didn't have time to be so much in control of our time and schedules. This may be difficult for others to understand, but I am telling you precisely how unhappy we were with NFP. Our greatest joy and gift has been our children.

The added stress may not be worth it.

Eileen struggled with her fear of motherhood.

> I didn't think I would be a good mother. The ironic part about NFP: The time your body is telling you it's interested in sex is the time you refrain if you don't want to get pregnant. The times I was not interested were also frustrating because I knew this act was not life giving. I began to feel used. Now, I appreciate this gift from God.

Though this mother experienced frustration, she was able to appreciate NFP.

NFP can be challenging when only one spouse is convicted that contraception is wrong, as this mother of ten realized:

I couldn't be open to God's will in my life and use contraception, too. Using contraception contradicted God's will. I simply reasoned that it is God's will that I bear children, or else he would have made me a man! When I stopped contraception, my husband insisted we use something; I insisted that it must be accepted by the Church. We were not taught legitimate reasons for using NFP. It was taught and practiced with the same mentality as birth control, only you might mess up and still get pregnant, so you were still open to life.

My husband did not like NFP. He didn't want to go through periods of time where I was unavailable. He made me feel guilty about my fertile times when we should abstain from intimacy. I tried to avoid activities that might trigger his desire so I wouldn't be put in the position of having to say, "Not tonight." We became distant and quarreled a lot.

Perhaps, if this couple had taken a class on marriage explaining NFP in context, they would have been spared some of this pain.

At first, one couple used contraception "because of our fear of our fertility. In hindsight I see using artificial contraception caused many burdens in our marriage. [Switching to NFP] I learned about sacrificial love. It was pivotal in my reconversion to my faith and led to my husband's joining the Church."

Two couples who switched from contraception to NFP discovered very positive relational changes. The first couple reported, "We had a much more loving, stronger relationship with mutual respect, and more admiration for Christ. We accepted the children openly and still live our life that way." The second couple, John and Barbara, affirmed a similar sentiment: "Together with the other aspects of our conversion, the switch radically improved our marriage."

The Church's teaching on openness to life has led some people to the Catholic Church. Here is one family's story:

I was born and raised in an Orthodox Jewish home in the middle of the Bible Belt. Being "witnessed to" for much of my life, I became a "closet Christian." Shortly after we were married, one of my ovaries developed a cyst and ruptured.

My doctor told me that he would probably have to remove the ovary, and with the endometriosis, etc., the probability of my having kids was slim. As I was being wheeled into the operating room, I "put out my fleece" and prayed to God that if I could have children in three to five years, I would dedicate my life and my child's life to him—and Jesus. Four months later I became pregnant and realized, even though the timing was askew, I'd better honor my end of the bargain. I entered the RCIA program and was fully sacramentalized that Easter.

Four years ago, we began hearing the words of our pope and the teachings of the Church on NFP and taking them to heart. Dear friends of ours in the Church were excellent role models on submitting our lives *totally* to God (and to each other) and trusting in him for life for our family. This was not easy, as our last two pregnancies were nothing less than "faith stands."

I had already had two premature births, five C-sections, and lots of problems during the last two times. (Several doctors had told us no way.) We struggled through five miscarriages, including two sets of twins. All looked hopeless; but we know nothing is impossible with God. (We also desired a boy—the four girls had already been praying for a brother.)

In November, I realized I was pregnant and the real fun began. I was on strict bed rest again ... bleeding and with a myriad of other problems and bad reports. We called our priest for Anointing of the Sick, took Communion, enlisted the aid of all the angels and saints (including St. Gerard), the Blessed Mother, and our friends' prayers. And I put my old pregnancy Scriptures into daily use.

We offered up the time, sacrifice, and *inconvenience* of the whole family [due to the pregnancy] for the unborn and for the "unsaved." Seven months of trials—the homeschooling really kept us together— and God was with us. From twenty-two weeks, I would go into labor if I stood or sat up for longer than a few minutes and was on IVs from home for the last six weeks.

Labor indeed came unstoppably six weeks early. As it turned out, my uterus began to rupture, and along with other complications, I came to the end of my natural childbearing years. The Lord did bless us with a wonderful four-pound baby boy, Max, named after [St. Maximilian] Kolbe, of course. God has been so good.

Though many trials came, this family is grateful to have lived this new conviction.

A couple from Wilmington, Delaware, realized God was not calling them to NFP: "After a short time we discovered that even NFP wasn't what God wanted for us. He wanted us to remain open to life and accept all children he wanted to bless us with."

Anne from Fairview Park, Ohio, and her husband summarized their experience: "Two pregnancies, two beautiful children—imagine if we used NFP the two months we conceived and ended up childless!"

One couple "switched from artificial contraception to complete acceptance of however many children God wanted to send us. This had a positive effect on our relationship. The fruits were obvious: Faye, Tessa, John, and Maria! The switch back to regulating birth using NFP has altered our relationship. The fruits aren't as obvious and much harder to produce—it's very purifying."

Another couple related circumstances in which NFP has helped them through difficulties in their service to life. In Paul's words:

My wife and I began to learn NFP about one month or so prior to our wedding. Although we had no problem understanding the process involved, it took some years for us to understand its value and its implications. We learned along the way that a couple could commit sin by using NFP for selfish reasons, too. Due to this, we reevaluate our motives for using NFP regularly.

We decided to use NFP when we got married, only because our family suggested it would be "smart" to allow some time for our marriage to grow before starting a family. We stopped using NFP after about six months or so of marriage.

Since my wife becomes very ill during the first two to three months of pregnancies (we now have three sons), we decided with lots of prayer to space the births of our children. Our sons are five, three, and eighteen months.

Over the past seven years, we have learned so much about one another because of our use of NFP. I have a better understanding of why my wife's behavior changes frequently. Earlier in our marriage, I took many of my wife's actions personally, before I became familiar with her physiology. NFP helped us to learn how to give ourselves to one another unreservedly, so that each time we come together we renew our marriage and must be completely open to life.

What a beautiful testimony of how NFP can be a helpful tool for difficulty.

The Brocks express the joy of openness to life, even in the midst of loss of their two-month-old baby. NFP helped them during that difficult time.

Since our second child was born, we let God have control over our fertility and we would be open to having the amount of children he wanted to give us. We have since that time (thirteen years ago) only had an occasion that was serious for us to use NFP for six months. Being open to life and generous with God has truly made our married and family life an exciting adventure.

We would have missed out on so many of his blessings had we stopped at four like we planned. I'm expecting our thirteenth child this September at age forty-one. Five of our children have gone before us to God. We feel our anti-child society has *so* many messages about the burdens of having children. It takes great courage and discernment to let go of the nonserious reasons to avoid cocreating one more soul and to be generous in a heroic manner.

If we embrace the truth about openness to life, embracing our spouse, we will share the Gospel of Life to all around us and for generations to come.

CHAPTER NINE

CAN WE BE OPEN TO ONE MORE SOUL?
ANSWERING COMMON OBJECTIONS

The delicate balance of priorities is a challenge for every marriage. How do we assess our physical reserves, our financial resources, our emotional reservoir, and our current psychological state? Can we imagine the possibility of one more soul as the fruit of our love?

When my children refuse to serve in some way, they rarely say, "No." Their refusals are usually much more indirect: "I'm not able right now." "I need to do something else." "My hands are full." "I can't afford the time." "I don't know how."

You get the picture. They are mentioning legitimate excuses. Nevertheless, they are refusing to help at that time.

Some of us have wrestled with the question of openness to life and are in the midst of finding a creative way to say *no* to our heavenly Father. We might have legitimate, serious reasons for declining the gift of a child right now, and we might not. How can we know?

First, we must pray for wisdom, for "if any of you lacks wisdom, let him ask God, who gives to all men generously and without reproaching, and it will be given him" (Jas 1:5). At the same time, we must place our trust in the Lord rather than in our own insights (see Prv 3:5-6).

Second, we know that whatever is not done in faith is sin (Rom 14:23), so we must examine our motivation: Is it faith or fear? Then we pray, "Increase our faith!" (Lk 17:5) And he will. Sometimes we do not realize that our vision of what our marriage can and should be has become clouded.

Third, we need the support and encouragement of the body of Christ to live our mission; we also need to offer it to others. Together, we can remove obstacles that block us from discerning and then doing God's will. New information and fresh insight into various concerns helps us clarify our motives and rectify our intentions.

Here are some quick responses to legitimate concerns we have heard regarding the Church's teaching on openness to life. These objections are not meant to be ridiculed, though there may be some humor in the answers. Let's consider together common objections to saying *yes* to receiving the gift of a new life, one more soul, in our family.

Physical Issues

Serious Harm or Death

Our medical condition may be very serious. We cannot discount a doctor's opinion that another pregnancy could cause serious harm or even death, just because we want more children. If the Pill or a hysterectomy is required medically, and it is not being chosen for its contraceptive effect, there is no sin.

Doctors may not be thinking through the spiritual ramifications when they advise us. A mother from Lockport, Louisiana, voiced her concern about repeat C-sections.

> I'm surrounded by well-meaning friends and relatives (and doctors) who continually remind me of the "dangers" of repeated surgery. I know they mean well, but [they are] causing me to question the wisdom of my willingness and desire to have more children. In my heart, I trust God to take care of me. But at times I wonder, how much longer can my body do this? How do I reconcile my desire to trust God, with my fear of pushing my body too far?

Certainly we should not intentionally compromise our ability to mother the children God has already given us; at the same time, all doctors do not share our views on openness to life. Their bias may play more of a part in their advice than we realize.

In Joliet, Illinois, two of my friends were given almost identical advice. One friend saw the doctor after her third delivery, and he discouraged her from having more children, reminding her, "Three children make a nice-sized family." Soon after, that friend spoke to a mutual friend who had just delivered her second child. The same doctor had discouraged *her* from having more children, saying, "Two children make a nice-sized family."

Both women wanted to get a second opinion. The second opinion, in both cases, revealed no medical reason for not having another baby.

Doctors do not know everything. One couple reported: "We were encouraged to have an abortion [after a stillborn birth of a child with severe abnormalities]. We were told we were likely to have a repeat of the anomalies present in our son if we were to conceive again. Two years later we used NFP to try to conceive—it worked! Anne is now three years [and perfectly healthy]. We still *desire* more—'Thy will be done.'"

Another mother shared her story.

There are times when a woman's health can be seriously compromised by a pregnancy. However, many times I've talked to women whose conditions were far less threatening than my own, yet they resorted to birth control or sterilization without NFP methods, or trusting in God. Most regretted their decisions.

When I was twenty-one, I was working in a hospital. I had lifted a patient and sprained my back. I was returning from the emergency room to the floor I worked on via the elevator. The elevator malfunctioned and I received a very hard jolt, which caused a disc in my lower back to slip. Then I was really injured. For the next two weeks I was on pain medication and muscle relaxers, and had numerous unshielded X rays because of the location of my injury.

I woke up one morning quite nauseated. I thought I might be pregnant. (Until this time I was not questioned or asked.) When I revealed my suspicions to the doctor, he did a pregnancy test. The results were positive. He then recommended that I have an abortion right away. He explained to me that the baby was "probably" deformed or mentally retarded because of the drugs and X rays I had received. I firmly refused his proposal.

He continued to say that I would "probably" be paralyzed from the waist down, if not from carrying the baby during the pregnancy, then during the delivery. When I still refused to abort my baby, he refused to treat me anymore and released me. He explained to me that he didn't want to be accused of keeping me home for "being pregnant" and not for a back injury. So I was dismissed, unable to walk, sit, or lie down without severe pain.

Since I was pregnant, all drugs for pain were discontinued immediately. I went on to face a pregnancy full of pain and fear. I kept wondering when I would lose the use of my legs. As the pregnancy progressed, I healed somewhat, and was able to return to work, assuming lighter duties. I worked up until two weeks before the baby was due with the aid of a great deal of Tylenol.

When I went into labor, I didn't know what to expect. I thought of the possibility of never walking again. I thought about the possibility of having a deformed or retarded child. I prayed (begged) God for the grace to accept and trust in him whatever his will was for my life throughout the pregnancy. Then came the time to know the results.

Our daughter, Sarah, is seventeen years old now. She is a healthy, beautiful, intelligent, and talented young woman. She directs the Kids That Care, is president of our parish CYO [Catholic Youth Organization], and is the Region Five CYO representative. She also is a cantor at our church. I am not paralyzed, either. As a matter of fact, I now have ten beautiful, healthy, wonderful children. I educate them at home. I know so much joy with my children that words cannot adequately describe the happiness they've meant to me, and to others.

We've formed a group called Kids That Care. They sing to and then visit with the elderly. They perform corporal works of mercy for those in need. It is my goal to raise my children to know, love, and serve God. There is no way I could have even guessed the kind of fulfillment and satisfaction I would receive from my children.

So the point of my story is this: If I had listened to that doctor eighteen years ago, I would have robbed myself of more joy and happiness than I could ever have imagined. I thank God for answering my prayers and granting me the grace to trust in him. That's the message I would like to convey to others!

Doctors offer their best advice, but sometimes they are wrong.

Sometimes doctors advise use of the Pill when a woman suffers from irregular cycles. Though it would not be sinful to utilize the Pill for a purely medical reason, there are other considerations:

Much cycle irregularity is self-induced—the results of improper diet, nutrition, and exercise.... *The Pill does not "regularize" irregular cycles.* It is true that the Pill will make "periods" (actually Pill-induced with-drawal bleeding) come at regular intervals, but this is completely Pill-controlled. The Pill does not assist the normal fertility cycle but com-pletely overrides it.... While sometimes a cross, cycle irregularity is bearable; it is frequently made more regular by improved nutrition, and it certainly provides no justification for resorting to immoral forms of birth control or sexual behavior.[1]

A couple from Mt. Carmel, Indiana, share their story:

Our original "plan" (as if it were ours to plan) was to have three or four kids. However, after our first two were born via C-section, the doc-tors started their usual pessimistic attitude toward further children. We were in a holding pattern. It was about this time the Hahns came to town, and we saw the light regarding being open to whomever God still had to send us. We immediately put the ball into God's hands, and Gabriel was born soon after. We always attribute his birth to the message God spoke through you at that conference.

After Gabe, of course, the doctors got really negative on us having another baby. But we now believed in trusting God versus birth con-trol, and Jacqueline was born two years later. After Jacq, the doctors started using words such as "life-threatening." However, as scared as we were (mostly Mom, since it was her life being threatened), we both felt there was at least one more baby for us, and Asher was born soon after, a real miracle.

We should not ignore a physician's advice, but we need to be sure they are giving medical advice and not a personal opinion.

Mary, from Elkhart, Indiana, records this testimony:

I am the ninth of thirteen children. When my parents were married in 1962, the doctors told them that because of some problems with their blood, they could at most have one healthy child. My parents prayed a lot to the Blessed Mother and to our Lord and put their future family completely in God's care.

From that time on, my parents have been blessed abundantly. Today, thirty-five years later, they have thirteen children perfectly healthy in body, mind, and soul. Not one of their children has ever had a serious medical problem. Not one has ever left the faith. We pray the family rosary daily. All of us go to weekly Mass and most of us go to daily Mass. My point is that God *does* reward those willing to trust his will and remain open to life—even when it is difficult.

Prayer makes a difference.

Sometimes God even does a miracle *through* the new little one, as witnessed by one woman when she was a teen:

My cousin Pat, the father of seven boys, came to see my mom for prayer and discernment. His wife was pregnant with number eight. She had been diagnosed with a heart condition the doctors deemed life-threatening, if she had this baby. They decided to leave the matter in God's hands. She had the baby, a girl, *and* the mother was totally healed of her heart condition. I was fourteen years old when this happened, and I never forgot it.

What a testimony for all involved!

Too Old

Feeling old and being old are two different things. One mother expresses her dilemma.

We are certainly not past our fertile years, but as we approach forty, having a teenager, homeschooling four children, and raising an infant, we are feeling tired. I wonder, how do we make sure we are being open to God's will for life in our marriage without answering the question with our own selfish needs in mind? I believe prayers are the only way to do this, although I'm afraid I may try to put the answer in my head and then convince myself it is from God.

She is not alone in this struggle.

If we notice signs of aging—beginning menopause, having miscarriages possibly from old eggs, or other physical difficulties—we might discern that the Lord is closing the door for more children. However, society cannot tell us we are too old to have a baby. Only God makes babies, and he knows our ages and abilities. We need to pray about whether or not this is a serious reason or just someone else's timetable.

If we can still conceive, who says we're too old? Late babies are a wonderful blessing. They used to call them bonus babies back in my mom's time. It was as if God said, you did such a good job, you get to raise one more! Think of the maturity we bring to the parenting process now—maturity to discipline with confidence and peace.

When we live in front of our children, day in and day out, the truth about openness to life, our teaching becomes concrete. They see many of the sacrifices involved. We have opportunities to teach our children practical information about care for children, and that increases their confidence around small children, better preparing them for parenthood.

When we have a baby as older parents we have more help. We know we can get a nap anytime, since there are older children around. That reduces some of the stress related to tiredness. Generally, there is more money to hire necessary help than there was when we began our family years ago. And our older children can even help us with some of the more physical tasks of chasing after little ones and bending over the bathtub, if need be.

When older children observe our delight in this new child, they are reminded of the joy we had anticipating and celebrating their birth. They remember the little songs we sang them, the way we cuddled and tickled them—and they feel deeply loved. By now we know how fast those early years go by. (Wasn't it just yesterday we held our first newborn?) Here's another chance to slow down and drink in the early baby and toddler years again.

Having a baby in the house is wonderful for teens. Teens still have a need for affection, but they may feel awkward being affectionate with siblings. Babies welcome affection and return it with few demands and little awkwardness.

Babies do not care whether or not the teens have friends or dates. They do not notice acne or bad hair days. They do not withhold a smile or a hug for bad grades, a scratch on the car, or a disappointing day at work. Babies just look up (and up, if the teen is really tall), raise their arms, and wait for the love to flow.

What a confidence booster for older children to see the effects of their teaching the new little one so many things, from counting toes and fingers, and singing the ABCs, to learning the names of every person and object in sight. They share the joy of such games as hide-and-seek and peek-a-boo, playfully giving of themselves a little each day.

At a time in their lives when it is more natural to have an inward focus, teens give generously of themselves to a baby sibling, lavishing their love on this precious family member. And at a time in their lives when teens are differentiating themselves from the family in many good ways, they are also being drawn ever more deeply by the cherubic face and outstretched arms of the littlest one.

Having babies in older age means no empty nest syndrome. By the time the last one's grown, grandchildren will have arrived. (Or grandchildren may overlap our children with aunts or uncles younger than nieces or nephews!)

Some people make us feel as if forty is a magical age after which we cannot justify giving birth to children. However, many parents testify that having a baby later in life kept them physically and mentally young. Two neighbor women, ages forty-seven and forty-eight, delivered in Steubenville, Ohio, just last year! In the movie *Father of the Bride, Part II*, Steve Martin holds his new daughter in one arm and his new grandson in the other, and says, "It doesn't get any better than this!" I'd have to agree.

When one couple over the age of forty discovered they were expecting, they were upset. It was not what they had planned. Since their four sons were all in school, the wife wanted to go back to college and prepare for a career.

In the midst of their struggle, however, they listened to our tape series *Life-Giving Love*. God used these tapes first to help them receive this baby as a gift, and second, to share the message with their prayer group. The result? The first couple gave birth to their first daughter; they were beside themselves with joy. And two more couples over the age of forty (from their prayer group) chose to be open to life and conceived.

Finally, it is awe-inspiring to see that our old(er) bodies can produce someone so fresh, beautiful, and new. What a special joy to create with God!

Too Young or Immature

If we are too young to have children, we are too young to marry. It's a package deal. When we give ourselves to each other in marriage, we vow to receive children from the Lord and to educate them in the faith.

If we are too immature to have children, we are too immature to marry. To be honest, no one ever feels completely mature enough to have children depend on us for everything, but having a child matures us. God gives grace in time of need.

Postpregnancy Body Changes

It's tough to look as if you had a baby, but you did. Perhaps it will take time to lose the weight gained. But carefully weigh (no pun intended) the alternatives: the value of a new ensouled being who will live for all eternity because of your willingness to have your body grow and change to accommodate your developing child, versus the value of being thin.

By the way, there are no scriptural texts that speak of thinness being next to godliness. Yet it may be a woman's greatest hesitation in saying yes to one more soul. What should our standard be?

In the movie *Gone With the Wind*, the lead female character, Scarlett O'Hara, makes a shocking decision. She refuses to have any more children or even to have relations with her husband just because her corset will not go back to its original measurement.

As absurd as that may seem, it is practically the example some women today follow. Instead of refusing to have relations, however, they refuse to have relations without contraception or sterilization because of the effects of pregnancy on their body. (Scarlett would be proud.)

Who says that we're supposed to look like prepubescent teens after we've had a baby? Why is the ultimate compliment "You look like you never had a baby!"

We want to get back in shape for a variety of reasons, but it is not right to pressure young mothers into looking as if they have never been pregnant. Gaining weight while pregnant is not the same as getting fat; it is nurturing the life within. In Italy, a curvaceous woman is considered a mature woman of beauty.

Proverbs 31:30 says, "Charm is deceitful, and beauty is vain, but a woman who fears the Lord is to be praised." When we *risk* all the permanent physical markings of pregnancy out of the godly desire to bear children for the Lord, we are truly beautiful. External beauty is a temporary thing, but a soul lasts forever.

The husband's attitude is critical here. One of my friends delivered the same day as I did—my first baby, her third. After the six-week checkup, I said to her, "It's kind of exciting to get the doctor's approval to resume relations, isn't it?"

She shook her head, chagrined. "I still have five pounds on my hips to lose. And my husband told me that until I lose it, he just can't imagine having relations."

Isn't that incredible? I still would like to slug him! How audacious of him to make her feel anything but beautiful and desirable after all she had gone through to give him his precious children!

In stark contrast, Scott looks at my body and says, "Your body says you have loved me enough to bear my children." He values me for who I am rather than what I look like. And that opens my heart to more children.

When I became disheartened at the number of stretch marks I was acquiring, my doctor told me to think of them as merit badges. He assured me that in some African cultures, women with stretch marks are honored because they are proof that women have borne children. Varicose veins can do a number on my ego, too, but my husband is the only one I want to look good for anyway.

There *are* many adjustments after the birth of a baby. The focus needs to be on meeting the needs of the baby through nursing; losing weight comes later. It is more important to eat well so that the baby eats well.

Tiredness also plays a role in our struggle with weight loss. We often eat when we are tired, and "a new study also suggest[s] that sleep deprivation may promote weight gain, at least for the short term."[2] Besides, it took nine months to acquire the weight; aside from an immediate ten-to-twelve-pound drop at delivery, it will take time to lose the remainder. We need to give ourselves time.

Sometimes our struggle with food has nothing to do with having babies. Our greatest hunger is for God. Maybe we need more time for prayer, reading Scripture, or going to Mass.

I highly recommend a program I have been working through with dear friends called *The Light Weigh* by Suzanne Fowler,[3] which combines spiritual growth with a weight loss program. It helps us focus on the Lord rather than ourselves, offering our sufferings for others. We have been challenged spiritually in a fresh way, we are enjoying time with friends, and we are losing weight, too, albeit slowly. Our goal is physical fitness, so we are better able to serve the Lord, not looking like we never had a baby.

"After all," Scott reminds us both, "in eighty to a hundred years our bodies arc just worm food anyway, so why not use them while we can to be open to the life-giving power of love?" Humorous though it may be, there's a point of truth in it as well. Or as a ninety-eight-year-old gentleman once said, "We're only here to get out of here." We need to retain an eternal perspective on why we have a body in the first place.

We'll Have Too Many

One friend having her second baby in two years said, "What if I have a baby every year?"

God rarely blesses a couple that much. How many families do we know personally or from history who boasted a family of that size?

God doesn't ask us, "Are you willing to have a certain number of children?" Rather, he says, "Will you be open to the next one?"

One of our friends was expecting her ninth child. I was curious about how she could think through being a mother to that many children. She replied, "Well, eight was seven plus one, seven was six plus one, and so on."

"OK, Carol, I get the idea. That's helpful; another baby is just the next one. The five we have is the four we had plus one more." Since babies usually come one at a time, it's not as difficult for me to imagine a larger number of children in our family.

Nursing is a great blessing in many ways. There is no guarantee that we will not conceive while nursing. However, most women who nurse completely in the early months experience a number of months of amenses, delaying a return to fertility.

At the six-week checkup following Michael's delivery, the doctor asked me what I was going to do about contraception since I should not get pregnant after a C-section for at least six months. I told him that I did not believe in contraception; I was going to nurse the baby and trust God. He confirmed that as long as I nursed full-time for the early months, my body would not return to normal until it had healed enough from the C-section.

I appreciated his encouragement and, in fact, I have had at least a year of amenses following every delivery.

Just because we entrust our family size to God does not mean we will have many children. We have conceived nine times, but due to miscarriage, we are raising only six children. A number of families in the Steubenville area where we live have been able to have only one, two, or three children in more than twenty years of married life.

Overpopulation

Overpopulation is a myth that can be traced back to the nineteenth-century English economist Thomas Malthus. He proffered dire predictions in the early 1800s about increases in population. Malthus was convinced that the human race might destroy our way of life based on our inability to control sexual drives.

In 1822, Francis Place, with thoughts based on Malthusian ideas, urged liberals to crusade against the problem of overpopulation. Birth control was presented as the solution to humanity's lack of self-control. Margaret Sanger used this misinformation to promote her agenda for birth control, abortion, and population control.

In 1968, Paul Ehrlich's book *The Population Bomb* exploded onto the scene. He fanned the flames of fear regarding population control. Though his solutions to the problem were radical, most of them are being implemented today. People tout these population control solutions as compassionate, but they are not. They cannot be implemented without interfering with a couple's God-given liberty to be open to life.

World hunger is not a problem of overpopulation but of technology—the challenge of making the land that exists more productive. This is why twenty thousand Native Americans sometimes suffered from starvation on the same land that today feeds millions of people. What has changed? Technology has been developed to improve tools and methods of farming.

According to Robert Sassone's *Handbook on Population*, there is much land yet to be developed for food production: more than three times the rain-fed land currently being used for food production is still available; developing countries could eventually produce ten times more food for the world than they do; the earth has more than one million years' supply of oil that is yet untapped; and only 11 percent of usable land is used by the six billion people in the world today.[4] In fact, Sassone demonstrates that a country that stops growing in its population begins to decline.

Poverty continues in so many places around the world. If the source of the problem is not overpopulation, what is it? The problem is political rather than economic. Many countries that struggle with extreme poverty have governments whose political policies interfere with economic growth. Governments prevent or destroy crops; they control the means of production; they impose heavy taxes; they debase currency; and they limit people within a caste or political system. By discouraging development of technology, they limit growth.

In addition, some people revere their food supply (grain or cattle) instead of consuming it. (One missionary in India watched a shopkeeper beat hungry children who begged for food and then allowed a cow to stop and eat.) Ethnic groups starve each other, destroying each other's crops in civil wars. Corrupt governments limit supplies to their people based on politics. Natural disasters interfere with food production. All these factors contribute to poverty and have nothing to do with population size.

In the name of compassion, people have developed policies to limit population growth: forced abortions and sterilizations in China, which have resulted in women being injured and dying; forced sterilizations in Peru in Tubal Ligation Festivals;[5] sex education materials that encourage homosexuality. These programs demonstrate why the Church opposes such policies. To remove civil liberties in the name of meeting society's needs is contrary to human dignity.

Who benefits from the myth of overpopulation? The abortion and anti-life industry benefit: people can more easily justify killing life if they are convinced they are helping the overall population problem. The sex industry benefits: homosexuality is encouraged; pornography flourishes since birth control and its backup, abortion, help people risk sex outside of marriage without fearing pregnancy. Hyper-ecologists and people who worship nature further their agendas by pitting people against nature.

Though overpopulation is a myth, many people perpetuate it today. Part of embracing the cross is embracing the suffering of being misunderstood in our culture. A dear friend, Anne, was sightseeing in Boston with her children when a man approached. Her three-year-old held her right hand, her two-year-old held her left, her one-year-old was in the backpack, and she was visibly pregnant with a new baby.

The man said, "It's people like you that are causing all the problems in this world!" With that, he spat on her!

If that had been me, I would have spat back. But Anne, being the gracious woman of God she is, just looked at him sadly and said, "I'm so sorry you can look at these precious children and think *they* are the problem." Rather obviously, the problems of this world relate more to intolerant attitudes toward children than to children themselves.

Psychological Issues

Newlyweds

Newlyweds are typically told, "Get to know each other first." Yes, there *are* adjustments to married life, such as learning to be less selfish and more giving. And just being male and female, we are radically different. The early years can be even more challenging, depending on how many major differences we have in our backgrounds. But if we do not know each other, we shouldn't get married.

One young mother writes about beginning marriage with a simple openness to life: "It was wonderful. We had a beautiful baby girl nine months later."

Another couple concurs: "Having a baby so soon has helped us to learn about sacrifice and selflessness from the beginning. We don't own a home yet, and we have clothes from discount stores, but God has provided."

Pam, from Vermillion, Ohio, advises young couples to be aware of the option of NFP, "but they need to be encouraged, exhorted, to only use NFP (to postpone pregnancy) for *serious reasons*. They may need to be encouraged to be open to life right from the start. We had a child ten months after we married—a blessing for our marriage."

One of the greatest blessings of pregnancy for us has been growth in healthy dependence on God and interdependence on each other. It brings out the best in us: I feel so feminine when I am pregnant; I am not as self-sufficient or independent because my needs are greater, and that draws the best out of Scott as provider, supporter, and encourager. We both need more grace from God, too, so we can serve each other and the family more. That's good for everybody, even if it is challenging.

Don and Michelle followed the advice of waiting a year before being completely open to life. After eight years of marriage that included periods of infertility and miscarriages, they have just delivered their second child. She told me, "Please tell young couples getting married, don't wait. You don't know what is ahead."

For some newlyweds, the adjustments to married life may constitute a serious reason to use NFP. But don't assume it is serious just because other people say it is. Remember: the Lord does not always bless couples immediately. Openness to life can allow for the joy of spontaneity and space for God to time the first child without the pressure of trying to get pregnant.

We Have Enough Children

After I gave a talk in Lincoln, Nebraska, a woman approached me to tell me her story.

> I already had ten children when someone asked me whether or not I was still open to life. I responded, "I already have ten!"
>
> My friend said, "You never know, but number eleven could be your special companion in old age." She was right. My husband passed away recently, and this special son, number eleven, is my heart and a dear friend.

What a blessing that this woman had such a bold, good friend.

When we think about having *enough* children, it is often in reference to other families. But we do not decide family size based on comparison.

When I shared the good news that one of my sisters was expecting, my son said, "Mom, come on! We're losing!"

I laughed (and said a quick prayer for his future wife). "Losing? Honey, this is not a game to win or lose—we *all* win when there is a new life. All we can do is ask God for the blessing of children and be grateful for the gifts he gives us. This is not a competition."

We wonder, what might the next child be or do? I have never heard of someone in later life wishing they had had one less child, but I have heard many people say they wish they had been open to at least one more child. As one father said to me, "I wish we had had two more children. I would love to know what they would have been like; whom they would have looked like; what their gifts, talents, and abilities would have been."

The Vatican II fathers noted:

Among the couples who fulfill their God-given task in this way, those merit special mention who with a gallant heart, and with wise and common deliberation, undertake to bring up suitably even a relatively large family.[6]

If the only children of value were number one and number two, how many of us would be alive, especially if we consider our place in the larger family tree? Our existence was dependent on the heroic generosity of many of our forebears; will we also be generous?

Emotional Limits

We may be at an emotional limit. Either spouse might have a serious reason to use NFP based on emotional or psychological health. Why do we feel we are at the end of our emotional rope? Sometimes we can better sort through the difficulties if we can identify the reasons for feeling overwhelmed. What needs to change to lessen stress?

If we are suffering from fatigue, could a sitter or mother's helper give us the time we need to exercise or nap? It may not be a major expense, but it could make a big difference. I remember being flooded with gratitude when a friend dropped by to take my oldest son to a park so that I could nap when the baby napped. Those two hours of sleep were desperately needed just to face the rest of the day.

I also found that lack of sleep was more difficult to cope with when I had our first couple of children. I panicked over whether or not I would ever sleep six hours in a row again. Now I have had enough children to know that months of night feedings are relatively brief. It has even become a special time for prayer and for cuddling the littlest one when time is so limited during the day to pray or cuddle.

Are there mothers who would be willing to mentor us in the area of home organization, if that is getting us down? They could point us in the direction of books, tapes, and videos that help with organizing the home, streamlining housecleaning, or assessing our overall vision for what we are doing as a wife and mom. Perhaps we need a game plan that includes our children on the work crew. Perhaps we can budget for hired help.

Are there women whom we respect in the area of discipline of children who could tutor us? We may not have grown up in a household that offered good discipline. Does our spouse agree with us about a strategy for discipline? Sometimes the frustration is caused by not knowing how to discipline children, rather than the number of children we have. There can be chaos with two and order with ten. Again, there are great books and materials to assist us to work together on this task.[7]

If there are serious marital difficulties, a priest or a counselor could be necessary. Perhaps a counseling group or a spiritual director could offer concrete ideas to improve marital communication. If the stress is related to finances, perhaps there is a financial counselor who could develop a strategy for budgeting and goal setting.

Help is available if we identify the problems. Let's remember to take one day at a time, or as Jesus says, "Therefore, do not be anxious about tomorrow, for tomorrow will be anxious for itself. Let the day's own trouble be sufficient for the day" (Mt 6:34).

Those of us with a number of small children may feel the need for a breather before heading into another pregnancy. The fragility of our emotional state can change when other circumstances change. Our spouse can offer greater emotional support. Our children will get older and be better able to assist. Lorraine wrote: "I feel more organized with four and a half children than I did with two, and I know it is because my focus has changed from 'my will be done' to 'Thy will be done.'"

We need to draw on the graces of the sacraments of Confession, the Eucharist, and matrimony. If possible, we can be rejuvenated by getting some time before the Blessed Sacrament, filling our heart and mind with love for our Savior in the midst of solitude. As we grow in Christ day by day, we will grow in the grace of Christ and the fruit of the Spirit.

Whatever our particular emotional need, we can find ways to meet those needs through counseling, support groups, reading, and prayer so that we can be the kind of wife and mother or husband and father God wants us to be. And, perhaps, we will have the mental and emotional health to be open to another baby eventually.

Fears

Many women face various fears: fear of a miscarriage or stillbirth, fear of severe vomiting or toxemia, fear of a normal delivery, fear of another C-section, fear of breast infections from nursing, fear of postpartum depression. All these fears are real; they cannot be wished away with a quick-fix pat on the back. Can we identify what fear is gripping our heart and why? In order to develop a strategy to combat the fear, we need to know what it is first.

I never knew there were so many references to peace in the Mass until I was pregnant with Jeremiah after my second miscarriage. I felt as if the priest was giving peace, people were sharing peace, and God was giving peace to everyone but me. I finally approached a priest for Confession.

When I revealed my anxiety, he listened compassionately. Then he said that though my concern was understandable, my anxiety was sin. Concerns are petitions to be prayed; anxieties are sins to be confessed. After I repented and he prayed over me, I was filled with peace. Only rarely did I struggle with anxiety about miscarriage after that.

Two passages of Scripture helped me a lot when I was in the grip of anxiety during Jeremiah's pregnancy (following back-to-back miscarriages). The first was this: "Have no anxiety about anything, but in everything, by prayer and supplication with thanksgiving, let your requests be made known to God. And the peace of God, which passes all understanding, will keep your hearts and your minds in Christ Jesus" (Phil 4:6-7). The second was this: "Cast all your anxieties on him, for he cares about you" (1 Pt 5:7). Prayer—with thanksgiving—is the key.

How can we tackle fear? First, we need to train our hearts in truth so that we can respond rather than react to the possibility of new life. We need to review the call of God in the vocation of marriage, the value of each child, the love we have for our spouse, the power of the grace of the sacraments, and the privilege it is to offer suffering in union with Christ.

Second, we need to develop a strategy. We need more facts about the situation we dread. What went wrong that we can change?

Are there medicines safe for a baby that could help us with high blood pressure? morning sickness? toxemia? Do we need a new doctor? Should we switch locations for the next delivery (home instead of hospital or vice versa)? Is there anesthesia that would work better? Can we find helpful materials on VBACs (Vaginal Birth After C-section) or postpartum depression?

Knowledge often lessens fear. Perhaps we can speak with people who have faced similar situations and find out strategies that worked for them.

A couple who had lost a child to cancer wanted to be open to more children, but their grief was too deep to imagine risking the loss of another child. They asked me if they should be open to another child, and I assured them that they alone could answer that; I could not tell them that their fears or concerns were not serious enough to delay a pregnancy. However, I prayed with them and told them I would continue to pray for them. A year and a half later I received a beautiful birth announcement expressing thanks for prayer and joy at the blessing of this new little one.

Jesus has paved the way for us by resisting temptation and gaining strength to face trials:

> For we have not a high priest who is unable to sympathize with our weaknesses, but one who in every respect has been tempted as we are, yet without sin. Let us then with confidence draw near to the throne of grace, that we may receive mercy and find grace to help in time of need.
>
> HEBREWS 4:15-16

There *will* be grace in our time of need, if we ask Jesus.

Criticism From Others

Get your spouse to help run interference by boldly stating the great news of the next child's conception. Or perhaps send in one of the children with the revelation. Rarely will a grandmother look into the shining face of a grandchild and lament a new baby.

If face-to-face contact sounds intimidating, announce the happy news in a letter and invite their joy. If there is a way to address their primary concern—health and well-being, finances, the closeness of the children in age—that might help them open their heart more to this child. On the other hand, if they have a preconceived notion that there *ought not* be more children, conversation about it with them may be a waste of time and energy.

We should share our news with enthusiasm. Sometimes relatives are tentative about their joy because they do not know how we feel about the news. One grandmother asked, "Are you happy?" Another queried, "Is this good news?"

Perhaps if they see our smiling visage, they'll be reticent to voice their concerns. Keep in mind St. Paul's advice to St. Timothy to be courageous, "for God did not give us a spirit of timidity but a spirit of power and love and self-control" (2 Tm 1:7).

Perhaps we need to support our husband, if criticism is directed against him. Following the announcement of their sixth child, the husband's business associate retorted, "Can't you control yourself?" His friend misunderstood openness to life as a kind of fulfillment of rapacious sexual desire. In reality, the father was taking true responsibility in his commitment to his spouse and all children who resulted from their love. (They have ten children now.)

A similar situation of embarrassment happened to Janet's husband.

While at a large party celebrating my father's seventy-fifth birthday, my father, who is not a member of our faith, stood and introduced my husband to all of his friends as "my son-in-law the sex maniac." Everyone roared with laughter, even though it is quite possible that my husband was the only man in that large gathering that had been virtuous before marriage, faithful in marriage, and faithful enough to accept the full responsibility of fatherhood. The world equates birth control with self-control—a perfect example of Isaiah 5:20-21.

It takes the courage of conviction to stand tall when others try to knock us down to size.

Sometimes people are just negative about children. We always looked forward to having a large family. Before we had children, some people warned, "Wait until you have one, then you'll think differently." After we had our first, we still wanted a lot more.

Others predicted, "Wait until you have another one. You'll change your mind." After we had our second child, people remarked, "Since you have two boys, you're probably still hoping for a girl."

Finally, after Hannah, people assumed we were done. When they found out we *still* wanted more children, they quit fussing with us because we would not be "reasonable."

This is *our* life, *our* marriage, and *our* family. We are the primary ones sacrificing; we will take full responsibility for each child. We must not let family or friends keep us from having another child just because we can't face the criticism. The gift of a child is too wonderful to let another's negativity control us.

It is natural to want encouragement from loved ones; however, let the Lord be the one who says, "Well done, good and faithful servant," even though we want to hear it from the people we love most. Sometimes we have to dare to be different, even if we are all Christians. Pray for those who oppose us to have a change of heart, to have the grace to see the eternal significance of what we are doing so they will support us in it.

Less Conflict With Fewer Siblings

People think if there are fewer children or they are spaced farther apart, they can avoid sibling rivalry. Yet rivalry happens because children, like their parents, are sinners in the process of being saved. Sure, if children are spaced far enough apart, there will be less conflict because they will have different interests, different schedules, and different friends. They will live mostly separate lives. Spaced far enough apart, there will be less conflict simply because there are fewer siblings!

In contrast, siblings who are born closer together share much in common: common interests, similar schedules, and often the same friends. In fact, children love having more children. Let's coin a new phrase: sibling revelry! Fewer children may minimize the conflict, but it also minimizes the joy. Rather than eliminating the children, let's eliminate the behavior that shows a lack of virtue in order to minimize the conflict.

Some people want fewer children because they are introverts or because they were raised in a small family. They anticipate that a small number of children could still feel like a crowd. Fewer children will give everyone more private space. But the Lord can help us develop coping skills to deal with a larger family.

Our children might also tend to be introverts, in which case, even a large family would not necessarily be a loud family. Rather than focusing on our limitations, we should focus on God's limitless grace and strength. A larger family may be outside our comfort zone; but if the Lord graciously blesses us with a number of children, he will give us the strength we need to embrace each child with joy.

Emotional Issues

Care for a Handicapped Child

Burke and Ruth's third child is a son with Down's Syndrome. When I asked them if that had affected their openness to life, they said yes. Their resolve was strengthened to surround this handicapped child with siblings who would love him with the unconditional love siblings have for each other. They anticipated that their children would be sensitized to the needs of other handicapped people since they would have met the challenges of serving their brother.

We have to face our own mortality. Our handicapped children are probably going to outlive us. Let's not be shortsighted. Let's give them siblings who will love them long after we are gone with the unique love of siblings combined with the compassion of children for someone who is hurting.

A woman approached me after I gave a talk in Anaheim, California, on openness to life. She explained that since she was an only child, she had not thought it unreasonable to choose to have only one child since her child has Down's Syndrome. "But now I want to go home," she began, through many tears, "and see how many loving siblings I can give this precious girl." She had a new vision for what God's blessing of siblings could mean for her little daughter.

Most of us who have had babies after we were thirty-five years old have been offered a battery of tests when we were pregnant. One woman related her story.

The doctor is pushing the triple check and amniocentesis. I asked her why? She said to find out if there are any birth defects, Down's Syndrome, etc. Then I asked, "If you find the baby has one of these, then what?" She said, "Then you would have an option to terminate the pregnancy." I said, "Oh, no! My husband and I are Catholic. We don't believe in murdering children, including the ones that aren't perfect. Don't bother with the tests; it wouldn't matter anyway."

We need to stand up for disabled people, born and unborn, and declare God's truth: Their lives are as valuable as ours because, like us, they are made in the image and likeness of God. He is the one who declares each one of us valuable.

When Scott and I were expecting our first baby, people would ask, "Do you want a boy or a girl?"

Our quick response was, "We don't care, as long as it's healthy."

One day, Scott asked me, "Does it have to be?"

I was brought up short. Here I thought our answer was so magnanimous; we had no condition about the sex of the child. But there was a condition: health. "No, I guess the baby doesn't have to be healthy," I said. Thereafter, our response to questioners was, "We don't care if it is a boy or a girl. We pray for health, but regardless, this child is God's good gift to us."

Some dear friends in Cincinnati have lived this truth. I want to share a portion of their account.

In 1961, our second child was born. We named her Carol Joy. Carol Joy was a breach baby, but other than that, there were no other problems. We did notice that she was very placid, cried very little, and was easy to take care of ... unlike Julie, who had been a real "live wire." But she didn't really seem to be responding. At her six-week checkup, our doctor suggested that we should see a neurologist.

After several conferences with doctors over the next weeks and months, we were told that Carol Joy was a microcephalic (small head). Part of the brain had not been formed properly. There was a chance that the brain could still grow in time, but they were not really optimistic about what she would be able to do.

We were devastated.

We were both Christians, and we trusted God, but this was hard to handle. We asked the same question everyone else asks: "Why did this happen to us?" We prayed continually that God would allow her brain to grow and permit her to live a normal life. So did many of our friends.

Betty and I decided that we would take Carol Joy home with us ...

and love her. That's what we did. We didn't want to place her in an institution; we wanted to keep her with us. It became apparent that there would probably be no change in her condition, and we would have to accept her, just the way she was.

Carol Joy could not walk, or talk, or react to us in any way. She was never really aware of our presence, although our friends assured us that she really did "know us." There was never any evidence of this, but we knew her and loved her.

During those years, God was making a lot of changes in our lives. While we were both Christians and attended church regularly, we needed more than that. We began to read the Bible more regularly. Betty began a Bible memorization program. She would sit in Carol Joy's room and go over her verses for the week. Carol Joy was a "captive audience." She heard a lot of Scripture verses over the years.

Betty and I decided to start an informal Bible study in our home for friends and neighbors. It quickly became obvious that young people really wanted to talk about spiritual values and how the Bible could actually change people's lives. But the most important person in our group was the little girl in the next room.

Carol Joy was always there. On the first or second time in our home, it was sometimes awkward for people to see her. They didn't know what to say. Most of them had never seen a child like this. But it wasn't long before they would look in on her, hold her hand, pat her head, and make sure she had her bottle of juice.

And surprisingly, people became different just by being around her. In a way, Carol Joy was a little evangelist ... a silent little evangelist. Even though she couldn't say a word, even though she was completely unaware of everything around her, she seemed to have the capacity to bring people closer to God. People around her were changed.

We learned lessons that we could have never learned before. We made new friends that we would have never known. Our priorities changed dramatically, and our lives were blessed tremendously because of Carol Joy, as were the lives of so many other people. It's hard to understand how a child so severely handicapped could actually make this a better world, but she did.

It is so common today, in situations like this, to ask, "Why does God allow this to happen? Was it just a tragic accident, or was there really a purpose?"

Looking back, it has become clear to us that there definitely was a purpose. Through this little girl, God was able to draw people to himself and make the rest of us more caring, more loving, and more compassionate to others.

After Carol Joy's death, several people confided to us that they had prayed for her recovery ... every day ... for twenty-one years.

But God said no.

Heaven will be a wonderful reunion. We have the assurance that she will be whole. For twenty-one years she was unable to walk, unable to talk, unable to really recognize us, completely unaware of everything around her. But now we know that she is up there walking and talking and dancing and singing and laughing ... most important ... laughing. And we can tell her that we love her, but I suspect that she knows that already.

As this testimony demonstrates, Carol Joy's life counted. Every life counts, because every life is a gift from our heavenly Father.

It can be difficult to imagine caring for more children when the needs of a handicapped child are so great. One mother recalled her family's experience:

In 1992, after many struggles with our two daughters' health, they were diagnosed with cystic fibrosis (CF), a genetic, fatal illness with an average life span of thirty years. We were devastated, to say the least. Previous to this time, we were casual Mass attendants, married in the church, had the children baptized, etc. But there was no zeal; the Lord was not an active part of our lives. However, with the onset of this illness and the challenges we faced with the maintenance of the girls' health, I found my way back to Mass, daily.

I hadn't been to the Sacrament of Reconciliation for many years. I prayed for help from our heavenly mother, and I think she led me by the hand to my pastor one morning after Mass. That was a turning point spiritually.

My husband and I took the girls to a supposed apparition site of the Blessed Mother. We had heard of healings there. We had no sparks or flames on that trip, but it was beautiful, and the most important thing was that we "relearned" how to pray the rosary. Upon returning home, I began to pray it daily.

I became pregnant about a year after that. People thought we were crazy to run the risk of having another child with CF, but I didn't feel that way. The Lord had done so many wonderful things through this suffering for our children that we knew everything had been in his hands all along.

I remember reaching a point when I said, "OK, Lord, I'm ready. If you are going to take them, I thank you for allowing me the time to prepare. It would be the most awful thing that I could ever feel in my heart, but they are yours anyway. To know they would be with you would be consolation enough for me."

Funny thing was, they began to improve incredibly. I learned about herbal formulas that greatly helped their condition. We administered them faithfully along with breathing treatments, chest physiotherapy, and the Eucharist. Life went on in faith.

Our third daughter, Noelle, was born in 1993, and after testing at six months of age, was found to be CF-free. Praise God!

I finally got up enough guts to talk to my husband and tell him I couldn't use "anything" anymore, except for abstaining during fertile times, God's will be done. He wasn't happy—brooded for quite a while. But he is really, truly, a wonderful man. He loved his family too much to let it become an issue and agreed. We weren't looking for it, but it has happened again. So we await this baby, our first boy.

As my husband and I continue to grow in faith and love, learning all the while, we are very aware of the blessing God has given us. The most profound of all is that a year ago last May, the girls were healed. They were retested at the pulmonologist's request and found to be free of the illness.

This is unheard of, of course. Many are not quite sure what to make of it. But I do know that four years prior, I was told by a visionary that the Blessed Mother said they would be all right; they were praying with her to her Son.

Sometimes miracles do happen.

It's Too Hard to Make My Children Live This

One of the most difficult things for any parent is to watch a child suffer. Our natural inclination is to shield them from any and all difficulties, but we have to supernaturalize that inclination to be sure we are all faithful to God. Living the Church's teaching on openness to life will include suffering.

When I gave talks on abortion, the toughest crowd to convince were women in their forties, fifties, and sixties. They would never have had an abortion; however, if their daughters were raped or carried a child who was deformed, they told me that they could not tell their daughter not to abort. Likewise, one of the greatest challenges facing us in America are the couples in their forties, fifties, and sixties who struggle with sharing the truth about contraception with their children.

Some young Catholic couples suffer because their parents pressure them to use contraception. Sometimes siblings support each other even when their parents will not.

> My two sisters and I, through the grace of God, have been led to the truth of this teaching and choose to live it. Both our mother and grandmother, very strong in their faith, think birth control is OK. It's kind of a paradox to be talking to your sixty-year-old mother and your eighty-six-year-old grandmother about the use of birth control being morally wrong. In most families it would be the other way around! They found a priest who led them astray, and they followed.

How sad that the very women who should give the greatest support and encouragement to these three young women actually oppose them.

Our faithfulness to God as parents includes obeying him regarding openness to life *and* urging our children to obey. Remember, our Blessed Mother did not tell Jesus *not* to go to the cross because it would be too painful for him. Rather she accompanied him to his death, praying for him and feeling his pain from a distance.

In imitation of Mary, we should not withhold the truth from our children. Rather we should accompany them throughout their arduous journey of obedience to Christ so that they may live lives worthy of the calling to which they have been called. We need to remember, and to remind our children, of St. Paul's admonition to us that we are children of God, "and if children, then heirs, heirs of God and fellow heirs with Christ, provided we suffer with him in order that we may also be glorified with him" (Rom 8:17). We must not try to spare our children suffering that comes from pursuing holiness. We want nothing less than heaven for them.

Concern About Hypocrisy

If we ourselves once compromised the truth with contraception or sterilization, we may feel disqualified to talk about the Church's teaching with our children. Is it hypocritical to teach our children to live truths we failed to follow?

The very opposite is true, provided we repent. Once we have gone to Confession, we train our children not only to obey the Church's teaching but also to receive God's grace through Confession when they are not faithful. It's humbling, but even that can be used by God for good.

Realize that it is not God who accuses us that we can't tell our children to live truth we have not lived flawlessly. Walking in forgiveness means teaching our children responsible moral behavior. We dare not withhold the truth from our children—we *have* to do better for our children, once we know the truth.

Desire for Spontaneity Without Pregnancy

Someone may say, "I want to be spontaneous without getting pregnant." Well, I want to eat at Dairy Queen whenever I please and never gain weight! But it ain't gonna happen.

First, Natural Family Planning, used correctly, has a higher rate of effectiveness (not getting pregnant) than any form of contraception. Instead of messy, difficult-to-use contraceptives, and without the uncomfortable side effects of the Pill or IUD, NFP helps clarify which days are fertile; all other days are available for spontaneity. (For more details, see chapter 8.)

Second, if we choose to be open to life without using NFP, we have two benefits: We can be as spontaneous as we want; and we don't fear pregnancy because we have already reconciled our heart to the possibility that it could occur. In fact, it is a real joy to get to the place where we simply say with our hearts and our bodies, "Lord, please make this act of love life-giving in your time."

Finally, spontaneity in lovemaking is not necessarily more passionate or tender than planned lovemaking. Often couples about to wed feel more strongly about spontaneity than do couples who have been married awhile. Most women prefer to have some idea about when intimacy will occur so they can prepare themselves.

Often a certain amount of work around the house and time for talking prepares a woman's heart for lovemaking more than a sudden lavishing of physical affection leading to a spontaneous marital act. This is certainly something for each couple to figure out for themselves. Unfortunately, our culture gives the impression that spontaneous lovemaking is the best, and, depending on the couple, that may not be so.

People Plan Families

Made in God's image, we imitate him with our rational cooperation and obedience. Animals copulate out of instinct. We, on the other hand, know we are giving ourselves to each other and receiving each other as gift. We renew our covenant with the act of marriage, and we take responsibility for new life that may result.

A current myth is that men, like animals, cannot control their passion for sex, so women had better protect themselves against pregnancy. Certainly, passions can be strong—for men or women—but self-control is a fruit of the Holy Spirit. Our desire is not for *sex* but for intimacy and union with the person to whom we have committed our lives. The habit of self-control that was developed before marriage is important for the times in marriage when we need to abstain from relations. Though sexual intercourse does help counter concupiscence, our goal is to love each other with complete self-donating love.

No one *plans* to have a baby; only God does. We do plan when we will be completely open to life, but whether or not we are abstaining, we acknowledge God has the best plan of all, which might be different than ours.

My Spouse Does Not Want More

It is very painful when one spouse desires a child and the other one does not. Sometimes the husband desires more children and the wife refuses. Sometimes the wife wants more children before it is too late biologically, yet the husband denies her.

The spouse who is closed to life, at least temporarily, needs to be sure there is a serious reason for saying no both to God and spouse. Possibly the spouse who desires another child is ignoring factors that constitute serious reasons.

We have to do the relational work to come to one heart and mind: sharing concerns, listening to each other's heart, praying together and for each other. Remember: "Love does not insist on its own way" (1 Cor 13:5). If we are still at loggerheads, we may need someone we both trust who can help us discern the issues involved. Even though it is a struggle, our marriage can grow in the process if we maintain respect and love toward each other.

Financial

Not Enough Money

We prayerfully balance St. Paul's teaching, "If anyone does not provide for his relatives, and especially for his own family, he has disowned the faith and is worse than an unbeliever" (1 Tm 5:8) with Jesus' teaching, "Don't be anxious for your life.... Seek first the kingdom.... Let the day's own trouble be sufficient for the day" (Mt 6:25-34). We work diligently, but we also trust the Lord to provide for us.

Can we imagine the response from a couple who lived two hundred years ago, were we to tell them we were too poor to have another baby? They might have a few questions for us: You have electricity and indoor plumbing? You have cars instead of horses? You have grocery stores (as opposed to farming for daily food)? They might well conclude, "The problem is that you are *too rich* to see your poverty of thought about children!"

Couples who are DINKs (Dual Income No Kids) often focus on building their careers rather than building a family. Recently, a young man arrested my attention with this comment: "We're on our way from being a DINK to being an OINK."

"What does that mean?" I inquired.

"We both used to work, and we didn't have any children. Now we've had four kids in the last five years. So now my wife is home full time and we are halfway to being an OINK: One Income Nine Kids!"

The Catholic Church has long supported a family wage for a man so that a woman can be home to mother the precious children the Lord has given them. To pursue that vision some good financial decisions have to be made:

Avoid debt as much as possible. If we are already in debt, we should get out of debt as soon as possible, remembering that "the borrower is the slave of the lender" (Prv 22:7).

When both spouses work before children, as much as is possible, they should try to live on the husband's salary, so it is not so difficult to forgo the wife's salary when a baby arrives.

Keep in focus that people are more important than things—we do not have to own a house before we have children.

Think long-term: The children will be home only a few short years. Remember to invest wisely; children are our real wealth.

Bottom line: We make the wisest financial decisions that we can. Then we entrust all our plans to the One who loves us best and knows what we need.

Desire to Provide Well

Often parents want to give their children their own room, a college education, or whatever the children desire. But if we want the best possible gifts for our children, what about siblings? After one of Scott's trips, he shared the following incident with me.

A young child was screaming as the plane began its descent. Scott turned around to the frustrated father, suggesting that the child would stop crying soon once his ears adjusted to the change in cabin pressure.

"Is this your first?" Scott asked.

The wife began to nod yes, but the father said, "No, she's our last! But we're gonna give her everything."

To which Scott quickly rejoined, "Everything but siblings." The dad looked chagrined, but the mom gave Scott the thumbs up sign.

Since when is giving our children everything they desire the best goal for them? That could actually backfire; we could set them up for failure in marriage and failure in life. Siblings, on the other hand, force them to share, to give, to serve, and to sacrifice.

Aileen reflected, "We are the parents of eleven children. We left the size of our family to God, and, of course, we had many trials, but God will never be outdone in generosity. So much joy came to us, and still comes, in our family life."

Our children develop virtue as they love, have conflicts, and resolve dilemmas together. They develop character by learning what it means to love others selflessly rather than collecting toys and trinkets selfishly. And when we are gone, they will have each other to help them complete this journey of faith on earth.

Siblings are the greatest physical gift, apart from the love you give your spouse, that you can possibly give your children. And unlike other gifts, they improve with age, as Mary from Elkhart, Indiana, confirms:

After my parents had twelve children, we took in foster children between the time they were born and adopted. During this time my mother had a miscarriage. After this difficult experience we received Johnny, our last foster child, whom we eventually adopted. He is black and we have received many criticisms from the world for bringing him into our white family. Yet we always knew, and so has Johnny, that God offered him as a special gift to our family, and he has added a great deal to our lives.

We may have worn hand-me-downs and eaten generic food, but our clothes were always ironed and our stomachs were full. We all received Catholic educations through college. Just at the moment when we had no money left, it came. God has never failed us; he always provides.

My father will never be able to retire. My mother will deal with some physical suffering the rest of her life because of the thirteen pregnancies and twelve births. Yet these things do not matter to them. My parents have embraced sacrifice wholeheartedly. These children are living monuments of their sacrificial love. They have been a wonderful example to the world not only of faith-filled saints but also of God's awesome generosity.

I can never thank them enough for all they have provided me: food, shelter, clothing, a two-parent household, a mom to stay home with me, a Catholic education, a great faith, and twelve best friends that will be there for me the rest of my life. The best gifts my parents could give us children, besides our faith, were siblings. For when the entire world is against you, your family will always be there to support, help, guide, protect, and love you.

From time to time we all need the reminder of how great a gift our children are to their siblings. Here's an incident that occurred in Pittsburgh.

I went into a Chuck E. Cheese restaurant with my husband, his parents, and our three children. At some point I was alone with our daughter, Hannah, along with another woman and her little girl. We were watching the two girls play when she said, "Do you ever think about having another baby?"

I answered, "Yes, I do. I think about it all the time."

To which she inquired, "Is she your first?"

"No, she's my third."

"Really?" She seemed surprised.

I continued, "I think a sibling is the greatest physical gift that I can give my children."

She grew quiet. "My husband is from a big family, so he wants more children. But I don't think I want another child."

"Do you have any siblings?" I queried.

She seemed pensive. "I just moved from Philadelphia, away from my only sister. I really miss her."

I restated my premise. "I think that siblings are the greatest physical gift we can give our children."

All of a sudden she got teary-eyed. She picked up her daughter and said, "I'm going to have another baby." And with that, she left Chuck E. Cheese. I never knew her name, but I'll bet her husband was glad we had that conversation.

Children are not the ones who say no to more babies, unless they have been coached. When visiting a friend with our new baby girl, my friend's two children seemed fascinated by her. I nudged my friend, "How about a third?"

She turned to her son, then four years old, and said, "Tommy, what do you think about another baby?"

Right on cue, Tommy parroted, "Debbie's enough. Debbie's enough." He had been coached well.

My friend handed me the baby and thanked her son for reminding her that, in fact, Debbie was enough. My heart was very sad at the thought that they had enlisted their son to protect his mother's heart from wanting more children.

When I was expecting our fifth, my eleven-year-old, Michael, said to me, "Everyone should have a baby when they have a kid my age. It's *so* exciting!" Our children count down the hours until they can hold the new baby in their arms.

Can't Afford More

According to some claims, raising a child is very expensive. The caption for one health insurance company ad picturing a newborn read like this:

> Three years of dancing lessons. Eight years of piano. It all adds up. Today, it costs $224,800 to raise your child to college age. And that's assuming she's going to like her nose.

$224,800? Who calculated that amount? "Like her nose"! Are they implying that caring for children's needs may include plastic surgery?

This is an unsubstantiated modern-day myth! Anyone who is paying that amount per child has not gone to yard sales, used hand-me-downs, had generous families, or resisted the temptation to succumb to advertisers for the latest fads. The question is, What do we value? What will our standard of living be? How sad to select between designer clothes for two children or sharing clothes and being able to afford a third child. What poverty to value things over people!

There are a variety of ways we can cut costs so that another child can join our family without breaking the piggy bank. Within families, for instance, aunts lend clothes for nieces and nephews, and grandparents often give assistance. Through yard sales, rummage sales, and Salvation Army Stores, people have purchased all kinds of baby equipment and clothes at a fraction of the cost of new. Often they don't even look used. We are reminded continually, "And my God will supply every need of yours according to His riches in glory in Christ Jesus" (Phil 4:19).

At one sale I found a good-as-new car seat and stroller for five dollars apiece. I asked the woman whether or not she really wanted to sell them, since her child was still so small. "What if you have another baby? Won't you need these things?"

She quickly countered, "I told my husband, 'If you get me pregnant again, I get all new stuff!'"

Her attitude amazed me. Her husband had been forewarned: He would pay for it if he got her pregnant. It is too bad she adopted an adversarial relationship toward her husband should she conceive again, but at least my family benefited from her selfishness.

One friend who was raised in a large family asked this question: Is it really possible to live in America and claim to be too poor to have children? Caley says:

> I wish more people would talk about the blessings of children instead of the burdens. I think the emphasis should be on what they give us. By the world's standards, John and I couldn't have afforded one child, much less four. But finances have gotten better with each child. We've learned to focus on each day and thank God for our tremendous blessings. People often make rude comments to us about our family because they don't understand how we could be so foolish as to have four kids a year apart. I guess we do look crazy with four car seats in a rundown old minivan. But we can smile back at them because we know we've found the secret to living life joyfully—our children.

All over the world people do with much less, yet they are rich in family life and they know the worth of their children.

A couple of old movies, *Cheaper by the Dozen* and *Yours, Mine, and Ours,* are fun-loving family films depicting how large families care for each other, sharing rooms and belongings, assisting one another, and working together. Aren't these the values we want our children to have? The fewer children we have, the more we tend to take care of things ourselves instead of requiring the children's help. The more children we have, the more all of us must give of ourselves for the good of the family.

Pope John Paul II offered Mass on the Mall in Washington, D.C., during his first visit to the United States. He said:

> Decisions about the number of children and the sacrifices to be made for them must not be taken only with a view to adding to comfort and preserving a peaceful existence. Reflecting upon this matter before God, with the graces drawn from the Sacrament, and guided by the teaching of the Church, parents will remind themselves that it

is certainly less serious to deny their children certain comforts or material advantages than to deprive them of the presence of brothers and sisters, who could help them to grow in humanity and to realize the beauty of life at all its ages and in all its variety.[8]

We can't afford *not* to be open to life.

Spiritual Issues

When a Priest Gives Approval to Contraception

No priest can authorize the unauthorizable. Perhaps Father is not fully aware of the Church's teaching, though he should be; maybe he deliberately dissents from openness to life, though that is not a legitimate option open to him. When a priest sanctions contraception or sterilization, *Casti Connubii* calls it, "the betrayal of his sacred trust."[9]

We must pray for our priests to be faithful fathers. My husband does not really care whether or not the children like him when love demands a difficult decision. If our children faced a choice between poison that looked like beautiful candy and good food that looked like mashed-up peas, he would take away the poisoned candy and offer the peas. He is not in a popularity contest. *That* is the price love pays.

Likewise, it is essential that our priests have the strength of spiritual fatherhood to say to their children, "Contraception is poison to your soul and to your marriage, and openness to life brings health to your soul and to your marriage." Priests can offer comfort and consolation for the difficulties a couple is experiencing, but they cannot condone sin in the name of compassion.

Church teaching has not changed, and it will not change. A priest in Ohio observed the great sacrifices involved when a local pastor gave up his career (and financial security) to become a Catholic. The priest said the man's sacrifices inspired him to risk preaching against contraception, though it might mean suffering for the sake of truth.

Even though a priest may have sanctioned contraceptive use, it is our own responsibility to form our conscience about the wrongness of contraception.

We have access to the *Catechism* and other Church documents. We can know God's truth as taught by the Church. Clericalism is not an excuse for error.

The Bible Was Written Before Modern Technology

The Bible is pretechnological; God isn't. He isn't bound by the conventions of any age. Though technology changes, God does not change and truth does not change.

Technology in and of itself is neither good nor evil. How technology is used and for what purpose it is developed makes the difference in whether or not it honors God. One godly purpose for technology is understanding more about God's creation. For instance, technology helps us explore the universe and plumb the depths of the oceans. Another godly use of technology can be to reverse or slow the effects of sin by providing cures for disease or by tracking down criminals. (There may be many more godly purposes for developing technology than these two.)

Birth control accomplishes neither of these purposes. It reveals nothing about God's creation nor does it reverse the effects of sin. Fertility is not a disease to be cured, nor are children the consequence of sin. (Even in the case of rape, any child conceived is still a gift from God and not part of the sin of the father.)

Some people imply that since we have developed the technology of contraception, we are obliged to use it. Otherwise, we are poor stewards of knowledge acquired if we choose to ignore it. But the question remains whether or not the technology should have been developed in the first place. One theologian proffered that a disregard for technology on this issue could lead to "a bondage to nature camouflaged by religion";[10] however, we need to take care lest we accept bondage to technology camouflaged by common sense!

Insofar as technology has assisted us in understanding how our fertility works, that technology has a good use. Natural Family Planning, for instance, utilizes a thermometer to chart a woman's cycle, enabling the couple to pinpoint times of mutual fertility. Looking at God's design, the Creator's intention is revealed: procreation cannot occur every time a couple engages in the act of marriage, whereas union can. Therefore, it is possible to abstain during times of mutual fertility while remaining open to life rather than contracepting and intentionally thwarting the life-giving nature of the act of marriage.

Prevention of conception is not a legitimate realm within which science should operate. (Currently, we face similar issues in the area of genetic engineering, for example.) To whom do we owe obedience: God or science?

More Time for Spiritual Commitments

Sometimes we want more time for spiritual things: holy hours, retreats, and apostolic work. As my mother says, there are seasons of life for everything. If God wants us on the mission field or in ministry, it will fit the priorities we have for our marriage and family life. Of course, God wants us to pray; but is the priority spending an hour or more a day in prayer while we have little ones who need constant care, or will that time come in a few years?

Selfishness can creep in even with spiritual goals. But as Blessed Josemaría Escrivá has observed, "He is our Physician, and he heals our selfishness, if we let his grace penetrate to the depths of our soul."[11]

One friend wrote that the corporal works of mercy *are* a mother's works. These works are reflected in Jesus' words about those who minister to him by caring for those in need.

> I was hungry and you gave me food, I was thirsty and you gave me drink, I was a stranger and you welcomed me, I was naked and you clothed me, I was sick and you visited me, I was in prison and you came to me.
>
> MATTHEW 25:35-36

Here's how a mother accomplishes such corporal works of mercy:
"I was …
"… hungry." Mom makes school lunches, snacks, and meals.
"… thirsty." She nurses; she brings cups of cool lemonade onto the driveway basketball court; she offers jugs of ice water to children gardening in the orchard.
"… naked." She dresses them; she covers them with blankets at night; she wraps them in towels after countless baths; she takes them to a sale in the mall.

"... a stranger." She welcomes them in the womb; she eagerly prepares their room; she brings them home from the hospital; she prepares for college break homecomings.

"... imprisoned." She listens with compassion when a teenage body holds so many emotions.

Sometimes I feel bogged down by the mundane tasks involved in being a homemaker. Am I making headway in holiness? Shouldn't I be doing more for God?

One night at Eucharistic adoration, I jotted down the following poem:

My Path to Sanctity
Where I am, I am to be.
This is my path to sanctity,
Though toil and strife—the affairs of life—
Draw my attention away from Thee.
I begin again, afresh, anew.
Today I choose to follow you.
Though others' demands require my hands
Clasped in prayer to open and do.

I want to make each task a prayer,
Each word—each thought—*your* love to share.
Though sins abound
Forgiveness I've found,
As the cross you've made for me I bear.

I ponder, at the close of day
On the manifold graces that came my way.
Through trials and pain and joy, I exclaim,
Where I am, I am to be.
This is my path to sanctity!

Our vocation to marriage is our call to holiness. Faithfulness in the myriad tasks that comprise marriage is our path to sanctity. Today we need this reminder: There are all the time and resources I need to do what God wants me to do today. (I may have unrealistic plans, but God does not.) As St. Paul declares, "I can do all things in him who strengthens me" (Phil 4:13).

Only for Catholics

Some say that these truths apply only to Catholics. Not at all. Before 1930, all Christians were united on this issue. This teaching is based on Scripture, traditional Christian teaching, natural law, human dignity, and conscience.

Are only Catholics eager to follow Christ sacrificially? No. Are only Catholics trusting in God's sovereignty? No. Are only Catholics interested in giving God everything, including their fertility? No.

A woman named Mary wrote to us recently and shared the following story:

> Because of the tapes Scott made, I became aware of your research into Protestant prohibitions against birth control. My sister-in-law, who is in some nondenominational Protestant church, was using the contraceptive pill. I found a book and sent it: Scripture about children versus birth control.
>
> She took it to heart. Because I sent the book, I now have a nephew! Because I was reading things to send my sister-in-law, I decided that we really did not have any substantial reason for avoiding more children ourselves, so we now have a fourth child.

Openness to life applies to every married Christian.

Good Protestants Disagree

We may know Protestant friends and even pastors who have been sterilized. If they seem more spiritual than we are—better students of the Bible or more prayerful—we may tend to assume that their actions must be OK for Christians.

We should not assume we are not smart enough or spiritual enough to understand their reasons; they may have been swept up by the culture of death without knowing it. Historically, Protestants stood with the Catholic Church in opposition to contraception until 1930. That could be a fact that our Protestant friends do not know.

Other Christians are under the same obligations we are to follow truth;

there isn't one standard for Catholics and another for other Christians. In fact, we have important information they need to have that will give them the clarity to live according to truth.

God Can Overcome Contraception

Some couples assume that if God wants them to have a baby, he can overcome contraception. After all, "accidents" happen. Some people even offer this objection after they have been sterilized: Since God can do anything, he can give a sterilized couple a baby.

First, let's offer a word other than *accident* to describe God's allowing a surprise gift of new life for our family. What's involved in an "accident" besides an unexpected occurrence? An accident is painful, debilitating, and sometimes deadly. It often involves suffering, and usually there's a mess to clean up.

How about this? Let's call an unexpected child a windfall: unexpected, yes; but a windfall is also a bonus, a blessing.

Now to answer the dilemma. Are we supposed to test God by saying, "God, if you want me to have a baby, you can give one to me, even though I am blocking the possibility with contraception or sterilization"? It seems as if we are daring God to make us faithful against our will.

We need to separate the questions. The question about whether or not to contracept has already been answered; it is an immoral act. The question about whether or not there is a serious reason to abstain during the fertile time still needs to be explored. If there is no serious reason to abstain, the couple remains open to life. In this way they can discover whether God wants them to have a baby; the answer is not always yes.

Spouse Insists on Contraception

We are obligated to follow the Church's teaching on contraception, whether or not our spouse agrees. It is a matter of objective truth, not one spouse's opinion over another's. What options are there if your spouse insists on contraception?

First, you can temporarily abstain from the act of marriage. As best as you can, explain to your spouse that for love of him or her, you cannot contracept. At the same time, you acknowledge that engaging in the act of marriage is a duty.

As much as you love your spouse, you have to love God first. Explain that you hope total abstention is only a temporary measure until a different solution is found. You are not trying to punish your spouse for contracepting, but trying to avoid participating in sin.

Offer up the real suffering this would be for the good of your marriage. If you go this route, it is essential that you demonstrate in other, concrete ways how deeply you love your spouse, so that in no way do you communicate rejection.

Second, you have the option to use Natural Family Planning. NFP could be a compromise without compromising your faith. If you follow NFP carefully, you could assure your spouse that there would be less of a chance of pregnancy resulting than if you were to contracept. Though some abstinence would be involved each month, there would still be many days for having relations. Hopefully, this is a compromise with which both of you could live.

Third, if your spouse threatens to have an affair or to divorce you unless you use contraception or agree to sterilization, you can allow a sterile act of marriage with great sadness to avoid this greater evil. But you must make it clear that you are not giving consent to it nor are you the one who will employ the contraception.

It is with great sadness that a spouse enters into the act of marriage with the other intending to sterilize the act. According to instructions given priests from the Pontifical Council for the Family, it is possible for a faithful Christian to have intercourse with a spouse who voluntarily renders the unitive act infertile when all three of the following conditions apply:

when the action of the cooperating spouse is not already illicit in itself;

when proportionally grave reasons exist for cooperating in the sin of the other spouse;

and when one is seeking to help the other spouse to desist from such conduct (patiently, with prayer, charity, and dialogue, although not necessarily in that moment nor on every single occasion).[12]

As the spouse who is faithful to Christ, *you* cannot use contraception, no matter how insistent your spouse may be, and *you* cannot be sterilized. However, at the risk of mortal sin, your spouse can, and you will not be guilty of his or her sin.

John Kippley concludes:

It is generally agreed by Catholic moral theologians that when a wife is threatened by infidelity if she does not allow her husband to have contraceptive sex with her, she may allow him to use her body in that way without her sinning. The idea is that she is allowing one evil to happen in order to avoid a greater evil.[13]

Permitting a sterile act of marriage is not the same thing as actively participating in evil, though we should help our spouse avoid mortal sin at all costs for his or her soul's sake as well as our marriage's success.

There is another critical consideration. "Furthermore, it is necessary to carefully evaluate the question of cooperation in evil when recourse is made to means which can have an abortifacient effect."[14] In *Evangelium Vitae*, Pope John Paul II speaks to this point:

It is never licit to cooperate formally in evil. Such cooperation occurs when an action, either by its very nature or by the form it takes in a concrete situation, can be defined as a direct participation in an act against innocent human life or a sharing in the immoral intention of the person committing it.[15]

As discussed earlier, some forms of contraception have an abortifacient aspect: the Pill, Norplant®, Depo-Provera®, and the IUD. If your spouse wants to sterilize your act of marriage with something that could mean you participate in taking the life of your child, you cannot cooperate.

As much as possible, try to explain that your sense of obligation comes from your love of God, your true love for your spouse, and your desire to follow Christ, no matter what the cost. You are not asking your spouse to agree with you, though that would be optimal. However, your spouse should not ask you to go against your conscience or your faith. Try to arrive at a solution in conformity with faithful marital love in a spirit of loving respect.

Jesus, the Model of Life-Giving Love

Any one of the concerns addressed above could cause us to close our hearts to another soul. It is my hope that these thoughts, testimonies, and Scripture texts will encourage you as they have encouraged me, so that we will keep our hearts open to the possibility of another child in our family.

The key is to keep our eyes fixed on Jesus. As *the* life-giving Lover, he has generously called us into existence, given us the gift of our spouse, and enabled us to imitate his sacrificial, life-giving love. Can we imitate him with generous spousal love and be open to one more soul?

V.
LOSS OF LIFE:
MISCARRIAGE, STILLBIRTH, INFERTILITY, AND STERILIZATION

CHAPTER TEN

MISCARRIAGE AND STILLBIRTH

One of the keys to facing any loss is understanding the love of God the Father. Meditating on God the Father helps us make sense out of suffering, the suffering of waiting for the blessing of a child or losing a child he has given us.

Any time we suffer, we wrestle with two facets of the providence of God: His love for us and his power to change anything. Either God loves us and is hurting with us, yet does not change our situation because he cannot; or God can do anything, and he is choosing not to change our situation because he does not really love us enough to care that we are suffering. Neither position is tenable; but both are ideas that rummage around in our souls when we are trying to understand why our suffering does not end.

God is our loving Father. As Father, he loves us as his children. There is nothing he would not do for us, except that which would not be best for us. As God the Father, he is completely able to change any circumstance; only love for us would prohibit him from changing it.

Our heavenly Father is not a miser, withholding the blessing of children until we beg him enough or jump through the right hoops to please him. Neither does he grant life whimsically, giving children to those who might spurn such a gift and denying them to those who really desire them.

As God, he has a perspective we cannot have. Isaiah says, "For my thoughts are not your thoughts, neither are your ways my ways, says the Lord. For as the heavens are higher than the earth, so are my ways higher than your ways and my thoughts than your thoughts" (Is 55:8-9).

We see our isolated circumstance. He sees our circumstance in the light of the rest of our lives: individually, as a couple, as a family, as a part of the Church, and in the light of time and eternity. He can be trusted to balance unconditional love for us and unlimited power. He has a greater plan than we can see for our holiness and for our part in the kingdom of God. Our heavenly Father is faithful, and he will never change.

Losing a Child in the Womb

Few moments in our lives can match the deep-seated joy when we realize a new child has been conceived. We rejoice together as a couple; we select the best time to tell loved ones; we anticipate the special days—and the years—to come.

But then there's the twinge of a cramp, a feeling that everything is not right, and bleeding. We wait, we watch, we pray; and then we grieve the loss of a person we never met, never held in our arms, and never will see this side of eternity.

The loss of a child is a painful experience. So many families have had at least one miscarriage that we can say it is a common experience. At the same time, it is an intensely personal experience. Sometimes people say and do just the right things that lessen the pain and ease the difficulty. Others suffer from foot-in-mouth disease—they are so awkward in their attempts to be helpful that they deepen our suffering.

The following are suggestions for what to say to a family that has lost a child. They are based on the experiences with loss many of us have suffered. If we take time to think through what we say and do, we can make this difficult time more meaningful and bless the family involved.

What Can We Say to a Friend Who Has Lost a Child?

"I'm so sorry for your loss."
That really says it all. This child who died was a real human being, regardless of size or age—a child who will be greatly missed. Consequently, the parents are in real pain. People in grief do not need quick solutions to fix their pain, though I hope the sentiments expressed in this section will be helpful. They need our sincere sorrow and love, a squeeze of the hand or a hug.

> "Miscarriage is real hush-hush because it's early and often at home. ...
> There is no death certificate, no record that a child, a child of yours,
> ever existed," said JoLynn Crouch, a determined Utah woman who
> endured multiple miscarriages and stillbirths on the way to becoming
> a mother of seven.[1]

When there is no body to hold or bury, people often underestimate the loss. This further intensifies a couple's feelings of sadness. By acknowledging their loss, we can lighten the load of grief.

We can communicate sympathy well whether or not we have experienced this kind of loss ourselves. Jesus wept at the tomb of Lazarus (see Jn 11:35) though he knew he would raise him from the dead. Like Jesus, we weep with those who weep (see Rom 12:15); yet we do not grieve as people without hope (see 1 Thes 4:13). One couple from Rialto, California, spoke of the comfort they felt when their parents and family recognized that they had actually lost a child.

"Did you name the baby?"

Encourage a couple that has lost a child in the womb to name the baby. It makes the reality of this young life more concrete for everyone. Remember the child's name for a future note or gift.

Our children have received comfort in being able to refer by name to the children we have lost: Raphael, Noel Francis, and Angelica Frances. We remember the children we have lost in a special way on the feast day of the saint for which they were named.

It is not too late to name your baby or to grieve your loss, no matter how long it has been since your loss. A grandmother called in to a radio show I had on the topic of miscarriage. Her loss had occurred fifty-three years ago, yet she wept fresh tears as she recounted the story. Only recently had she discovered the healing that could come if she named her baby and let herself grieve.

"How are you?"

Give your friends an opportunity to share about how they are and about the child they lost. Give them a sense that you are not in a hurry. Sometimes people are so afraid that it will reopen a wound, they do not ask. That can make people who have just lost a child feel as if others are not acknowledging their child's life or death.

Ignoring the topic, rather than giving your friends a chance to share thoughts and feelings, can make them feel shunned or neglected. One mom wrote, "I was twenty-two weeks pregnant at the time. I finally got a dear friend to listen and to ask questions. I needed to talk, but most people were too afraid to say anything to me." Diane, from Long Beach, California, was grateful that people "asked me about it and let me talk."

A couple from Nassau, New York, had a sudden loss. "We had a beautiful stillborn baby girl. We were helped the most by persons who came to the house immediately and a lot. Some sent cards that said to trust in the Lord, etc. Others spoke to me about it and asked how I was. They let me talk about her." We need to have others recognize our immense loss.

One woman had the trauma of discovering she was pregnant out of wedlock, and then, two months later, she hemorrhaged. She recounted what happened:

Nobody has ever lost a baby [in my family]; it had not occurred to me. But I did lose her. I never felt her move inside me because she wasn't old enough. I never watched my stomach grow, because it didn't have a chance to, but I always had the knowledge that she was there and I loved her.

My mom said, "You'll have other children." What she didn't understand then and still doesn't today is that that would be the equivalent of saying that any one of us is replaceable.

For seven years not a day went by that I didn't think about my daughter. And no one seemed to understand my pain or my loss. I heard a lot of "it wasn't meant to be," and it only added to my pain. If what they said was true, not only were my pain and loss not real, but neither was my daughter.

Nobody mourned her, only her mother. One Mother's Day, one sister bought me a gift. I wrote, "A Mother's Day gift for a childless mother."

At a prayer meeting, a woman asked me if I had a child. I told her yes, and she said, "God wants you [to know] that your baby is with him in heaven." I was on my knees in an instant. I cried so hard but mostly tears of joy. My baby was real; she had a soul and is a person; to mourn her was OK.

This woman's suffering was intensified by her family's failure to acknowledge her loss and pain.

Though husbands and wives may grieve differently, we must believe that our spouse is grieving without making him or her express it the same way we do. Fathers are often overlooked. One grieving father shared his frustration.

"I had questions continually about, 'How's your wife? How's she doing?' But never about how are *you*," said Chuck Lammert, an engineer at a power plant in St. Louis.

"I was offered some consolation when I came back to work, but it was mostly about getting on with business. And I tried. I didn't know of the significance of the events unfolding," said Lammert.[2]

Mr. and Mrs. Lammert help lead SHARE, a national network offering support for grieving parents.[3]

Another father addressed the difficulties that grieving dads face.

"A great many of us end up running from it. We throw ourselves into work or drink a tad more or go fishing," said Michael Donnen, a therapist who conducts grief workshops in Seattle. "Society says we're supposed to be strong for our wives, that they can do the crying for both of us."

But it's a setup, because while the wife might be crying she often is also seething…. Doesn't he share this grief? The divorce rate among couples that have lost a child is significantly higher than the norm.[4]

Just because men and women grieve differently does not mean that either spouse is not in grief. It is also important that grieving parents allow their children to express their grief, so that the family can share the loss together.

People in grief can have good days and bad days; it can be an emotional roller coaster. Try not to figure out a timetable for them to be better. Much grief comes in waves, triggered by due date or death date anniversaries, holidays, and special songs.

"Your child is with the Lord."

If the goal of Christian parenting is getting your children to heaven, then we have already succeeded with this child. Our child will live forever. We have often said to our children, "Raphael, Noel Francis, and Angelica

Frances are with the Lord. We intend to join them, by the grace of God. You guys make it a complete family, OK?"

Heaven will never be the same again. I remember the strong sense that I had not just had another loved one die; a part of me had died. Heaven is dearer because a part of me is there.

St. Paul says, "For to me to live is Christ, and to die is gain" (Phil 1:21). Though it is agony for those of us who remain, the truth is our children are better off with the Lord. They have been spared the pain, suffering, and sin in this world.

Though our plans were awesome for this child, God had a better plan. "We know that in everything God works for good with those who love him, who are called according to his purpose" (Rom 8:28). Although we cannot see it quickly, it is still true. We ask God to show us blessings from such tragedies.

Susan Erling shares a poem she wrote following the death of her unborn child.

Just Those Few Weeks
For those few weeks ...
I had you to myself.
And that seems too short a time
To be changed profoundly.

In those few weeks ...
I came to know you ...
And to love you.
You came to trust me with your life.
Oh, what a life I had planned for you!

Just those few weeks ...
When I lost you,
I lost a lifetime of hopes,
Plans, dreams, and aspirations.
A slice of my future simply vanished overnight.

Just those few weeks ...

It wasn't enough time to convince others.
How odd, a truly unique person has recently died
And no one is mourning the passing.

Just a mere few weeks ...
And no "normal" person would cry all night
Over a tiny, unfinished baby,
Or get depressed and withdrawn day after endless day.
No one would, so why am I?

You were just those few weeks, my Little One.
You darted in and out of my life too quickly.
But it seems that's all the time you needed
To make my life so much richer
And give me a small glimpse of eternity.

We take comfort in knowing that this child's life was not cut short; the psalmist says that the Lord knows the length of the unborn child's life (see Ps 139:16). There were purposes for the child's life, as short as it was, and there are purposes in his or her death.

Furthermore, this is not all there is. He or she will continue to live for all eternity, and God has a plan for that phase of his or her life as well.

"Perhaps your child, as part of the communion of saints in heaven, could be a special intercessor for your family."
Certainly, a child's love for parents and siblings would be perfected by Christ. I believe I am a different wife and mother because of my children's intercession. A mother from San Diego, California, wrote: "I had seven miscarriages and one tubal pregnancy. (Now I only have one tube.) We conceived repeatedly, but they would die due to premature labor. I felt alone and brokenhearted. The most helpful thing someone said was my spiritual director's comment: 'You sure have lots of children praying for you in heaven.'"

A couple from Lake Orion, Michigan, wrote: "The knowledge of the communion of saints is very consoling as we can ask prayers of our children who have gone before us. We truly believe we have received many blessings from the intercession of our children in heaven over the years."

One of my sisters and her husband have lost eight of the fifteen children they have conceived. How do they face such enormous loss? She quotes Matthew 6:19-21:

> Do not lay up for yourselves treasures on earth, where moth and rust consume and where thieves break in and steal, but lay up for yourselves treasures in heaven, where neither moth nor rust consumes and where thieves do not break in and steal. For where your treasure is, there will your heart be also.

Kari concludes, "Children are the only treasures we can store in heaven."

Marianne and her sister nursed their mother during her last few days of life. (Her mother had delivered eight babies and had miscarried seven.) As she was dying, she kept asking her attending daughters, "Can you hear them singing? I can hear them. The babies are singing to me." Though the world might think this woman ridiculous for having risked, and seemingly lost, so much, yet her own testimony as she left this world was that she was rejoining those who had gone before her to enjoy them forever with the Lord in heaven.

"Mass is the one time our family is united in a powerful way."
We have found great comfort in knowing that in the Mass, the heavenly liturgy, our family on earth is approaching the same throne of mercy in front of which all our loved ones who have died in Christ are right now worshiping him. This has strengthened our hearts as we have grieved for the loss of loved ones, including our unborn children.

"I am praying for you and your family. Any specific prayer intentions?"
I have received great comfort in knowing that people were praying for us as we have gone through our miscarriages. Our first miscarriage—a tubal pregnancy with which I had been hemorrhaging internally for three days, probably from rupture—was January 22, 1989. We requested a blood test to check for HCG levels to be sure the baby had died, but the doctor said no technician was on hand. "In the time it would take to get someone here," he insisted, "you could be dead. We are going to surgery now!"

Hours later I awoke to tremendous pain. No small incision had been made, but rather a full vertical C-section cut. The doctor came in and said he had found a sack in the tube and had baptized it before removing it; I was to recuperate for four days on the maternity floor (no children permitted for visits).

I have never felt so empty. I felt the deep emptiness of knowing our child was no longer residing within me. I felt physically gutted; the surgery seemed excessive for such a small sack. And never had those first walks to the bathroom been so painful. All that pain with no baby to show for it!

I felt so alone. No one within me, and no one in the room, since Scott had to go home to be with our three young children. As I wept, the Lord brought to mind Hebrews 12:1-2, which speaks of our being "surrounded by so great a cloud of witnesses."

All of a sudden I realized that as I lay there feeling alone, I was actually in a very crowded room. Not only was Jesus there but also the saints who had gone before me, who had experienced much greater suffering than had I. And they were not there as silent observers, ready to be critical of my lame attempts to bear up under my suffering. Rather, they were surrounding me like spectators in a stadium, cheering me on in my race as champions who had already won the gold in this event. They were *for* me!

For the first time I understood the Church's teaching on the communion of saints—including one new encourager, my beloved child. How deeply grateful I am to know about the gift of these brothers and sisters!

Some people offered me special meditations or prayers. When it was difficult to formulate a prayer, due to grief, it helped me to have a prayer I could read out loud. Prayers for me to say and prayers of others buoyed my spirits.

A mother from Boone, Iowa, reflected, "I have miscarried four times. While recovering in the hospital, I could grieve, but I could not despair, because whenever I closed my eyes, I saw myself floating on a white cloud supported all around by hands folded in prayer."

When we were on pilgrimage in Jerusalem, we visited the Garden of Gethsemane. There is a beautiful church built over the rock on which we believe Jesus prayed and sweat drops of blood before his death on the cross. I brought with me there the grief from our third miscarriage six weeks previously.

As I meditated on Jesus' agony, I was reminded of a messianic prophecy: "Surely he has borne our griefs and carried our sorrows" (Is 53:4). Part of what the Incarnation means is that Jesus has entered into the pain of our sorrows as surely as he has borne our sin. As I wept on that precious rock, the Lord healed my grief.

The Brocks had a child suddenly die.

Meditating on the Seven Sorrows of Our Lady was the only thing that got me through the death of our two-month-old. Mary—Our Mother of Sorrow—truly held me close, and when I thought my heart would break, I'd look up and remember the hope of heaven. No matter how sad I felt or how much more suffering we would endure, there was a limit of [perhaps] forty more years, and then the hope of being reunited.

As our Lady of Sorrows, Mary's mother-heart draws us close to her and to her Son.

Monica, from LaCrosse, Wisconsin, reported that they "lost two early pregnancies after our second child. Then I did a novena to St. Maximilian Kolbe and asked for twins, who were conceived three months later on Ron's birthday!"

"When you lose a child, you realize how fragile a gift is our fertility."
When you conceive your first child, you usually don't think about miscarrying; you think about what Christmas will be like (pregnant at the time Mary was expecting Jesus) and the time you are due and what life will be like for years to come. That's further reinforced when you have babies without any difficulties.

Our first miscarriage happened after we already had three babies. What a shock! We were incredulous. We assumed it was a fluke.

Since our miscarriage was a tubal pregnancy (where the baby implants in the tube instead of the uterus), an ultrasound with our next pregnancy allayed our fears of a repeat: the sack was in the right place. We relaxed; we thought we were past the critical point of the last miscarriage, never suspecting that in a few weeks our baby would die.

Christmas was right around the corner. It was December 18, 1989. We were packed for our annual homecoming, but I had begun to spot, just a little. The week previously Scott and I had taken the children with us to hear the baby's heartbeat, but when the doctor could not find it with the doptone, he assured us that it was probably due to the baby's size.

But that was before I began spotting. We dropped off the children with friends and headed to the doctor's office. He examined me and said, very sadly, "Kimberly, your uterus is smaller than last week. That's not a good sign. We need to have an ultrasound." He had such compassion; he and his wife had suffered a recent miscarriage.

Our hearts were pounding as we wended our way to the local hospital, my bladder feeling every bump in the road since I had drunk the fluid required for a clear ultrasound picture. Surely the baby was OK. It couldn't happen again—not after waiting so long to conceive, not back-to-back losses, not at Christmastime.

The technician barely looked at us. "There's a sack, but there's no baby."

We could hardly breathe; it was over before we had a fighting chance to do something, anything, to save our baby's life. And the ordeal didn't end there. It was more than two weeks before I finally went into full miscarriage, with my body still giving signals of pregnancy with nausea and tiredness. (Talk about kicking someone when she is down!)

We had no idea our fertility could be this fragile. Would we ever have another baby to hold?

The Brocks discovered how fragile life can be.

We had two miscarriages before our son was born at term. It was a great grace for me to turn my heart back to my Creator and realize he alone is the Author of life. Before the miscarriages I had a cocky attitude that having children was a given. I was trying to plan my conceptions around the comfortable seasons to be pregnant. God in his mercy allowed the miscarriages to open our eyes to see how privileged we are to carry life at all.

This is a new realization for many of us who did not have problems with our first pregnancy as well. Theresa writes:

When we conceived baby number seven while I was nursing baby number six, my husband became angry. He eventually accepted this pregnancy (after a week or so), but a few weeks later this baby was stillborn. Through this suffering we learned how incredibly precious human life is, and he vowed never to be upset, no matter how many children God chooses to send us.

This couple just delivered their eleventh child, thanks be to God.

"Are you finding practical medical help to avoid repeatedly miscarrying?"
Due to repeated miscarriages, like so many other women Debbie was labeled a "habitual aborter." Doctors discouraged her from having more children, but did not offer to help resolve the cause of the miscarriages. She and her husband were left to find a solution on their own, if one existed.

After my fourth miscarriage, an NFP instructor recognized by my charting that I probably had a progesterone deficiency. That could be a factor in the cause of so many of our babies' prenatal deaths. I connected with Dr. Thomas Hilgers long distance, and, after some blood work, he diagnosed me with that problem. I grieved when I realized that so many babies could have made it had Dr. Hilgers' research on miscarriage been put into effect with us. Most of our doctors and midwives shrugged their shoulders and said nothing could be done when I was miscarrying. Now I know that's not true. I've had absolutely no bleeding this pregnancy and hope to deliver our "miracle" baby in seven weeks.

This baby was safely delivered on time, thanks be to God.

Dr. Thomas Hilgers has helped to develop The National Center for the Treatment of Reproductive Disorders.[5] This center has assisted many couples in their quest to resolve difficulties with fertility.

"You might consider recording your thoughts, feelings, and prayers."
Journaling helps a couple individually or together to record their thoughts, feelings, and any meaningful poems, sentiments, or psalms that helped them walk through their grief. It may be hard to imagine, but the pain will fade, and with it the memories of specific ways the Lord brought comfort and strength.

It is such a blessing to be able to reread a journal and get a clear sense of God's guiding hand. What are your memories of your child? your pregnancy? your delivery, if you had one? Karen Edmisten expressed her prayer in a poem.

Fiat
You said that we
Would have a child.
So I, in love, welcomed new life
And smiled
With each wave and sea
Of morning sickness,
Caught up in this
Miracle-to-be.
"For you, Lord," I said,
And offered each tiny suffering
As a gift to Thee,
Incomparable to the gift of life
You were giving to me.
And so I reeled,
Stunned and shaken
At my baby's death.
I was forsaken.
Anger rose and built a case
Against misinterpreted signs of Grace.

I was so wrong—
"Here is a child," you said,
Or so I thought.
But my arms are empty, bereft.
There is nothing left
Of my trust
When I listen for your Voice.
How can I trust when I was so wrong?
How will I again be strong?

I quiet myself and turn to you,
O Ancient Beauty ever new ...
I ask you, my truest and deepest Love,
For an answer, some comfort,
A sign from above.
There is silence,
And my tears ...
Tears of a mother's grieving love.

Then, in your kindness,
Your encompassing Love,
You embrace me and speak:
The words from above
Flow through an earthen vessel.
A man of God
Who listens to me
And tells me I can—I must—
Dare trust, for *all is as it should be.*
The mystery that is my child
Is in your hands,
Your Sacred Heart.
The part I play
Is to surrender and be free.

When next I quiet myself
To pray,
"My grace is sufficient for you,"
You say,
"For my power
is made perfect in weakness."
The words play again and again
In my mind,
Like a record left to skip ...
They rip
Into the core of my grief
And leave me no choice

But to drop to my knees
And offer you my child.

Oh, heal my heart, Lord,
Bitter and spent,
Be perfect in my weakness,
My Pearl of great price.
Though I offer it, Lord,
Imperfectly and poorly,
My life is yours.
Let your grace suffice.[6]

What a powerful prayer!

"Take good care of yourself physically."

When we feel such deep grief, it is difficult to think about taking care of our bodies. However, for us to cope with our loss and with the demands of our marriage and family life, we need physical energy. Experts say we need a good diet (junk food will not strengthen us); we need lots of good fluid (caffeine and alcohol are not recommended); we need some activity each day for exercise, though a doctor may recommend we wait (especially if we have had surgery); and we need adequate rest, even if we have difficulty sleeping.

It is especially difficult if you look still pregnant when you have miscarried. People who have not heard the news stop you in the store to ask when you are due, and you choke back tears as you explain, trying not to become completely undone in the middle of Wal-mart. On the one hand, do not push yourself with a strict diet and too much exercise simply to diminish onlookers' questions about impending birth; on the other hand, put away maternity clothes and, if need be, buy some larger size clothes that won't look maternity. (Perhaps this is a practical thing someone can do: lend you postpartum clothes so you can save the money for new clothes you want to fit you long-term.)

Try not to make too many demands on yourself. Ease back into life; you do not know day-to-day how you will feel physically or emotionally. You may want to schedule a physical exam about four months after experiencing a loss, just to be sure you are in good health. Physical fitness strengthens coping skills.

"Grief is very individual—trust your own sense of what to do as you grieve."
People can be so quick, especially religious people, to hurry us along in the grieving process. They want to tell us what we should or should not be feeling. They want us to follow a timetable with which they are comfortable. Try not to let others tell you what you need to do.

We experience a wide range of emotions as we grieve: shock or disbelief, feeling overwhelmed or numb, deep sadness, guilt toward ourselves, blame toward God or others, anger, depression to the point where it is difficult to function, and relief. (By the way, suicidal feelings are not normal or healthy. Get help if this is your struggle.)

These feelings can come in waves, like the ride of a roller coaster. Just because you've felt anger and you don't now does not mean those feelings will not resurface, for instance.

These are emotions any human being feels; religious people are not exempt, though we have access to grace through prayer and the sacraments that will preserve us from despair. God can absorb the anger that comes from pain and frustration. Our challenge is not to combine sin with anger.

St. Paul says, "Be angry but do not sin; do not let the sun go down on your anger, and give no opportunity to the devil" (Eph 4:26-27). God's love for us and for our babies is so great that he brings a child home only because he has a better plan.

Our son Joseph was conceived on the first cycle after our third miscarriage. Joseph has said, "I'm sorry that baby died, Mommy, but this way you get both of us: one in heaven and one on earth. Otherwise, I would not be alive."

This path of grief is one we must travel. To grieve deeply does not mean that we lack faith but rather that we have loved deeply and feel the loss acutely. It might be prudent to avoid major changes for a year due to your stress level and your family's.

If we ignore our grief, pushing it down as we think a "good Christian" should, it will come back to harm us later. This work of grief has to be done, in faith, and through it we will grow as Christians and as human beings. You can and will heal.

"I have miscarried before. If you want to talk about it, let me know."
Availability is so important. We should offer to share without imposing our grief on others who are in the midst of their own pain. We should not offer to share to trivialize their situation but to let them know they are not alone. Sometimes it helps to know that others have lost children and survived.

"Here are some resources I have found helpful in the grieving process."
Your local hospital may offer a service; if not, your pastor may have a local resource to recommend. Here are a couple of support options no matter where you live.

The Pregnancy and Infant Loss Center provides both immediate and long-term resources through our referral and support services, a vast array of literature, the Loving Arms publication, educational and awareness programs, and bereavement and memorial products. Parents, relatives, friends, coworkers, corporations, institutions, and care providers can all benefit from our many services.[7]

For a resource that is specifically geared for Catholics, there is Morning Light Ministry.

Morning Light Ministry is for bereaved Catholic parents who have experienced the death of their babies through ectopic pregnancy, miscarriage, stillbirth, or early infant death, including up to one year old. This death may have happened recently or several years ago.[8]

They also offer a monthly support group, individual help by phone, and a library on bereavement.[9]

What Can We Do for a Friend?

Consider these suggestions for taking action to help those who are mourning the loss of a child.

Offer a Mass or a rosary as a family for them.
Let the couple or family know in a card that you have said special prayers for them. A mother from Altoona, Pennsylvania, wrote, "I felt extreme consolation from them when they told me they said prayers, the rosary, or Masses for us."

Acknowledge the baby through a card or a little gift.
Barb had already purchased a gift for my child before I miscarried. A week after I lost the baby, she still gave it to me in memory of that child. Her kindness touched my heart. I still have that guardian angel picture as a reminder of that particular baby.

One year I had an artist friend make a watercolor of Jesus surrounded by five children, different ages, for my sister and brother-in-law who had miscarried five children at that time. The artist looked at photographs of their children so that the children in the painting would look like their family.

Send flowers—or better, send a plant that will live for a long time.
Be sure to send them to the couple or the family, not just the mother. We have received planters before. They are beautiful living reminders of the child. Sometimes people have planted trees in the child's memory. Recently, one family began an orchard, naming it after their two-year-old who had died.

One woman usually offers a white rose with the following explanation:

I hope in sharing this rose and my thoughts you will understand how deeply I also share your grief. After the death of my first child, his father presented me with a single white rose. Each part of this rose has a special significance to me:

Long stem—reminds me of the binding love, mine joining with the Lord's, that makes this child of both heaven and earth.

Thorn—sorrow whose pain is only dulled with time, but never forgotten.

Bud, beginning to open—my dreams for this child coming to full flower in eternity.

White—this child's innocence before God.

Single—my loneliness, never knowing the warmth of his body in my arms.

Beauty—the beauty of God's love seen in me and shown through me in my child.

When we take time to acknowledge someone's loss, we share the burden of grief in some measure.

If there is a body to hold, encourage the couple to hold the baby and take photos.

Some people are in shock, so they do not think to ask. Afterward, they regret that they missed that opportunity to say good-bye. Sometimes nurses will dress the baby and wrap him or her in a blanket so that the family can take pictures. More and more hospitals are sensitive to families and offer suggestions about saying good-bye.

A male nurse, who was also a deacon, observed the distress of a couple who were losing their baby in the emergency room of the hospital without much care or concern from the staff beyond basic medical care. After doing what he could to comfort them—staying near them, helping them through the labor, and baptizing the baby—he realized that more needed to be done. With another nurse, he helped write the "Patient's Bill of Rights" and the "Child's Bill of Rights."

Some of those rights included keeping the whole family together rather than keeping children or grandparents in the waiting area; having clay available to make an impression of the foot or hand; asking the couple if they want the assistance of a religious leader; treating the baby's body with dignity; taking photos of the family with their baby; and helping the family collect any mementos belonging to the baby as keepsakes. Many hospitals have adopted similar ideas.

Encourage the couple to gather mementos (crib card, baby beads, wristband, ultrasound photos, a lock of hair, footprint or handprint, record of weight and length) to have for the future. While the grief was fresh, one family put the photos and mementos of their stillborn daughter in a box on a high shelf. Later, when they were ready to look at them, they took down the box.

One grandmother keeps a photo of her stillborn granddaughter with photos of all her other grandchildren on her mantle. She is able to acknowledge her loss, too.

Encourage the family to bury the baby.

The family can request the remains of their baby from the hospital or doctor's office, if they lost the baby there. That way they can bury the remains themselves. Depending on the local laws, they might have to get the baby from a funeral home.

One family buried their baby on their land and built a special garden there. Another family buried the remains in a garden designated by their church for such burials—consecrated ground next to the church to which they can return even if they move away.

Try to attend the funeral Mass or burial, if you are invited.

It could be a very private moment for the family, but if you are invited, taking the time to be physically present, rather than just sending a card, can be a special way of loving them. Monica and Edmund said, "We buried the remains of our first baby, and about ten people attended the funeral."

On Memorial Day and on the feast of All Souls, there is a special service at the cathedral in St. Louis for all who have died recently. They read the names of all of the people who have died in the last six months, including miscarried babies. They light a candle as they say the name, and the family gets to take the candle home.[10] Those who have had miscarriages are given a Certificate of Commendation with the names of the parents and the child on it.

Offer to make meals or to coordinate meals.

If their family life is in upheaval, this may be a helpful offer. On the other hand, the family may wish to be left alone, trying to resume a sense of normalcy. If a lot of family members offer help initially, you may want to wait a month and then offer a meal.

Offer to take the other children.

Perhaps you could offer to take the children for an afternoon, or during the time the couple needs to be at the hospital. Or you could offer to bring the children to the hospital, if the mother will have to stay and the children are allowed on the floor.

One of the most painful aspects of my first miscarriage was that my children were not permitted on the maternity floor. I had never been away from my one-and-a-half-year-old daughter. There is something about miscarriage that made me ache to touch my children's flesh and to see their faces. It increased my suffering to have to wait five days before I could see them. (I hope that hospital policies have changed since then.)

If you are a homeschooling family, and the couple who miscarried homeschools, perhaps you could include their children in your homeschooling to allow the mother time to recuperate physically. One couple who had a stillborn child recalls: "We were homeschooling six at that time, and people graciously took our children in and included them in their homeschooling classes for a week. Others made meals." This additional practical help enabled the mother to rest more for a week before resuming normal family activities.

Note the due date and death date of the child.

These dates are very important. Let your friends know you are thinking of them and praying for them on the anniversaries of the child's due date (if the child was miscarried), the child's birthday (if the child was born), and the child's death date.

Drop your friends a note just before the due date to let them know you are thinking of them. Or note the death date and send a card near the anniversary of the child's death. These are significant dates for your friends—they could be times that are made more difficult if no one seems to notice.

Mary from Leesburg, Florida, remembers: "We miscarried a little angel at seven and a half months. We remember her on her birthday each year."

Share the Church's teaching about unbaptized babies.

A mother from Monroe, Connecticut, described her losses and some of the things she had done to deal with the grief.

In 1980, I gave birth to a beautiful premature son. He died shortly after. A year later, we had a little preemie girl who also died soon after she was born. These were our first two children. In the flurry of medical activity trying to save their lives, I don't think they were baptized before they died. And in the emotional state I was in, I didn't think to ask for their baptism.

We have since moved to a different place and God is so great—he blessed us with four more beautiful healthy children (ages ten, eight, five, and two). Time helped resolve our grief over the deaths of Michael and Ann, and I arrived at a place in my life where I stopped remembering them with pain and sadness. I thank God for those little short lives and deaths. In the time they were with me, I learned more about life and love and priorities than anything or anyone could have ever taught me.

I remember them with a smile now and have done so for a good number of years. On their birthdays some years, I pull out a picture I have of each baby and the tiny inked footprint that I have. I show my other children, and we talk a little about Michael and Ann. It is never morbid or depressing, usually more sentimental—musing at the tiny size of the footprint, or that Michael had lots of dark hair like his brother did at birth, etc. I have always been open and honest with my children about it all, and they are quite comfortable with this knowledge.

I myself struggle with the idea of limbo for these two babies who did nothing in their little lives other than bless mine. It's hard to believe God would create those two precious souls who, through no fault of their own, were destined to be separated from him because I or the nurses failed to have them baptized.

Belief in limbo, as a place apart from heaven, is not required by the Church as an article of faith. What does the Church teach about unbaptized babies? Let's turn to the *Catechism*:

> As regards *children who have died without Baptism*, the Church can only entrust them to the mercy of God, as she does in her funeral rites for them. Indeed, the great mercy of God who desires that all men should be saved, and Jesus' tenderness toward children which caused him to

say: "Let the children come to me, do not hinder them," allow us to hope that there is a way of salvation for children who have died without Baptism.[11]

The babies of believers might be covered under baptism of desire. If there had been any way we could have baptized them, we would have.

Help for the Holidays When You Are Grieving

Consider these suggestions for coping with the holidays and the special sense of grief they can bring.

Acknowledge that there is a conflict of emotions.
You have joy, yet you feel sad; peace, yet you feel unrest and fear; faith, yet you have questions and doubts. You have gifts, yet you feel loss; hope, yet you feel empty and depressed. It is better to recognize such competing emotions rather than suppress them.

We can feel isolated even in a crowd.
Whether we are in a crowd at the mall, bustling about, or at large family parties, we can feel very alone. Family gatherings usually are anticipated with joy, but they could intensify the sadness, especially if our loss is ignored or if others are in the midst of pregnancy or celebrating a new baby.

We have to assess reasonably where the holidays should be celebrated.
When we were in the midst of our second miscarriage, with bags packed to go home for the holidays, the doctor encouraged us to go ahead with our plans. We assured him that we were willing to stay, but it would be a greater loss not to go. And it would be a blessing to be there. It was very hard to take out my maternity clothes, especially a dress I had just made, and replace them with normal clothes, but it was still better for us to go.

For some people, however, drawing your smaller family together may be more peaceful and comforting. To be with the larger family might be more stressful, because you might feel as if you are under scrutiny for how you are handling your loss.

We may want to limit some of the holiday activities we normally do.
Perhaps another family member can host the larger family this year. Or maybe your family will not go caroling with the church group or bake cookies for a large cookie exchange. Other years the holidays may be less difficult. Be good to yourself by limiting what could add stress.

Perhaps you can let the children do some of the baking or decorating that you normally do. Talk over your plans with your spouse and children.

Perhaps a special memorial would be helpful.
Could you give a gift in memory of your child to a special charity? Or could you make a special donation to a charity with the money you would have spent on that child's gifts? Perhaps you could adopt a needy family and provide their Thanksgiving or Christmas.

Consider signing your Christmas cards "… and in loving memory of _____" to include the child you do not want to be forgotten. One of the most special gifts I have been given is two Christmas ornaments with the names of Raphael and Noel on them. My sister inscribed them and had them when we came home the Christmas I was miscarrying. They are precious reminders to me, and every year I place them on my tree and share their stories with our children.

Perhaps you could purchase a living evergreen as your Christmas tree, and then plant it after Christmas in your child's honor.

What Not to Say

Well-meaning people have either lessened the grief or increased it through thoughtful or thoughtless words and actions. As one person with experience noted, "Friends and family may tiptoe around it, afraid of coming too close…. Or [they may] trample over it, bombarding grieving parents with useless, if well-intentioned, observations."[12] Here are some things to avoid saying.

"It's common; it happens a lot."
Perhaps—but it's still a unique event in this person's life. Some people may find comfort in finding out how many people have experienced loss. Often

people share their stories of loss while they are offering words of comfort. However, the fact that it's common doesn't lessen the pain.

A couple from Baltimore, Maryland, had a miscarriage at six to eight weeks. They recall: "The doctor remarked so coldly, 'This is common if you get pregnant with the Pill being involved.'" That was a very hurtful comment.

"You'll probably have another baby."
This is false comfort; no one knows that a couple will conceive again. Even if they do, one child does not replace another. Nevertheless, another child may diminish some of the pain of this loss, especially if the couple conceives soon after.

"Don't fuss–at least you have one!" or, "Be happy with the ones you have!"
Of course we are grateful for any living child. What does that have to do with our loss? This comment is as pointless as saying to someone who just lost a parent, "Be grateful you still have another parent." Of course, but one parent does not take away grief for the parent who just died.

Gratitude for existing children does not preclude pain for the loss of another child. In fact, when we love our living children so much, we long to be with the child we lost—to know that child and the similarities and differences that child has in comparison to the others. There is no question that loss strengthens our love for existing children, especially when we realize anew how fragile life is. However, one child does not replace another.

This comment is meant to shut someone up, politely. A mother from Chicago who received such a comment got the message: "I kept my sadness in because it was expected."

"At least you weren't very far along," or, "At least you know you can get pregnant."
These statements do not acknowledge pain and loss; they minimize it. Granted, loss earlier in pregnancy is less painful than later; however, it is still a *real* loss. The child may have been only 30 percent grown, but he was 100 percent our fully human child. Since we are pro-life, we believe that the child was a special individual from conception on. A real person, regardless of size or age, was lost.

One mother wrote:

When I told people that I had miscarried and the circumstances, they thought it strange that I would even mention it—pregnant one day, the next day, not. I guess you have to be a certain number of weeks along before you can receive condolences. (This was not true of our pro-life friends.)

Some people make these minimizing comments because they are older, and in the old days many babies died. The day my youngest brother was born, my mother called from the hospital, very upset. The nurses said he appeared to have pneumonia and they had taken him to intensive care; he might not make it. My grandmother's response shocked me: "At least she hasn't held him yet."

I felt numb. How could my tenderhearted Grandma sound so callous? Actually, she wasn't being hardhearted; in her day, many babies died after birth. She herself had lost a baby at one and a half years old, so she knew my mom was spared that kind of pain. Still, whether or not my mother had held her baby in her arms yet, she had held him under her heart for nine months. Thanks be to God, he was fine.

"Just use birth control. You don't have to keep going through this!"
If we suffer multiple losses, some people tire of hearing about them. Actually, *they* are the ones who do not want to keep going through it with us. Their solution is not helpful. First, birth control is not an acceptable alternative. Second, others should offer comfort and strength, prayer support and wisdom. This comment reflects none of that.

Ruth and Joe experienced this problem. "Five times I miscarried, once a set of triplets. Each time I was treated poorly by family and friends, urging me to use birth control."

"As a doctor, there is nothing special I can do to help you."
Sometimes doctors or nurses lack sensitivity. Many times, one or two miscarriages are so common that no diagnostic help is offered until there are a number of miscarriages in a row. Even three is still considered common enough not to warrant special tests to discern a problem that might be solved.

I had bled off and on, lightly, for weeks at the beginning of my pregnancy. When the bleeding stopped, I resumed light activities. One day I had more blood. I called the doctor, in tears, only to hear her say rather matter-of-factly, "The baby's probably dead. Come on in for a D & C."

I requested an ultrasound. Stunned, I called Scott, and a friend drove me to the hospital. There, before our amazed eyes, was our son, swimming all over the place. We wept to see such beautiful confirmation that, in fact, our precious son was fine. I immediately switched to a doctor with better bedside manners.

Three of my six pregnancies that have gone to term have involved some bleeding. Approximately 30 percent of all pregnancies that end in deliveries have some bleeding, and often the doctor does not discover why.

Perhaps doctors and nurses can be sensitized to their patients' needs in this regard. Following one miscarriage requiring surgery, the doctor placed me on the maternity ward. I had to walk by rooms with babies just to get to the community shower. When I told him it was difficult for me to be surrounded by babies when I had just lost one, he told me that he thought it would help me get over it faster. He was not very sympathetic.

Sometimes we have to request tests. Don't wait for the doctor to initiate the process, since he or she might not think enough children have been miscarried yet to warrant the extra help. Be proactive; do research. Check with friends who have also had miscarriages or stillbirths and find out what resources they recommend, or perhaps what doctor is more likely to be compassionate or pro-life.

One couple in Minnesota had a difficult situation.

I have miscarried twice. It was very, very traumatic. The doctor kept calling my baby "the product of conception." In the second instance, when I was bleeding very badly, we called the emergency room. The OB on call said, "Come on in and I'll clean you out." We went to a different hospital, and the doctor there (a Christian) said he wouldn't touch me, just in case the baby was still alive!

I was bleeding at thirteen weeks with each of my children, so in every pregnancy there was the threat of miscarriage. I've had few experiences more horrifying than the discovery that my babies were in danger.

The most supportive [medical staff] were the ones who cried with me and felt my pain, not the ones who said, "You'll probably have another baby." I didn't know if I'd ever have another baby. I just knew I'd lost one and I was really grieving. I can still cry for the ones I never knew.

We could not conceive (without miscarrying) for more than two years. Again, it was very traumatic, since the first conception was easy and quick. I had a terrible doctor who told me I had no right to fuss about miscarrying—that I should be happy with one child. I found another doctor, a Swede, who had left Sweden because he would not do abortions. He was wonderful, fully supportive of helping me find out why I couldn't conceive. He did some tests, gave me some pills, and now we have Jody. I thank God for him.

This couple's experiences with doctors reflect the kind of care many couples have received. Certainly when doctors have been involved in abortions, it is more difficult for them to want to fight for the life of an unborn child.

"As a priest, there is nothing I can do for you."

Talk to the priest about why it is important to you to mark the death of your child. Could he say the Mass of the Angels rather than offer a Mass for an unbaptized child? If he refuses to say a Mass for the baby, inquire why; maybe there is confusion that can be resolved. Maybe there is a different kind of memorial service he can offer that will minister to the family.

Rachel spoke to a number of women about this. "So many women have told us that their priests were not open to saying a Mass. One critic of the Church's pro-life stand even said to me, 'You say you are pro-life, yet you won't even care for your own who lose a baby.'"

Don't say nothing.

Your coworkers may not handle the loss well. They might even ignore the loss altogether. But isolation does not diminish the pain. Or they might try to "cheer you up," but that is not the same as comfort, compassion, and consolation.

A molecular biologist at a major pharmaceutical company related his situation.

We had three children and then lost two about halfway through the pregnancies. While we were going through that experience, my colleagues could not understand the grief that we both felt over the loss of these two children. It was just a fetus to them, nothing to be mourned. It was a very difficult time for us. The next pregnancy was filled with anxiety, but we were blessed with our fourth child. She is now four years old, perfectly healthy, and we appreciate her and our other children even more than had we not gone through the loss.

People who do not share our value of life ethic may not know how to respond other than to ignore the situation. They may feel awkward; they do not know what to say. It would be better for them to say, "I don't know what to say," than to say nothing.

"There was probably something wrong with the baby."
There is no consolation in this statement. It negates our pain. It says, in a sense, that we should be glad, not sad, that we're better off without this handicapped child!

The day after I miscarried, a male college student I had never met before commented, "It's nature's way of getting rid of an unhealthy child." He was not ready for my answer.

"Do you know what you just said?" I snapped. "You're telling me that my baby was probably in greater need than my healthy children, and I should thank God my baby's dead because now I don't have to take care of a handicapped child? Don't *ever* say that to a woman who has just lost a baby!" (I'm sure he won't.)

If anything, parents feel even more helpless when they imagine a child who had something wrong. Nature doesn't get rid of problems; nature is not in control. God is. We are not discussing an object (like getting rid of a car that keeps breaking down) but my child.

Even when people do not feel helped when they miscarry, years later God can bring healing. Ingrid from Pound Ridge, New York, recalled:

Years later, when I became involved in the charismatic renewal, during a prayer meeting someone talked about how the healing of the hurts from miscarriage and stillbirths could be brought about through prayer and celebrating a Mass in memory of these babies.

My babies became real people to me; I often ask for their interces-sion. I tell them how much I love them and am looking forward to hugging them in heaven.

Celebrating a Mass in memory of a baby you lost could bring great conso-lation.

"People miscarry because secretly they don't want the baby."
One mother who had miscarried was present when this comment was made. "This tore my heart!" she says. "I thought it was very cruel." False guilt can really get to us; if only I had done this or that, I would not have lost this baby.

When I had our second miscarriage, I was searching for a reason. I asked the doctor if painting the front porch could have caused the miscarriage. He assured me that this was not possible. "If it was that simple," he said, "those who do not want to be pregnant would paint a room or exercise strenuously rather than have an abortion."

"This miscarriage will give you better spacing between children."
This is hollow help. I would much rather have the baby than have more space between children. When someone "complimented" me on the spac-ing we have between children, she caught me at a mischievous moment. "Yes," I replied, "but a few had to die to make it happen." (I should proba-bly not have been that blunt.)

Be aware of those around you; remember their situations.
One mother of a large family introduced herself at a conference as "some-one who has been more generous with God than most." True, a woman who continues to practice openness to life, even after being blessed twelve times, *is* a very generous woman. However, no one can be more open than open.

Seated next to me, listening to the speaker, was a woman who had been married just as long as the speaker. She and her husband had been open to life their whole marriage, yet they had only two living children out of the six they had conceived. This mother had practiced at least as much generosity with God as had the speaker, especially since the pain of multiple miscarriages was so great for her.

I could feel her wilt when the speaker gave her introduction. The truth is that both women have been heroically generous with God.

"Time will heal."

No, time does not heal. But God does use time to help lessen the intensity of the pain. Unless we deal with our grief, time will not do anything more than dull the pain. To be healthy spouses and parents we will have to grieve. And, in time, God can heal the ache in our hearts.

"I know what you are going through."

Grief is so individual that it can seem shallow to say we can relate. Rather than claim inside knowledge of another person's pain, struggles, questions, and sorrow, we can relate our losses and allow the other person to see the similarities. It can be therapeutic for us to share and cathartic for them to respond, but we cannot elicit more of another's inner thoughts and feelings about loss than they want to share.

"You'll get over it," or, "You shouldn't feel that way," or, "Try to get back to normal," or, "You need to stop thinking about it."

This is not a bad haircut; *this* is a loss worthy of mourning. Life may never get back to normal, the way it was. Activities may help distract someone from grief, but filling the schedules may simply delay the grieving process. Friends cannot tell us what we need; *they* need to come alongside us while we grieve and pray hard for true words of wisdom and comfort. There is no quick fix for such heartfelt suffering as grief.

"Others have had it worse."

Yes, others have had worse situations. And we can be genuinely sorry for anyone going through more pain than we are at the moment. However, our pain is very real, and someone else's pain does not diminish our own.

"Maybe God doesn't want you to have another baby."

Every child who is conceived has a plan of life from God, though it may be a very short stay on this earth. There is no guarantee more miscarriages will not occur, but be assured you cannot make a baby God has not planned.

"Maybe God is punishing you for doing something wrong."

This is the tactic of Job's false friends, whom God clearly condemned for being accusers rather than comforters. Try to forgive them for increasing your pain and let love cover a multitude of sins. A mother from Michigan admitted, "I suffer from forced sterility.... Did I have cancer due to multiple sex partners? How God has poured his mercy on me after offending him with my gift of fertility!"

Whatever sins we have committed are forgiven, if we have confessed them. The Lord will not take our baby to punish us. On the other hand, he may not keep us from the consequences of past sins, which could include difficulties getting or staying pregnant.

How Do We Risk Loss Again?

We need a strategy. We need time to grieve; however, part of the grieving process is training our hearts again in truth. This is what the Lord says to his people (this includes us) about restoration after they have experienced tremendous loss in exile: "For I know the plans I have for you, says the Lord, plans for welfare and not for evil, to give you a future and a hope" (Jer 29:11).

Consider this strategy for becoming ready to risk loss again:

We should take time to grieve.

This is a matter for you and your spouse to consider prayerfully. Depending on the intensity of your grief and fear over another miscarriage, you might have a serious reason to use Natural Family Planning. If the doctor advises you to wait for another pregnancy so that your body can handle it, listen closely to his advice.

On the other hand, we have found great comfort in conceiving soon after a miscarriage (it happened only the third time). Perhaps another pregnancy could help you to heal. Talk and pray over your decision.

We must place our trust in the Lord.

This is an act of our will: We choose to trust God with our future plans.

> Come now, you who say, "Today or tomorrow we will go into such and
> such a town and spend a year there and trade and get gain"; whereas
> you do not know about tomorrow. What is your life? For you are a mist
> that appears for a little time and then vanishes. Instead you ought to
> say, "If the Lord wills, we shall live and we shall do this or that."
>
> JAMES 4:13-15

The Lord can give us all the grace we need to risk being open to new life
(and new loss).

**We must fill our hearts and minds with the wonderful truths about God's
design for marriage and the meaning of life-giving love.**

These certainties are like well driven pitons for a mountain climber—they
provide safety to help us regain our bearing when our footing falters. One
of these pins in the rock is our understanding of the value of redemptive
suffering. Christ's suffering on the cross makes our suffering meaningful;
his suffering makes sense out of ours. We can offer up our physical pain
and emotional distress, united to Christ's self-offering, and the Lord will
use our gift to strengthen the body of Christ (see Col 1:24).

We want to help build the kingdom of God. Through our broken bodies, he *is* building it, one soul at a time.

We can harness the host of heaven through the communion of saints.

We can risk loss again because we do not face it alone.

> Therefore, since we are surrounded by so great a cloud of witnesses,
> let us also lay aside every weight, and sin which clings so closely, and
> let us run with perseverance the race that is set before us, looking to
> Jesus the pioneer and perfecter of our faith, who for the joy that was
> set before him endured the cross, despising the shame, and is seated
> at the right hand of the throne of God.
>
> HEBREWS 12:1-2

We are, right now, surrounded by our older brothers and sisters in the faith, who actively cheer us on in this great race. Like Jesus, they intercede on our behalf if we ask them. We can also specifically petition saints such as St. Gerard, patron saint of pregnancies, and Blessed Gianna Beretta Molla, the mother who laid down her life for her unborn child.

We can pursue necessary medical assessments.

We may need to switch doctors if our current doctor does not take our losses seriously. Perhaps we need to contact the Pope Paul VI Institute or local Couple to Couple League teaching couples for help. Sometimes suggestions from friends, advice downloaded off the Internet, or ideas from our own research can provide answers to some of our questions.

We have to be proactive in looking for help. According to one report, "at least 70 percent of women who experience pregnancy loss do go on to have healthy children."[13] Perhaps some forms of alternative medicine will give us more information with which we can make decisions about the future.

Tap into the intercessory prayer of others.

In the Kirk clan, we celebrate two events: conception and birth. We have learned that if we hold off celebrating the new life—waiting to tell family and friends in the hopes that our pain of miscarriage will be less—we may miss our days of joy and feel, if we lose the child, as if we grieve alone. Collectively, we have lost at least thirteen babies by miscarriage.

Conception is worth celebrating! By the generosity of our love and God's gift, we have conceived. *This* child will exist for all eternity, no matter how brief his or her life on this earth. If we take this baby to term, then we will celebrate his or her birth.

Certainly, this is an individual decision. In some families, due to the number of their losses or the number of small children who feel those losses acutely, a couple may delay sharing the news of conception within the family. Nevertheless, the couple still needs the support of prayer.

We wanted to tell everyone about our new baby in person, so we briefly delayed calling about a new pregnancy in 1998. The day before Thanksgiving, I began to bleed. In tears, I called our parents and each of my siblings and shared that we were probably miscarrying.

My brother Tim spoke with great compassion: "Kimberly, let me say first, congratulations on this new baby." I was surprised, but relieved he had taken a moment to acknowledge this new life before consoling me.

After we spoke briefly, he led me in a prayer for our child's safety. As it turned out, David Timothy Bonaventure was fine, and I delivered him eight months later. How grateful I am for the response of our parents, siblings, and their families as they stormed heaven with us for his life.

We need to differentiate between concern and anxiety.
It is normal to have concerns about pregnancy, especially after you have experienced loss. Concerns are legitimate requests that we bring to our heavenly Father, asking for his help, trusting that he hears us and will answer. Faith grows as a consequence.

Anxiety, on the other hand, is our trying to carry the burden of our concerns rather than entrusting them to God. We fear and become overwrought as a consequence. When we become anxious, we need to go to Confession. We need to give our concerns to the One who can carry them.

We must love our spouse and let God bring new life, if he so chooses.
Here is a beautiful testimony of the McMenamans, a couple who risked again.

After four beautiful daughters, God sent us two beautiful healthy twin boys. We never had any twins in either family, so we never thought of having any. When they were four and a half months old, our second twin, Patrick, was suddenly called home to heaven. He did not have the immunity to fight off a cold, and spinal meningitis devastated his little body. Only our faith and everyone's prayers helped us survive that heart-wrenching time and enabled us to bathe in God's healing love, as no words could help us.

Immediately upon Patrick's death, our first twin, Paul, became very sick and had to be rushed to the hospital several times with six middle ear infections, pneumonia, and frequent spinal taps, checking to make sure that he did not have spinal meningitis also. His little body was so broken, as were our hearts.

After one and a half years of our son's being soaked in so much prayer, God in his mercy allowed him to survive and be healthy and strong. My husband, after much prayer, relayed to me that since the last child I gave birth to died, he felt God wanted to bless me again with a new life to nurture. He knew already how hard this concept would be for me because of losing one son and almost losing another, but gently he related it anyway. He did not push the idea, but I'm sure he prayed for me.

About six months later, my heart began to change. And I became open to new life again. I prayed for the grace to trust God and my husband's wisdom and actually found my heart overflowing with joy at the prospect of another baby—a miracle.

My husband saved the news till last that he felt God would send us a boy, and God did, nine months later! I thank God for a faith-filled, prayerful husband who loved me enough to speak a hard word that pulled me up and out of the fear-filled world I allowed myself to be in. And I thank God for his wisdom and mercy that enabled our hearts to be open to the new life that allowed our son Paul again to have a brother to share life with.

We are well aware of our little saint all the while interceding for all of us and who will be there someday to bring us home—a comforting thought that because of our yes, he is experiencing the beatific vision right now. Thank you, Jesus!

It is worth it to risk again.

CHAPTER ELEVEN

INFERTILITY

Most of us assume that as soon as we stop trying to postpone pregnancy we will conceive. Sometimes we have to wait a few months or a few years or longer. It may seem as if couples all around us are conceiving, while we wait in the wings to enter the stage of parenthood. In many ways it can become a grieving process, characterized by sadness, anger, bargaining, depression, and, to varying degrees, acceptance (of the wait, for some; of long-term infertility, for others).

Permanent Infertility

When is a couple permanently infertile? Apart from tests that prove sterility, there is no specific time after which a couple is considered permanently, as opposed to temporarily, infertile before the onset of menopause. Even if the infertility has lasted years, there continues to be some hope that the next cycle could be *the one* in which a child is conceived. However, the longer it takes to conceive, the more intense becomes the emotional struggle.

The process of exploring medical help, seeking wisdom, and grieving the lack of children is a time-consuming, energy-expending, and emotion-spending task. The couple wrestles with how they can experience a fruitful marriage apart from bearing their own children. They may consider adoption.

This struggle is intensely personal. For some couples, any discussion of it, apart from close family members or friends, is an invasion of privacy. People feel their suffering increase when others fail to acknowledge their ongoing sense of loss. At the risk of offending those who think a woman with children should not address the subject of infertility, I want to share these thoughts, collected from others who have struggled deeply with infertility (primary or secondary), so that we all can better care for our brothers and sisters who face this difficulty.

Temporary Infertility

It took only nine months of trying for us to conceive our first child, but during those nine months we never knew how long it would be. As I tried to explain the difficulty to a friend, the following analogy came to mind.

Consider what it would be like to have a wedding postponed month to month. It would be as if every month my father would say, "Honey, I know you love this guy, and he's right for you. I just don't know whether it's the best plan to get married this month. I'm going to think about it, and I'll let you know in a couple of weeks."

That's much how it was as I waited to conceive. My hopes would soar around the time of ovulation. I would wait the two weeks. Then my period would come, and it was as if my father advised, "Don't get too discouraged. Maybe next month. I'm going to think about it, and I'll let you know."

"Hope deferred makes the heart sick, but a desire fulfilled is a tree of life" (Prv 13:12). At times, my disappointment was that kind of heartsickness. However, two weeks later, my hopes would once again pick up, thinking, this could be the month my heavenly Father says yes. And so the cycle would go.

The wait for other children has also been difficult, sometimes lasting up to four years, but no wait was as difficult as waiting for our first. Currently, in the United States, one in five couples is experiencing at least temporary infertility.[1]

Possible Causes of Infertility

Usually couples have to try to conceive for a year before a doctor will get involved. Without any intervention, about 5 percent more couples will become pregnant the second year. However, there are various reasons why couples have difficulty conceiving. The biological factors contributing to infertility are evenly divided between men and women (about 35 percent of the time for each). The rest of the time the cause is either mutual infertility or an unknown factor.

Infertility can be caused by internal, external, and societal factors, some of which can be identified and addressed and some of which may never be identified. Though I am no expert on these issues, I want to share what I have learned in the hope that a suggestion gleaned and shared here can assist you or someone you love. Let's take a look at several identifiable causes with possible suggestions for remedies.

Internal Factors

Currently more than five million people of childbearing age in the United States are experiencing either primary or secondary infertility. Internal causes of infertility for women include lack of certain vitamins and minerals that could strengthen a woman's reproductive system, low thyroid function, a lack of iodized salt, cervical mucus that reacts to rather than works with sperm, failure to ovulate (release an egg), and an overactive thyroid (for which you need to see a doctor). The following information includes a number of self-help suggestions. At the same time, I would encourage you to get medical attention as early as possible, especially from pro-life medical personnel.

Changes in nutrition can have a great impact on fertility, according to the experience of nutrition counselor Marilyn Shannon. In *Fertility, Cycles and Nutrition*, Shannon gives many suggestions for diet improvement, including consumption of iodized table salt and the right amount of oil daily for improving irregularities in cycles and in mucus patterns. She highlights the positive impact of vitamin A, all of the B vitamins, vitamin E, zinc, and selenium, especially in regard to hormone balance, endometriosis, and thyroid problems. (A single carrot a day could increase a person's intake of vitamin A sufficiently to have a positive impact on mucus patterns.)

In a truly remarkable study, vitamin B6, a critical nutrition for PMS sufferers, was given in doses of one hundred to eight hundred mg/day to fourteen women who had normal menstrual cycles but also had PMS and infertility of eighteen months to seven years' duration. Ten of the fourteen had never borne a child; the other four were experiencing secondary infertility. Twelve of the women conceived, eleven within six months of the B6 therapy![2]

It may be a matter of weight. Some women are underweight; they may need to gain a few pounds to have at least 20 percent body fat. Others may be overweight; they may have too much fat in comparison to their muscle.

Overweight women may need to set a modest weight loss goal and then lose weight at a reasonable rate. Perhaps a goal of twenty pounds lost could be attainable, and it might make the difference. If you are having secondary infertility, what was your weight when you conceived before? Maybe that would be a healthy, fertile weight for you.

An unusual remedy for thick cervical mucus can be found at the local grocery store: "an over-the-counter cough syrup containing guaifenesin, an ingredient which liquefies bronchial mucus—and has the same effect on cervical mucus, thus sometimes assisting sperm migration."[3] The recommendation is to take it from the end of the woman's period until the second day after ovulation.

Physical concerns for men include a lack of testosterone and sperm with poor health or movement. Vitamin A, zinc, and selenium are recommended to strengthen the husband's overall health, including his fertility. Vitamin A helps the cell lining in the testes where the sperm develop. Zinc, for instance, increases the testes' ability to synthesize testosterone. An improved diet could also help.

Vitamin C is critical for the production of testosterone. A remarkable study demonstrated the impact that Vitamin C can have on a man's fertility. There were twenty-seven male participants who had the difficulty of spermagglutination (in which the sperm clump together rather than moving forward successfully). The patients were divided into two groups, one of which took a supplement of one thousand mg/day of Vitamin C in addition to calcium, magnesium, and manganese.

Following the sixty-day regimen, all subjects were reexamined for evidence of change. The wives of each of the twenty men who received supplemental ascorbic acid [vitamin C] had become pregnant during the study period. In contrast, no wife of any subject in the group which did not receive supplemental doses had become pregnant during this time period.[4]

This program of supplementation significantly improved sperm quantity, morphology, and motility, and reduced spermagglutination. A subsequent study used pure vitamin C (two hundred or one thousand mg/day) and confirmed the beneficial effect of this nutrient on the same measures of fertility in men with spermagglutination. In only one week, sperm counts for those receiving one thousand mg/day of vitamin C rose an average of one hundred and forty percent![5]

You may not have the time to do the needed research to discover the best levels of various vitamins and minerals that would strengthen your fertility. A well-balanced multivitamin and mineral supplement may be all you need. Consult your physician before you make any drastic changes.

External Factors

External factors that increase the possibility of infertility for men and women include caffeine, alcohol, prescription drugs, harmful toxins from work, and tobacco. Sensitivity to light during the night may be a factor for women. Sensitivity to heat to the man's scrotum can affect the viability of sperm. Even gravity can work against you.

In the late 1980s two independent studies confirmed what had previously been suspected through anecdotal evidence: caffeine consumption affects fertility.

In a 1988 study, women who used more than the equivalent of one cup of coffee per day took significantly longer to conceive than did those who used less, and high caffeine users experienced longer delays in conceiving than did lower level users. This finding was quickly confirmed by other researchers who studied a large number of women.[6]

Improvement was seen in women who cut back to one cup of coffee per day and in men who cut back to six cups per day.

Alcohol in moderation does not seem to be a factor, but heavy drinking interferes with fertility. "Alcohol decreases levels of testosterone, ultimately contributing to lowered sperm production *which may be irreversible.*"[7]

If you are on prescription drugs, ask your physician if they could have an impact on fertility. Some cold and allergy remedies work well because they reduce mucus in nasal passages. If their overall impact is to reduce mucus, they could have an adverse impact on cervical mucus.

Are either of you being exposed to toxins at your workplace? Perhaps you should check with your physician to find out whether or not you are being exposed to something that is now interfering with your fertility. If you can confirm that, ask your supervisor for a different place to work.

A government study showed that male smokers are "fifty percent more likely to suffer from impotence than non-smokers."[8] Smoking by women can cause them to have much longer periods of infertility than nonsmokers, especially if they began smoking before they were eighteen.

Women who smoke are estimated to have only seventy-two percent of the fertility of non-smokers; they are three and one half times more likely to take a whole year to conceive. Smoking one pack of cigarettes per day is enough to impair fertility; starting to smoke before age eighteen also has negative effects on fertility.[9]

If quitting smoking could increase your chances of getting pregnant, it would be a good idea to quit. Once you get pregnant, you do not want to filter all that nicotine through your tiny baby's body anyway.

Some women are sensitive to night lighting. Hall lights, bathroom lights, lamplights, and even the lights from digital clocks can interfere with the hours of darkness a woman needs for deep sleep. For those women who have to work during the night, they may want to invest in special blinds to darken the bedroom better for sleep during the day.

Men, on the other hand, are not sensitive to light but heat. Sperm take about seventy days to mature before they are released. They are stored in the scrotum, which has an ability to adjust a little closer to the body when there is a lack of heat and to adjust away from the body (somewhat) when there is too much heat.

If a man enjoys soaking in a tub of very hot water, or taking very hot showers, he may be damaging the sperm. In fact, some men have found that changing from briefs to boxers has made a difference. The scrotum can do its job better with boxers when the body gets warm than in briefs that might hold the scrotum too close. If a change is made in this way, be patient; fresh sperm will not be mature for a couple of months.

Without thinking about it, many women go to the bathroom right after making love. Unfortunately, this lets gravity work against the sperm that are trying to migrate to an egg. But gravity can be harnessed: After making love, the woman can elevate her hips by placing a pillow under the small of her back for fifteen to thirty minutes. It may not be the most comfortable thing to do, but it may assist sperm migration.

The materials I found suggested making love every other night, rather than making love every night, so that the husband's sperm count might be higher. You might want to vary the time of day—try morning, skip a day, try afternoon, skip a day, try night. Sometimes couples have discovered a highly unusual pattern works best:

> Have a second coitus about forty-five minutes after the first. In some men, apparently, the first ejaculation opens up the pathways, so to speak, and the second delivers the sperm with a much higher sperm count than the first. This is the opposite of what happens with men of normal fertility. Or possibly the semen of the first ejaculation has many older or less motile sperm while the second has fresher, more motile sperm.[10]

This strategy may be worth a try.

Societal Factors

Societal factors include delayed childbearing and the consequences of promiscuity.

Delayed childbearing can be the result of a couple not discovering each other until they are older, or a married couple waiting awhile to have a child so they can establish a career or a home. Sometimes pressure is brought to bear on a couple from other family members to wait. Consider this:

To avoid disappointment, any couple is advised not to delay, too long, the decision to have their first baby. The peak of fertility for both men and women wanes after the age of twenty-five. The use of any contraceptive beyond this period for a couple who has never conceived may be lost opportunity for those who unknowingly possess low fertility potential.[11]

Is there a good reason to delay? If not, it may be best to live openness to life right away.

Another result of delayed childbearing can be endometriosis. "Endometriosis causes infertility in one third of the women who develop it; infertility specialists sometimes call endometriosis the career woman's disease."[12] Endometriosis is a very painful disease. It often lessens in severity if a woman becomes pregnant; however, the infertility that can result has the added effect of making the disease even more painful. Talk about adding insult to injury!

Promiscuity can play a role in infertility.

Abortion, the IUD, the Pill, sexually transmitted diseases (STDs), and early and promiscuous sexual relations all can reduce fertility and even cause permanent sterility. The IUD can cause sterility through scarring of the uterus and pelvic inflammatory disease; the Pill can cause a woman to be infertile for months after discontinuing it; chlamydia and gonorrhea are among the sexually transmitted diseases that can leave a woman permanently sterile.[13]

These can be the sad consequences of a pre-Christian lifestyle.

Resources Are Available

Infertility is a physical condition, not a psychological one. Though some couples' fertility will improve without pursuing treatment, couples can do more than just hope and pray things will improve. There are resources available on the act of marriage that are based on scientific research *and* respectful of Catholic teaching.

Dr. Thomas Hilgers and his associates at the Pope Paul VI Institute of Human Reproduction have developed the Creighton Model Fertility*Care* System as "a new, uniquely American model of advanced procreative education."

The System allows for the first time the opportunity to network family planning with reproductive and gynecologic health maintenance. ... *NaProTechnology*, which refers to the use of the *natural procreative technologies*, is defined as a science which devotes its medical, surgical, and allied health energies and attention to cooperating with the natural procreative systems.

Because it also is a system that accurately monitors reproductive and gynecologic health, it can be used to assess chronic discharges, perform targeted hormone evaluation and treatment, identify ovarian cysts (and treat non-surgically), evaluate the effects of stress, and treat premenstrual syndrome, evaluate and treat reproductive abnormalities such as infertility, miscarriage, ectopic pregnancy, stillbirth, prematurity, etc. It can also be used to evaluate and treat unusual bleeding (decreasing the need for hysterectomy).[14]

Rather than offer medical treatment that could damage or alter the woman's cycle, Dr. Hilgers uses this approach in cooperation with a woman's cycle. (The institute also offers training for physicians in Medical NaProTechnology.)

In *The Art of Natural Family Planning*, John and Sheila Kippley discuss two medical tests that are licit for Catholics: the Huhner Test and the perforated condom. The Huhner Test involves collecting sperm from a wife; the perforated condom is used by the husband during the act of marriage. Some sperm can get through, but what is trapped in the condom can be used for analysis. These are the only morally acceptable ways I know to gather sperm for testing purposes.

Whether or not you discover the reason for your infertility, do all that you can to keep your hearts close to the Lord and each other. Resist the temptation to reduce the marital act to making babies, so that neither of you begins to feel used by the other. Support each other; encourage each other. Try not to question the efforts of your spouse to solve the difficulty.

Infertility, temporary or permanent, is a major life crisis. It complicates life much more than others know. It is challenging to follow diets, meet with doctors, discuss strategies, and undergo tests. It can be exhausting, especially given the hormonal ups and downs of even a normal cycle. I pray the Lord will give you a sense of his grace for this moment.

What Can We Say to a Friend?

What do we say to couples who struggle with infertility? Here are a few suggestions. Don't take them as a script with which to approach someone with the problem. We need to be sensitive to the specific needs and situations of our loved ones. We don't want to make trite comments; we want to share our hearts and tears, encourage them with our support, and pray for them.

"I am so sorry it has been this difficult to conceive."
In a day and age when our culture ignores the value of the life of the unborn, people can be callous toward those who deeply desire a child. Some people are casting off their young like so much garbage, while others plead with God for just one child to call their own. Acknowledge that their infertility, whether temporary or permanent, is a real problem.

One couple said, "The most helpful thing people did for me when I couldn't conceive was agree that it was a *problem*. The doctor who cared that I'd miscarried, cared that I couldn't conceive, and took me seriously, was a great blessing."

Brenda, from Marion, Ohio, agrees.

> The people who loved us anyway were the most helpful, the people who didn't come up with pat answers or formulas or "your faith is too small" sorts of sermons for us. That was what sustained us, and pointed us to God, gave us the ability to face the pain and allow him to bring good out of it.

It is important to keep channels of communication open. We want to be available as a listening ear without intruding on an area of such privacy and pain.

"I'm praying for you and your spouse."
We pray for the couple right where they are to have the grace necessary in the midst of the struggle to endure and even to grow through it. We need to be supportive. It can be a very stressful time, trying out every remedy suggested. Make love daily, make love at different times of the day, make love every other day; jump up after the act of marriage and walk around, or don't move except to put your legs on the wall; take these vitamins; try these drugs; and whatever you do, *relax!* All the while they are trying to ignore the biological clock as it ticks ever more loudly.

Don't just *offer* to pray for them; really *pray* for them. Pray for them to be strengthened in their marriage as they endure adversity and as you pray that they conceive. One of the greatest struggles a couple can face is misunderstanding each other while they wait for a child. This can be a time of drawing closer together through the difficulty—or feeling pulled apart.

An example of this problem is the dialogue between Rachel and Jacob recorded in Genesis.

> When Rachel saw that she bore Jacob no children, she envied her sister; and she said to Jacob, "Give me children, or I shall die!"
> Jacob's anger was kindled against Rachel, and he said, "Am I in the place of God, who has withheld from you the fruit of the womb?"
>
> GENESIS 30:1-2

Certainly the conflict was intensified between them because he had another wife, Rachel's sister, who was fertile. Thank God we do not face this dilemma today (except, perhaps, in the case of divorce and remarriage).

Jacob correctly redirects Rachel to God—in essence, he says, "I'm doing my part; if you have a problem, take it up with Someone who can change things, God." Her husband is not unsympathetic, but he is unwilling to take the blame. Though some women can relate to the desperation Rachel communicates, they need to recognize the trouble she gets into when she tries to take matters into her own hands.

Sometimes the husband does not understand the depth of sadness his wife feels in the midst of their struggle with infertility. Since he does not go through the hormonal shifts throughout the monthly cycle as his wife does, he is not as tuned in, day to day, to the possibility (or not) of pregnancy.

The example of Hannah is poignant in this regard.

Hannah's pain from infertility was exacerbated in two ways by one woman, Elkanah's other wife, Peninnah. When Elkanah, his two wives, and their children went to the yearly sacrifice in Shiloh, there were problems.

> On the day when Elkanah sacrificed, he would give portions to Peninnah his wife and to all her sons and daughters; and, although he loved Hannah, he would give Hannah only one portion, because the Lord had closed her womb. And her rival used to provoke her sorely, to irritate her, because the Lord had closed her womb. So it went on year by year; as often as she went up to the house of the Lord, she used to provoke her. Therefore Hannah wept and would not eat.
>
> 1 SAMUEL 1:4-7

First, Hannah suffered because her husband's second wife had been blessed repeatedly ("sons and daughters"), while she remained infertile. Think how many years she endured the pregnancies and upbringing of a number of children! Second, the other wife taunted her, year after year. Who could bear such tortuous suffering?

Further, she essentially bore her infertility alone, because her husband *did* have children, through his other wife (a particular suffering today for those who marry someone who already has children). That may be why he pleaded with her to relax about it with this comment:

> And Elkanah, her husband, said to her, "Hannah, why do you weep? And why do you not eat? And why is your heart sad? Am I not more to you than ten sons?"
>
> 1 SAMUEL 1:8

For him to ask the question belies how little he understood about the situation. How could he ask why she was sad? (And he probably should not have pressed the "ten son" thing—he might *not* have been worth more to her!)

Rather than stay and argue with her husband, who lacked empathy, she took her cause to the Lord, the One who could actually do something about the situation.

After they had eaten and drunk in Shiloh, Hannah rose. Now Eli the priest was sitting on the seat beside the doorpost of the temple of the Lord. She was deeply distressed and prayed to the Lord, and wept bitterly.

And she vowed a vow and said, "O Lord of hosts, if thou wilt indeed look on the affliction of thy maidservant, and remember me, and not forget thy maidservant, but wilt give to thy maidservant a son, then I will give him to the Lord all the days of his life, and no razor shall touch his head."

1 Samuel 1:9-11

Not only did Hannah deeply desire to conceive and bear a child, but she knew, if God gave her a child, that child could be the answer to many other prayers, prayers for godly men to lead their nation. She knew how wicked were the sons of Eli, the priest in Shiloh—everyone knew—and how desperate was the need for prayerful leaders.

Hannah had not allowed bitterness to grow in her heart. She did not approach God demanding her rights. Her vow was not a bargaining chip—if you give me a son, I'll give you a son—but a pledge from her heart. She yearned to be a part of building the kingdom of God through the gift of new life.

Sometimes not only husbands but also priests misunderstand the agony of the heart over the issue of infertility.

As she continued praying before the Lord, Eli observed her mouth. Hannah was speaking in her heart; only her lips moved, and her voice was not heard; therefore Eli took her to be a drunken woman. And Eli said to her, "How long will you be drunken? Put away your wine from you."

1 Samuel 1:12-14

Hannah's grief was expressed so strongly as she prayed that the priest mistook her for someone who had drunk excessively, and he rebuked her. Here was Hannah pouring out her heart to the Lord, only to be mistaken for a drunk. Yet Hannah refrained from reacting defensively toward the priest for misjudging her; consequently, her response actually brought out the priest in him.

But Hannah answered, "No, my lord, I am a woman sorely troubled; I have drunk neither wine nor strong drink, but I have been pouring out my soul before the Lord. Do not regard your maidservant as a base woman, for all along I have been speaking out of my great anxiety and vexation."

1 Samuel 1:15-16

The priest was cut to the quick. He knew he had completely misjudged the situation. He did not berate her for expressing such agony; godly women (and men) can pour out their hearts in grief without fearing reproof. He heard Hannah's heart and then he gave her the word of the Lord in answer to her prayer.

Then Eli answered, "Go in peace, and the God of Israel grant your petition which you have made to him."

And she said, "Let your maidservant find favor in your eyes." Then the woman went her way and ate, and her countenance was no longer sad.

1 Samuel 1:17-18

Hannah believed the word of the Lord. She had taken the matter to him and believed that he was answering her prayers. She went forth in peace to love and serve the Lord. And the following year she delivered a son who would be a great prophet and the one who would anoint the first and second kings of Israel.

"I am praying for you to have a baby."

Infertility can be temporary. "He gives the barren woman a home, making her the joyous mother of children. Praise the Lord" (Ps 113:9).

Keep praying for the blessing of a baby; don't give up. Remember Elizabeth, Mary's cousin: "And behold, your kinswoman Elizabeth in her old age has also conceived a son; and this is the sixth month with her who was called barren. For with God nothing will be impossible" (Lk 1:36-37).

One friend who had been married a year said she was unsure whether she should ask the Lord for a child. She did not want to be selfish. I assured her that that is a good and right prayer for a couple in a sacramental marriage. There is nothing selfish about the desire to have marital love issue forth in new life.

Gloria, from Encinitas, California, wrote about a gift that meant so much to her as she struggled with infertility:

> One kind gesture was made to me by a woman from the local crisis pregnancy center. Though we had been acquainted for a couple of years, she had recently learned of our plight. A few hours after our tearful conversation, I found at my doorstep a beautiful, professionally wrapped gift with all the trimmings. Inside was an adorable newborn dress laced with ribbon and ruffles. The card read:
>
> I know that it can feel like no one else understands the pain that you're feeling. But you're not alone. I understand … I understand what you're going through. I've been through it, too. Maybe some of the things are different, but I've felt a similar loneliness and experienced a similar pain. But more than that, because we are friends … I know how you hurt. And when you hurt, I feel it, too (and pray for you). And right now, I hurt for you. And I care so much about you.
>
> Personal note: I know one day you too will hold your precious baby in your arms. Don't give up hope. God is faithful as he promises. Look at this "faith gift" every day and thank him for your baby. We did this and got ours.
>
> Obviously, the dress was not a good luck charm, but at that moment in time, her gift and note were a lifeline. I was not alone.

This gift became a daily reminder to pray for a child at a time when Gloria was struggling with hopelessness. When the Lord brought Sara into their home through adoption, Gloria put that dress on Sara and celebrated the answer to so many prayers. Then she gave the dress as a prayer reminder to someone else.

"Having a baby is a right desire, but it is not a right."

Many people are unaware that the Church has guidelines about which medical procedures in diagnosing and treating infertility are morally acceptable. Marriage is the right context for conceiving a child. "Nevertheless, marriage does not confer upon the spouses the right to have a child, but only the right to perform those natural acts which are *per se* ordered to pro-creation."[15] If a couple has a renewed sense of hope that they can achieve pregnancy through medical intervention, they could feel abandoned by the Church when they find out they cannot have that medical help.

This information is important to share, and it is *essential* to share it the right way. If we share the truth without sensitivity to the blow it could give them, we could close their hearts to us and to the Church. If, on the other hand, we share the truth in love, in the larger context of the Church's teaching on marriage, we may soften the blow that infertility wields.

People assume that since the Church encourages people to have children, any measure that enables people to have children is allowed. That is not the case. The Church is not out to make all the babies it can; not every way that exists to create a baby is licit. The Church's teaching needs to be understood in the larger context of the purpose and meaning of the act of marriage as an integral act, one that respects the dignity of husband and wife. That is why with infertility, some medical measures are licit and some are not.

The marital act must remain whole. We are not to separate the procre-ative aspect from the unitive by using contraception. Nor are we to separate the unitive aspect from the procreative by collecting sperm or eggs for arti-ficial insemination by the husband or a donor.

> Techniques that entail the dissociation of husband and wife, by the intrusion of a person other than the couple (donation of sperm or ovum, surrogate uterus), are gravely immoral. These techniques (het-erologous artificial insemination and fertilization) infringe the child's right to be born of a father and mother known to him and bound to each other by marriage. They betray the spouses' "right to become a father and a mother only through each other."[16]
>
> Techniques involving only the married couple (monologous artifi-cial insemination and fertilization) are perhaps less reprehensible, yet remain morally unacceptable. They dissociate the sexual act from the procreative act. The act which brings the child into existence is no longer an act by which two persons give themselves to one another.[17]

Artificial insemination, whether by husband or donor, and embryo transfer are not moral options. *Donum Vitae* summarizes the Church's concerns about such procedures:

> Such fertilization entrusts the life and identity of the embryo into the power of doctors and biologists and establishes the domination of technology over the origin and destiny of the human person. Such a relationship of domination is in itself contrary to the dignity and equality that must be common to parents and children.[18]

It is essential to understand these guidelines before consulting doctors.

An adoptive mother from Andover, Massachusetts, observed:

> Just as people need to hear the truth about birth control, they also need to hear the truth about artificial and assisted reproductive technologies. Because this technology removes the unity component of the marital act, it is wrong, even though the goal is to procreate. Many people don't understand the teachings of the Church on this matter. I certainly did not and pursued some treatment. It wasn't until the doctor wanted to do *in vitro* fertilization that I started to ask questions.
>
> You can virtually forget about finding a parish priest who knows anything about it. Fortunately, I live in the Boston area and was referred to the Pope John XXIII Center for Medical-Moral Research.[19] It was there that I met with a priest who explained it to me, and very gently, but firmly, spoke the truth, as I held back my tears.

It is important that priests teach this truth, even though it is difficult for people to hear that they cannot have access to some techniques available when the pain of their infertility is so great.

One woman from Indianapolis, Indiana, assumed *in vitro* fertilization was acceptable as long as she and her husband attended Mass each day of the process. Sometimes people, unaware of the Church's teaching, have opted not to use *in vitro* fertilization due to their pro-life convictions.

One couple questioned the validity of *in vitro* fertilization for Christians.

During fertility treatments as Protestants we were faced with the option of *in vitro* fertilization but did not take that step because of the possibility of too many fertilized eggs. Now as Catholics we appreciate the guidelines for these procedures and understand the reasons not to go that route.

Another woman recounted the situation with her sister.

My sister was unable to conceive through "normal" means due to severe endometriosis. She knew the Church's teaching on IVF; however, her local priest encouraged IVF and said that under this circumstance it was OK. She "felt" God thought it was OK because she and her husband prayed about it—after all, it would be hers and her husband's baby.

I did try to bring to her conscience concerns about all the embryos that were fertilized—ten the first time and seven the second time, with two now frozen! I asked her how she felt about them—to realize they are all her babies—and what about the dilemma of the frozen ones? She did have twins from the second try and is not sure if she'll try IVF again.

I know she will need tremendous healing one day. It's just a shame that now she can feel justified because a representative of the Church said it was OK. There must be consistency from priests who are the ones teaching the people.

Sometimes doctors are unaware of the moral dilemma in which they place their patients. Maria, from Milwaukee, Wisconsin, admitted, "We had a lot of trouble finding a doctor who would perform some of the infertility tests in a way morally acceptable to Catholics."

Pray with couples and for them about those temptations. It is so painful to feel as though the Church is withholding the key that could unlock their fertility. Mary Kay, from Virginia, describes the difficulty of following the Church's teaching but the blessings that resulted.

After waiting to work with one doctor, then another, we found ourselves in a fertility clinic, firmly explaining to the specialist that we would use none of the artificial reproduction techniques. I prayed constantly for strength against the temptations that surrounded me in this office.

We agreed to use a drug that can "jumpstart" a stalled system such as mine. We conceived in that first month! We indeed have been rewarded for our constancy, faithfulness, and obedience!

Although I am grateful for the life that I carry within me, I also experienced gratitude during my journey of the past few years. The difficult path my husband and I have traveled has been a gift from God to learn so many difficult lessons of faith. I came to realize that I was not being punished by God; I had been given some wonderful opportunities to exercise my own trust in him while also carrying the message of his love to some other women as well.

The medicine that helped Mary Kay is a result of research that is benefiting many couples. According to the *Donum Vitae*, this kind of research, which helps couples overcome their sterility, is welcome, provided that it is "at the service of the human person, of his inalienable rights, and his true and integral good according to the design and will of God."[20]

Archbishop Charles Chaput of Denver offers these pastoral thoughts.

No prayers go unanswered, and all suffering given over to the Lord bears fruit in some form of new life. I encourage them to consider adoption, and I appeal to them to remember that a good end can never justify a wrong means. Whether to prevent a pregnancy or achieve one, all techniques which separate the unitive and procreative dimensions of marriage are always wrong. Procreative techniques which turn embryos into objects and mechanically substitute for the loving embrace of husband and wife *violate human dignity and treat life as a product*. No matter how positive their intentions, these techniques advance the dangerous tendency to reduce human life to material which can be manipulated.[21]

Children are not a right but a gift. If any one has a *right* it is the child, who has the right to be conceived in marriage and in the marital embrace.[22]

Our focus needs to be more on giving ourselves and receiving the gift of our spouse rather than on trying for a baby. This can be difficult, but we need to love God and each other and trust God for the timing of children.

"Your infertility is not a punishment from God."
God does not withhold the blessing of children as punishment for our sin. "If we confess our sins, he is faithful and just, and will forgive our sins and cleanse us from all unrighteousness" (1 Jn 1:9). God forgives completely when we repent. Nevertheless, he may allow us to experience the natural consequences of our sins, such as sterilization resulting from venereal diseases, contraception, or abortions.

One woman shared, "My sister and a best friend both had abortions with their now-husbands years ago. Neither is able to become pregnant after spending much money and time with doctors. The pain is unbearable!"

"We have a monthly healing service at church. I can get you the details, if you might be interested in going."
Infertility is *not* a faith issue but a physical difficulty; however, miracles still happen today. An invitation to a healing service must not imply that all the couple needs is a little more faith to get pregnant. Sometimes it is God's will that people embrace the cross of infertility; through their suffering, grace is released powerfully. However, sometimes it is God's will that people receive physical healing through the laying on of hands and prayer.

A mother from El Paso, Texas, shares her story:

> Between my third and fourth child I quit menstruating for four years. At a Catholic charismatic conference a woman prayed for my husband for healing, then prayed for me. I started menstruating soon after. At daily Mass a reading from 1 Kings said, "This time next year you will be suckling a son." The next year I had a baby boy and for the first time successfully breastfed.

There is no guarantee, but it is possible to be healed of infertility.

"God has a plan for your marriage right now. Family life is not on hold until you have a child."
Jesus said, "Seek first his kingdom and his righteousness, and all these things shall be yours as well" (Mt 6:33). The goal is priority living. First, we become part of the kingdom of God by becoming his sons and daughters. Second, we discern our vocation within the kingdom of God, and if it is

marriage, we commit our lives to each other. Finally, we prepare ourselves to welcome children, if the Lord opens the womb.

Every man and woman who covenant themselves to each other in marriage have formed a new family. "Therefore a man leaves his father and his mother and cleaves to his wife, and they become one flesh" (Gn 2:24). As *Donum Vitae* reminds us, "marital love is always life-giving when spouses give themselves honestly to each other, even if a child isn't conceived."[23]

For our spiritual health and the health of our marriage, it is important to place our trust continually in the Lord. He has a wonderful plan and he is working that plan, day by day, in our lives. In *Gaudium et Spes*, the fathers of Vatican II address this issue: "Therefore, marriage persists as a whole manner and communion of life, and maintains its value and indissolubility, even when despite the often intense desire of the couple, offspring are lacking."[24]

We hope and pray that plan will include children. But the plan will not begin when there are children. It has already begun.

We do not want to waste this precious time before there are children; it could end in a month. What does God want us to do with this time? Ask him.

Should the focus be getting out of debt? Or is there a short-term mission we could do better without children? Should we pursue a college or a graduate degree? Let's dare to pray and dream with our spouse about the possibilities.

"I know you are experiencing suffering at many different levels."
The struggle of infertility, whether it is temporary or permanent, is difficult. We need to recognize the additional sufferings that accompany infertility: trying not to be jealous of others' pregnancies, especially those who don't want the children; struggling with depression because the couple has waited so long for the right relationship and children have not come yet; being misunderstood by family members and friends who have never had the same struggle. As with miscarriage, people often want others to handle their pain privately.

A couple from Milwaukee experienced a range of emotions while they waited and hoped for a child.

After using NFP to postpone pregnancy for eight months, we tried to conceive for eighteen months. During that time it became increasingly difficult for me to let others know we had been trying for so long. I requested that my husband stop talking about it with other people and just not say anything. I was probably a little depressed. I could not really be joyful at news about other people's pregnancies. Never did I become really angry at God; I just didn't understand.

When people around them complained about being pregnant, it was difficult.

One friend who was struggling with infertility worked in a crisis pregnancy center. She and her husband were more than willing to accept whatever difficulty might be involved in a pregnancy, unlike others who almost held the gift of a child in contempt. After a while, she had to quit. It was too painful to talk to women who were ready to cast off their children as if they were so much garbage when her longing for offspring was so great.

Some couples suffer from being misunderstood as not being open to life because they have not yet had children. They can tell that people wonder if they are pursuing personal, selfish goals and putting off the possibility of children. People talk about how wonderful children are in the hope of inspiring the couple to want children, not realizing that they increase the pain of infertility. They *know* how wonderful children are; that's why they desire them so much!

More than that, the couple knows the comments are a gentle probe about the couple's loyalty to the Church without coming out and asking whether they are open to life. Sometimes people forthrightly ask if they are using contraception. Here's the dilemma: Does the couple reveal their very private and personal struggle, so friends will understand and pray for them, or do they keep their pain private?

There are additional sufferings within larger family contexts. Sometimes siblings of the infertile couple do not want the children they have conceived, and they complain about it, or perhaps hint about wanting cousins for their children. Parents who want to be grandparents may complain about waiting for grandchildren, not knowing their children are doing all they can to give them at least one grandchild.

One woman wrote about the "small talk between the people who have and the people who don't. Public questions about a very private matter.

Whether the inquiries are polite or downright crude, the insensitivity is enormous."[25]

When people share the blessing of a large family, they need to be sensitive to those around them who have not (yet) been blessed with a large family. It can seem boastful to those who are struggling. One mother who had had one baby but now seems to be infertile made this appeal:

> Please advise good Christians not to judge other couples. I rejoice in others' pregnancies, especially crisis babies that are not aborted. Many large Catholic families boast of their children and pregnancies, making it hard to bear when you are infertile. I've accepted my barrenness but am still hopeful for another birth.

It is not easy to share the joy of our next pregnancy while sincerely communicating sadness for a couple experiencing the challenge of infertility. We have to find the way to avoid minimizing the pain they feel while being positive about another baby.

Sometimes a woman aches to hold a baby. One woman remarked how much it meant to her when her friend offered her baby to hold. When people gave her a chance to help them with their child(ren), she felt very blessed. On the other hand, another woman said that there are times when she cannot look at a baby, let alone hold one, because her own sense of loss is too acute at that moment. Offer your child only if you sense openness.

Don't Say Stupid Things Real People Have Said

So much damage can be done by insensitive comments made to infertile couples. Here are some comments real people have made.

"You must have all the time in the world to do the things you want!"
Probably the person saying this is frustrated that he or she does not have time to do the things he or she would like to do. However, people who are struggling with infertility desire to give themselves in a meaningful, sacrificial way to their own child. They do not want to be patted on the back for getting to live the selfish life that others want to lead.

"It must be such fun shopping alone," or, "It must be so nice and quiet around your apartment."

Yes, and the silence is killing me, the infertile couple want to shout! Perhaps someone offers this thought because he or she is overwhelmed by the amount of noise and mess that can come with children. But the lack of it is not comforting to someone who longs for a house bustling with the commotion of children.

Sure, shopping without children can be easier. But as one friend told me, "Do you have any idea how difficult it is to go to Wal-mart and see rows of baby things and children's clothes right away? Everyone else shopping with their children is an additional reminder that I am alone."

"You're not working [outside the home]? What do you do all day?"

Though our culture barely gives women the freedom to be home with their children, it is uncomprehending of women who are home without children. Being a homemaker is more than being a mom. The implication of a comment like this one is that if you aren't caring for children, you aren't pulling your share of the weight of finances; and if you aren't busy with the responsibilities of caring for children, there could not be much work at home. Yet homemaking for a wife is a beautiful and complex vocation all on its own.

"Pulling weight" does not necessarily mean earning a paycheck. Some women may choose to work while they wait to get pregnant. But for those women who look forward to quitting work to focus on homemaking, it is an additional suffering to feel as if they can justify being home only if they have children—children who somehow are not being conceived. Besides, sometimes women have found that if they slow down the rigors of their career, pregnancy becomes more of a possibility; stress and hectic work schedules can affect fertility.

"Now that you've adopted, you'll get pregnant."

Just because some people have adopted and then conceived does not mean that this will happen to others. The idea behind this comment is that sometimes couples are trying so hard to get pregnant, their increased stress may be working against them. But now that they have a baby, the stress is lessened and perhaps they will conceive more easily. Even so, the hurtful underlying message is that the child who has been adopted is not good enough, not a real child; this child is more of a jump start to get a real child.

"No children? This committee needs people ... and since you've obviously got time to do it, you'd be perfect for it!"
Don't assume that just because a couple is childless they have lots of free time. It is good to let people know how much their assistance is needed, but they have goals for their lives, too, that go beyond filling in for all the gaps that busy parents leave empty.

Rather than putting people on the spot about volunteering, as if it is an obligation for couples without children, why not invite them to participate in a ministry or activity that you know they would enjoy? Then they can decide whether that is the direction the Lord wants for them.

[To someone in secondary infertility:] "Just relax! God will bless you with more children. You got pregnant once."
Infertility is not a psychological problem but a physical difficulty. It is not a matter of relaxing. Having one child means that the couple was not permanently infertile; but it does not guarantee that they will ever have another baby.

"At least be thankful for the one(s) you have."
The desire for another child has nothing to do with ingratitude for the child(ren) the Lord has already given a couple. In fact, the very opposite is true. The joy of life with a child increases the desire to share life with another child.

The Gift of Suffering

For four and a half years one family prayed every novena in the book before they conceived their first child. They ended up with a total of eight children, including one set of twins. In retrospect, the wife said they needed that time to pray and prepare for the family that God gave them.

Sacrifices offered in union with Christ's self-offering may help others see the blessings they are overlooking. Two different situations I recall led to a similar conversation, one with a family member, one with a friend: "Maybe I shouldn't get my tubes tied after all, after seeing what you're going through." You may be used by God to call others to holiness as they see you suffer.

Another couple prayed throughout twelve years of infertility. Though they still have not conceived, they now have children through adoption. They adopted a sibling set of five from a foreign country; the children spoke no English, and the couple didn't speak their language. They attest to the fact that they needed those years of prayer and yielding to the will of God to be prepared for the journey their family would take. The time of waiting was not wasted.

We can strengthen our prayers for others by offering up some of our difficulties for the intention of their fertility. A couple from Rocky River, Ohio, said, "We didn't have our first baby for nearly five years. Many people prayed for us. After the birth of our first child, Annie, we were able to conceive [again]."

A dear friend, Gloria, had a dramatic experience of healing in Medjugorje, Yugoslavia; her healing was spiritual, not physical.

> When you are numb with bitterness, the cross of infertility seems even bigger, darker, heavier than anyone else's. When I walked out of that church, I had a new frame of mind: My infertility was a blessing and a joy, not a curse. How blessed and privileged I was to be chosen to share in Christ's cross. Jesus considered me worthy to carry it, to share it with him. I am forever grateful for the suffering he allowed me.
>
> If anyone had told me that I'd be joyful in my suffering, I wouldn't have believed it. What a gift! I would not be the person I am today if I had not had the journey I have had.

In addition, there is the sadness some couples bear when their infertility comes after having one or two children. They hear their children beg God for siblings and wonder aloud why God seems silent. This can be especially difficult when aunts and uncles are conceiving. Not only do the parents have their own heartache, but they bear their child's heartache as well.

We believe—and we remind our children—that no prayer goes unanswered. But the answer is not always what we request. This is where we need to have a solid relationship with God our Father so that we can guide our children's hearts to deeper trust in him through the suffering rather than a rejection of him because of what they think is "unanswered" prayer.

All this misunderstanding and hurt, unintended though it may be, needs to be brought to the cross. Jesus wants us to do what we can to keep a root of bitterness or resentment from growing in our hearts. He will help us keep our hearts soft toward him and our spouse, rather than becoming hardened in our pain.

Jesus himself felt the pangs of grief, being denied spiritual children by the religious leaders of Jerusalem. Just before his crucifixion, he wept while he spoke of yearning to gather his people like a mother hen gathers her chicks. But he was denied (see Mt 23:37). One friend said that Jesus' weeping over a kind of barrenness brought comfort to her heart as a spouse bereft of children thus far.

The Adoption Option

Since the age of the early Christians, the Church has been a witness to the value of human life. At a time when Romans frequently cast off unwanted young and left them to die by exposure, Christians gathered the children and brought them into their families. Believers founded orphanages and hospitals for two millennia, receiving babies without question and providing them a refuge.

The language of adoption is used to describe the sonship that we receive when we are incorporated into Christ. Our adoption in Christ has truly made us his children. It is not a legal fiction but a fact.

In the same way, if we adopt children, they really and truly become our children. One woman who adopted a child experienced a deeper understanding of her own adoption as a child of God: "It has confirmed the truth and the glory of the Church's teaching to me, and my awareness of God's goodness, love, and mercy."

Some people have been given an amazing gift to love children. Their struggle with infertility can make excruciating the frustration of not being able to share that gift of love. However, adoption can be the means of combining a large heart, eager to love, with a child or children in special need of that love. Adoption can be a beautiful way of embracing the teaching of the Church.

One adoptive mother said, "Our understanding of openness to life impacted our decision to adopt. As a mother I wanted the opportunity to give of myself to another human being by making her part of our family and nurturing her."

Adoption is not an easy decision. It may or may not be God's will for a couple. Or both husband and wife may not be in the same place emotionally to take that step. A woman from Wheat Ridge, Colorado, expressed some of the concerns she and her husband have had with regard to adoption.

> We have had various obstacles to adoption. I'm too young (thirty-three) to be considered by some agencies, and my husband is too old (forty-five) for others. Health is a concern. The cost was high: The home visit alone is around five thousand dollars, which we are about one-third of the way to saving up. And we fear that what the state gives, the state can take away.

These concerns demonstrate why some couples have difficulty adopting.

Age can be a factor, depending on the state in which you live. Find an expert on adoption in your state so that you get the facts straight. How much time is involved in the process? How much money? Are there restrictions on medical or psychological problems?

When someone has an adoption fall through, it can feel like a miscarriage or a stillbirth. The loss is so great. When a couple has longed for a child and is promised one, only to discover the birth mom has changed her mind, it is devastating. A couple from Encinitas, California, wrote, "When we had a failed adoption, I could not imagine a greater pain. But something as simple as a sympathy card or flowers from a friend would have been helpful."

The struggle with infertility is not a question of whether or not a marriage will be fruitful but how. The *Catechism* teaches:

> The Gospel shows that physical sterility is not an absolute evil. Spouses who still suffer from infertility after exhausting legitimate medical procedures should unite themselves with the Lord's cross, the source

of all spiritual fecundity. They can give expression to their generosity by adopting abandoned children or performing demanding services for others.[26]

Anne echoes these sentiments in her testimony: "Our daughter, Mary Joy, is adopted. She is a true gift of God. Finally letting go of the dream of the child of our union was very difficult, but in my obedience I was blessed abundantly."

When a couple adopts, rejoice with them! Since adoptions are not finalized for a period of time (laws vary from state to state), people can hesitate to celebrate the newly adopted child. But we need to welcome this life into their family as we would any child. A mother from Encinitas, California, remembers:

When Sara was born and brought home, we received one floral arrangement. Most people are unsure when to send something. The thinking was, wait till the adoption is final. In some situations that could be a year! So for someone like me, who waited seven years for a child, there was sadness in the way others celebrated Sara's birth. Without a doubt, she was the prize; but as a new mom, I wanted to be treated like other moms—showered with flowers and cards.

Let's be sure to celebrate every new life, and every new mom and dad.

Gloria and her husband, Julian, discovered a new depth to their understanding of their relationship to God through the adoption of their two daughters.

Our adoption experience heightened our spiritual senses in so many ways that I could not begin to list them. Our understanding of infant baptism, becoming children of God and being welcomed into the family, no questions asked, meant profoundly more after adoption. (It has also helped in our discussions with non-Catholics regarding infant baptism.) Surely we did not wait for our daughter to understand everything it meant to be a part of our family before we gave her our name. The responsibilities that came with that would be taught and nurtured later.

Some people have experienced the joy of adoption from the standpoint of being adopted themselves, as Sally has.

I was adopted at four weeks from an unwed French girl who took me to a wonderful set of parents. I highly recommend it. If I had been conceived twenty-two years later, I could have been aborted, so naturally I realize how important each life is! And my parents appreciate it too.

Those children who have been adopted have a particular challenge to issue to those who are considering having an abortion, as Maria observes.

Three of my siblings are adopted, two of them after *Roe v. Wade*. Through them we are constantly reminded of other people's advice for life, and we praise God because of the decision of the two women we never knew.

In a beautiful way God has continued to use these adoptions. My sister had a friend who became pregnant and was strongly considering abortion. My sister was the person who changed her mind by using her and the choice her biological mother made as the example.

Others, like Patricia and William, have deeply thankful hearts for mothers who loved their children sacrificially enough to give them up for adoption.

The gift of our son John is incomparable. We cannot express enough gratitude for his precious life. Since his entry into life, we have been stunned by the peace in our hearts. We are grateful to his biological parents but now feel that his first parents have missed something extraordinary. I know the world would not be as wonderful if John's mother had extinguished his life. And for that fact, we stand in her honor!

The Lord has brought children to some of you through adoption. These children might otherwise never have had the opportunity to hear about the faith, yet through you, they have been baptized and taught the faith at great sacrifice. What a beautiful expression of the gospel of life!

A couple from Winfield, Illinois, share an account of their journey:

We were married ten years and had no children. Through Catholic Charities God has blessed us with children! In 1990, we adopted two beautiful girls who are sisters, ages five and two. Then we received another pair of sisters, ages four and two. A four-year-old, our first son, came this past September. Life has become very, very full.

Then the Lord shocked us: On October 28, the feast day of St. Jude (saint of hopeless cases), we found out that I was pregnant. I guess the Lord seems slow at times, but he is never late! We are so thrilled and thankful for all his blessings. He has given us all we ever prayed for and much more.

Many of us struggle, at one time or another, with loss: miscarriage, still-birth, the death of a child, or infertility. Our losses can actually be among our greatest spiritual gains, provided we entrust them to our heavenly Father. Our openness to life can bear much fruit when our hearts are yielded to him. Perhaps our sufferings united to Christ's will release life-giving love in a special way in the body of Christ.

CHAPTER TWELVE

STERILIZATION

Once after I gave a talk about the Church's teaching on openness to life, a man approached me. "I know the Church is against birth control," he asked. "But is the Church against sterilization?" (He had had a vasectomy.) I had to answer him honestly. If sterilizing a single act of marriage is serious sin, how much more is complete sterilization!

In the Old Testament, a man who was sterile could not be a part of public worship with the other men. "He whose testicles are crushed or whose male member is cut off shall not enter the assembly of the Lord" (Dt 23:1). This was an occasion of shame, yet today, men (and women) proudly announce they have been sterilized as if they have done a good thing.

The Teaching of the Church

The *Catechism* is unambiguous on this point. "Except when performed for strictly therapeutic medical reasons, directly intended *amputations, mutilations,* and *sterilizations* performed on innocent persons are against the moral law."[1] Sterilization is a mutilation of the body.[2] What other part of our bodies would we even think of mutilating because we refused to serve God with it ever again: hands? feet? legs?

Any sterilization whose sole, immediate effect, ... is to render the generative faculty incapable of procreation is to be regarded as direct sterilization.... It is absolutely forbidden, therefore, according to the teaching of the Church, even when it is motivated by a subjectively right intention of curing or preventing a physical or psychological ill-effect which is foreseen or feared as a result of pregnancy.[3]

This teaching is clear.

Dr. Joseph Stanford described his concern about sterilizing as a matter of course. "With regard to sterilization, I also recognized that fertility is a part of health, not a disease, and so there is something fundamentally contradictory about doing a surgery to remove a healthy and fundamental function of the body."[4] As the saying goes, If it ain't broke, don't fix it!

After five years, Pam and Burnie had a change of heart about vasectomy. They found a doctor who

> has quite a practice of men seeking reversals from vasectomy after God performs a reversal of the heart....
>
> He prayed with us before surgery, asking *God* to guide his hands and give him the strength to perform the surgery. And he asked God to bless us again with children.
>
> My dear husband suffered through this procedure to "fix" what we had willingly broken several years before. [The doctor] skillfully performed his task, and after giving us last instructions, we were home the next day. The entire process of surgery and also the "heart reversal" made us so happy to be back at home with the four blessings God had already bestowed upon us!
>
> Burnie and I purposed that even if God saw fit to never give us another child, we would know we had done the right thing by putting that decision back into the proper hands, his hands.[5]

Pam and Burnie have had one child since their reversal.

Sometimes people have not heard a clear teaching on sterilization. They approach Church teaching as if they have options regarding obedience. Sometimes even Catholic hospitals take a similar approach. But Catholic hospitals are not permitted to participate in contraceptive sterilization.

> For the official approval of direct sterilization and, all the more so, its administration and execution according to the hospital regulations is something of its nature—that is, intrinsically—objectively evil. Nothing can justify a Catholic hospital co-operating in it.[6]

Is this guideline being followed by administrators of Catholic hospitals?

Societal Pressure for the Ultimate Contraceptive

The pressure in our society to be sterilized is considerable. Undoubtedly, some of that pressure comes from the people who have already been sterilized, and as many as two-thirds of married people over the age of forty five have been.[7]

Sometimes the Ob-Gyn office is the place where these issues are raised. One woman reported, "My husband told the nurse [who suggested sterilization after the birth of their fourth child] that we loved and wanted this child and any more God would send. She did not think much of our statement."

Mary, from Long Island, New York, felt badgered by nurses about sterilization after she delivered her fourth baby. "Yes, after child number four, and also after number five and number six—and they gave up at child number seven! When I was going for prenatal visits for child number seven, one particular nurse would come in and, before taking my blood pressure, would start about sterilization. I'd get agitated and of course have high B.P. After that, I wore a pin that said: "BLOOD PRESSURE—TAKE, DON'T TALK.""

Others, like Ruth and Joe, succumbed to the pressure of a doctor's insistence. "During my eleventh pregnancy (I was thirty-nine years old), the doctor virtually insisted that my husband be sterilized because of my health and five miscarriages. We decided to go to Planned Parenthood. He had the vasectomy. The vasectomy was a big mistake. A thousand times I've felt he should be reversed."

Sometimes a couple is asked right on the delivery table. Recalls one mother: "When we delivered our fourth, I had a C-section. The doctor said, 'I have your tube right here (I only have one tube). I'll just snip it.' I said, 'Leave my tube alone!'" She is now a mother of twelve.

Another bold woman, Brenda, from Houston, Texas, forthrightly shared her values. "I told the OB that I was Catholic, and sterilization was against the Church's teaching. I also mentioned the effectiveness of modern NFP."

Sheila, from El Paso, Texas, responded differently.

After four (vertical) C-sections, the doctor led my husband and me to believe I could possibly bleed to death the next time. (The doctor is Catholic.) I had a tubal ligation. I have since discovered that the probable worst-case scenario would have been a hysterectomy. Needless to say, I repent that I didn't trust God more.

Doctors have a great deal of influence. Stephanie, from Lancaster, Pennsylvania, recalls her situation:

I was a victim of unwanted, unasked-for sterilization. To shorten this long, painful story, let me conclude by revealing that during my third pregnancy I developed gestational diabetes and in my ninth month a sonogram revealed that my baby was in great distress. She was delivered three weeks early by emergency C-section on the very day of that frightening sonogram. I was distressed and scared, to say the least.

The physician who delivered her "strongly recommended" I have a tubal ligation—while I was on the operating table under anesthesia! This had not been discussed prior to that day, nor did my husband or I desire birth control, let alone sterilization! But the truth was, this doctor seemed so concerned for my well-being and he was so "heroic" at that moment, having saved the life of my baby girl, he convinced Jim and me that this was *the* option—we had no other choice.

The doctor praised us for being intelligent people who already had three children and who couldn't risk losing me, their mother, through another pregnancy. He performed a tubal ligation after the C-section. I was and am sick at heart.

It is essential to know what we believe, and why, so that we can make sound judgments even during stress-filled situations.

For some people, fear of the consequences rather than conviction is enough to keep them from making a permanent decision. Rachel recounts a conversation with her husband.

He discussed a vasectomy but "forgot" to go to the doctor! He rationalized that this was too permanent and we were so young. (I was twenty-eight and Matt was twenty-six!) We also knew by now that I had Multiple Sclerosis (MS), and Matt, having such long-term vision, tenderly told me one night that he did not want to get a vasectomy:

"Rachel, you have MS. You might die, and I might want to get married again, and my new wife might want to have kids!" It was priceless!

Now Rachel and Matthew have a conviction against both contraception and sterilization.

Sometimes people try to live what they know is right only to feel pressured by their loved ones and even priests they respect to do otherwise. A couple from New Castle, Pennsylvania, experienced this problem.

Eight years ago we began to learn and understand more about our faith, but not knowing much at all about NFP, we quit contracepting and tried the rhythm method. I got pregnant. I was not too concerned. I felt God would see us through, but my husband was devastated, feeling a great burden had been placed on him.

He spoke to his parents, who urged him to have a vasectomy. He spoke to a priest, who told him not to have the surgery—he could always put any future children up for adoption! This, of course, was no help; it made my husband feel his only option was surgery. I sat silent. I was scared and didn't know what to do.

My husband had the surgery, and immediately following, he suffered a great depression. He had to wait three months before he could have it reversed.

Young couples need support from their loved ones to do right rather than pressure to do wrong.

Sometimes pressure to sterilize comes from a spouse. Sue wrote:

Ardie was sterilized, mostly at my insistence, because I thought *I* had gone through the "pain and work" of pregnancy and delivery. We had our three kids and we were "done," so it was his turn now.

However, once I opened my heart to God and saw my error, I realized the horror of our mistake and the need for the reversal. So I gave subtle hints to and prayed constantly for Ardie to be open to see the truth in the Church's teaching.

While preparing a talk for a church retreat on the Father's loving care in the area of discipline, Ardie had an eye-opening experience. He remembered how when growing up, if he did something wrong, his father would say he was disappointed in him. Ardie would have done anything to right the wrong and get back in his father's graces. As he related that experience to the relationship of God, his heavenly Father, he realized how he had disappointed his heavenly Father and wanted to do anything he could to regain his grace. He realized the need to be made whole again and to be "truly fixed," so he had a reversal.

That was about three and a half years ago. We have since had a beautiful son and are expecting another blessing in November. The reversal has brought God's grace more fully into our lives. We now see the blessing children are, not the problem. Ardie and I relate differently in our marriage. We see the need to evangelize others who haven't been taught well or who are caught up in this secular culture, so that they can receive the wonderful gift of joy we have received.

Sometimes the husband is the one who insists on sterilization.

As Protestants, we stopped using contraceptives only because I had a hysterectomy at age twenty-nine. It was an emergency situation. Had surgery not been necessary, my husband would have had a vasectomy. He was strongly against having more than two children; it was the *only* thing we could not resolve in the early years of our marriage. I wanted a big family; he did *not.* He didn't think it was wise.

Now this couple has come into the Church with their children, and they are united on the Church's teaching about openness to life.

Just because a couple has not been tempted to consider sterilization does not mean that such temptation will not come. One mother explained their situation.

Two years ago this month, our youngest daughter was born, our fifth Caesarean birth in ten years. We had practiced Natural Family Planning for most of our marriage and were convinced of its merits, and in the process were convinced of the Church's wisdom in condemning artificial birth control and sterilization. We had never considered sterilization after the other children were born. When, late in the last pregnancy, our doctor asked a second time if we were considering a tubal ligation, I was surprised. I believe he did not ask for any reason other than genuine concern for my well-being and our children's welfare.

We asked our priest if this was ever allowed. He said that given our intention—the preservation of my life and health, risk to an unborn child (something I already worried about more with each pregnancy), and the loss to our children if I should die because of a uterine accident—we "could in clear conscience make the choice to have the tubal ligation."

After agonizing over it, we did so, although I did not finally decide until the baby was born. Three other priests had given us similar counsel. One priest friend, whose counsel we have always valued for his wisdom and adherence to the truths of the Magisterium, was written to but was away.

He answered us with a letter and booklet when he returned. These arrived in the mail several hours after the baby's birth, however. What he found in his sources all said no. We've struggled with this for months. I'm still not at peace with this.

Sterilization was not an option. "Legitimate intentions on the part of the spouses do not justify recourse to morally unacceptable means (for example, direct sterilization or contraception)."[8] Though their intentions were noble, the means of sterilization was not moral. Sadly, the very spiritual advisors who should have pointed this out to the couple failed to do so.

Health insurance companies add their own subtle pressure. For example, in Maryland, the CareFirst Blue Cross/Blue Shield Company lists pregnancy and delivery under illness in its employee benefit guide. Benefits include contraceptives, voluntary sterilization, and abortion. Under exclusion: services to reverse a voluntary sterilization procedure; services for sterilization or reverse sterilization for a dependent minor.[9]

There are those in our society who believe, for the good of society, that we should sterilize mentally or physically handicapped people. The Church speaks to this point clearly.

Sterility induced as such does not contribute to the person's integral good, properly understood, 'keeping things and values in proper perspective.' Rather does it damage a person's ethical good, since it deprives subsequent freely-chosen sexual acts of an essential element.[10]

We must show greater concern for the human person.

Long-Term Consequences

As a fifty-year-old woman reflected on her life, she recognized sterilization as one more wrong step she had taken.

> I had a daughter out of wedlock at age twenty. I married a different man at age twenty-two and always contracepted because I had never really dealt with the loss of giving my daughter up for adoption. Pregnancy meant shame and pain to me. When things went rocky in our marriage eight years later, I had a tubal ligation. My husband and I divorced shortly thereafter.
>
> Several years later I obtained an annulment. My current husband and I went back to the Church and the sacraments. By the time I had grown enough spiritually to realize how wrong sterilization was, I was in my forties and reversal wasn't much of an option. The sterilization was the worst decision of my life, and I can only do my best to help others' lives now and trust in God's great mercy.

Another couple similarly see ongoing negative consequences in their family due to a vasectomy.

> Twenty years later I see clearly the harm: when the sperm were removed from the act, the hormones were imbalanced. His desire decreased; my desire decreased. Sexual activity was minimal. Children observed no more pregnancies; they took on a birth control mentality. All six of our children became sexually active before marriage—even though I had taught them minimally it was wrong. Three of our

children have divorced, one of whom had to get married. I believe it all traces back to the misuse of our sexuality and vasectomy.

These consequences are painful.

The pain from sterilization is increased when one spouse does not want it to happen yet the other goes ahead. Karen shared their story.

After our third child, Jay had a vasectomy. After all, our Catholic friends had had one after their second child; hey, we had number three! Wow!

It broke my heart down deep, but I tried not to mention it and was very ashamed of it. I tucked a baby T-shirt in my top drawer for four years. When I saw the T-shirt, I prayed Jay would have a change of heart and maybe we could adopt. He had been reading *Rome Sweet Home*. Together we had been studying very hard all the teachings of our faith.

In January 1995 Jay developed a hernia. When we went for his checkup, I couldn't believe what came off my lips: "When you go in for the hernia, could you reverse the vasectomy?" My face was hot and red and I think Jay was shocked, too. I knew two things: We weren't insured for a reversal, and we didn't have the money. (I had called a doctor, who said it would cost seven to eight thousand dollars to reverse it.)

The doctor said, "I can't, but while you're out on the operating table, we could have another doctor come in." We were both ecstatic and drove to see him two days later. On Friday he said he could do it, and since Jay would be out already, the insurance would pay all hospital costs. We would pay only his fee of three thousand dollars, and we could make any payment schedule we could afford!

We went to Mass together at the hospital and thanked God for the opportunity to restore Jay to the way God had made him and for his forever patience and forgiveness with us.

John Luke, our fourth child, was born April 25, 1996. He was nine pounds, thirteen ounces and a sign of God's mercy on Jay and me.

The Lord is kind and merciful.

Jim and Debbie, from Vista, California, also faced the dilemma of one spouse having been sterilized against the wishes of the other.

The pregnancies with the first two were tough, and my wife was bedridden six months with our second-born. After our second child was born, I discussed the prospects of a third pregnancy with our doctor. He advised that a third pregnancy would most surely cause severe and permanent damage to my wife's back. Against my wife's wishes, I obtained a vasectomy in 1987.

We both still wanted more children. My wife made great gains in strengthening her back, which included an operation. We decided that I should get a vasectomy reversal.

In 1997, I obtained a reversal. Alas, I am permanently sterile (great lesson here) and remained infertile after the reversal. God's blessing, though, allowed us to adopt a baby in April 1998. We are blessed with three children now and look forward to adopting more.

Though Jim's fertility did not return, they experienced great blessing from the Lord for undoing the damage done earlier.

Increased Health Risks

Much heartache could be avoided if married couples remembered St. Paul's teaching about our bodies. First, our bodies belong to the Lord as temples of the Holy Spirit, so we have to honor the Lord in how we treat them. And second, our bodies belong to our spouse as part of our covenantal exchange of persons. "For the wife does not rule over her own body, but the husband does; likewise the husband does not rule over his own body, but the wife does" (1 Cor 7:4).

As a Protestant, Valerie, from Chillicothe, Ohio, did not know the Church's teaching on sterilization. "I thought it was normal [to be sterilized] after two or three children. We looked into [reversal], but it was very expensive and I was over forty. I had known and respected other Christians (men and women) who had themselves sterilized and thought it was OK."

Valerie and her husband were received into the Church at Easter, 1997.

"Several years went by before the enormity of what I had done hit me. I grieved for the children I did not, and would never, have. I have found absolution in the Church, but I still grieve. I wish I had had more children."

Risks of Sterility

Many men and women do not know the number of health risks to which they expose themselves through sterilization. For women, side effects include many more difficulties than the common outcome of hysterectomy. Post-tubal ligation syndrome can lead to these difficulties:

Existing menstrual problems are often worsened
Severe cramps and much heavier periods
Longer periods or irregular periods
Dysfunctional uterine bleeding, sometimes lasting for years
Lack of ovulation
Infections
Abnormal hormone production
Pain during intercourse
Pelvic pain
Cervical cancer
Hormonal imbalances
Ovarian cysts or tumors
Endometriosis
Emotional imbalance.[11]

Other potential consequences have been identified as well:

The consequences of tubal ligation are very real. Between twenty percent and forty percent of women suffer from post tubal ligation syndrome, which means that women are experiencing increased pain with periods, abnormally short or long menstrual cycles, severe PMS, and pelvic pain. In addition, women who have undergone a tubal ligation end up having a hysterectomy much sooner than women who were not sterilized.[12]

When those who have been sterilized pressure others to follow their example, rarely do they mention these possible side effects.

Men also experience pain with sterilization. Dr. Whit Oliver offered his wife a proposal. "When we had our fourth child, I chose vasectomy sterilization as the best way to prevent further pregnancies—my gift to my wife, my pain as payment for hers endured with childbirth and child-rearing."[13] Nine years later, however, he got a reversal.

A number of diseases have been increasingly observed in men who have had vasectomies. Nancy Campbell, who compiled an anthology of stories by couples who have undergone sterilization reversals, urges couples to weigh the possible consequences. Based on research by Dr. J.J. Roberts, she reports increased risk for

thrombophlebitis and pulmonary embolism

infections of the prostate gland, epididymis (a tube leading to the testes), kidney, blood, heart valves

abscess of the liver

abscesses of the skin

auto-immune diseases

narcolepsy (sleeping sickness)

multiple sclerosis

migraine and related headaches

hypoglycemia and diabetes

emotional disturbances

impaired sexual function

kidney stones

tumors and cancer (especially of the prostate).[14]

Many studies attest especially to the increased risk of prostate cancer in vasectomized men.

Giovannucci, et al., reported statistically significant increases of prostate cancer in both a large prospective cohort study (1993a) and a large retrospective cohort study (1993b) of vasectomized men in the United States—viz., 10,055 and 14,607 subjects respectively. The overall risk increased by fifty-six percent but rose up to eighty-nine percent among those who had undergone vasectomy twenty-two years or longer. Such risk did not appear to be related to diet, level of physical activity, smoking, alcohol intake, educational level, body mass index, geographical area or residence, or detection bias in these carefully conceived studies.[15]

Another study reported in the *American Journal of Epidemiology*, December 1990, reveals a 70 percent higher risk of prostate cancer for those who have had vasectomies.

Researchers from the Brigman Women's Hospital in Boston advise men who have had vasectomies and are over fifty years old to have a yearly rectal examination and blood test. They state that vasectomy could raise the longer-term risk of prostate cancer by between 56 percent and 66 percent according to American studies with 73,000 men.[16]

Besides various physical side effects, some men deal with depression as well, as revealed by one couple: "The reversal was successful, but the depression lingered for quite some time. I felt awful for not trying to stop the initial surgery. We made it through that dark period, and our bright spot from that time is our beautiful sweet son Brendan."

Remedy for Injury

We heard of one Protestant couple who reversed a sterilization, and after they had a baby, the husband had another vasectomy! How can that be? After speaking to Ardie and Sue, a Catholic couple who had reversed a sterilization, I understood.

The first couple's motivation was to have another baby. Once that was accomplished, they sterilized again. There was no recognition of sin for the sterilization and therefore no repentance. Ardie and Sue, on the other hand, came to a conviction that they had sinned through sterilization. Their motivation was to undo the damage they had done, whether or not they ever conceived again.

The first couple was still motivated by wanting to control the outcome; the second couple wanted God to be in control of their fertility. The first couple checked with a doctor and had the procedure reversed. The second couple went to Confession as the first step toward restoration. There could hardly be a greater contrast.

The Church requires repentance for a restored relationship with the Lord. However, due to the financial burden of reversal and possible physical risk, the Church does not require a reversal of the operation. Yet one couple from Rialto, California, wanted to do more than repent.

> We had already been to Confession and knew that we didn't have to have the operation. Because our health insurance didn't cover reversals, we knew we would have to pay for it on our own. We began NFP, abstaining following my cycles, etc. During this time Richard experienced angina. As it turned out, he ended up having double bypass surgery after an angiogram revealed blockages. God knew which tubes to fix first!
>
> I began to get cold feet about the reversal after Richard went through the other surgery, but Richard was firm. He asked how soon following recovery he could reschedule his reversal. And then God did something truly wonderful. He arranged Richard's reversal to happen on Richard's birthday, January 7, the beginning of a new year.
>
> It's been five years. Richard is fifty and I'm almost forty-seven. We've been married twenty-two years. We have four children, none since the reversal—the cost of our own pride.

A reversal does not come with a promise of new life.

A self-described "blessed mom" from Midlothian, Virginia, succumbed to peer pressure to prohibit new life.

> The first time we were approached about sterilization at delivery was after my third son was born. We were horrified.
>
> But after my fifth child, I had my tubes cut. I felt I was so young to have all these kids, a husband who traveled all the time, left at home alone, etc.... I felt pressure from others to stop and enjoy the fruits I had; I had to consider the economics of everything. I had done my duty above and beyond!
>
> I considered reversing for three years after I did it. I prayed. I talked to people. I prayed some more. It wasn't until our second son, Bryan,

died from cancer at ten and a half years old that I knew what I had to do. I had to ask God for forgiveness—for not knowing the gifts that he had given us and realizing the gift that had been taken from us; and that if I was to reverse my surgery, to please give me the monetary means to do so or to take the want and idea and the guilt away from me.

The decision was *not* to replace Bryan, the child we lost; but to make a wrong right—to make me whole again. If we didn't have any more children—OK. That was God's choice, not ours. Something so strong inside me drove me to correct it.

On the day before my surgery, I called a friend. Maybe I shouldn't do this; it costs so much.... She told me to take a deep breath, close my eyes, and ask Jesus and Mary to be with me and listen to my heart.

Six months later I was pregnant with our sixth child, and on May 17 we were blessed with our daughter, Paige Elizabeth. I can say I've never regretted it.

When we bring our brokenness and sin to the Lord, he not only restores us, but he blesses us in new ways.

My husband, Tom, and I have been on an exciting spiritual journey for the last eight years as we have fallen deeply in love with our Lord and the Church he established. Each time we discover a new teaching, it is as if a light bulb turns on within the depths of our souls as the fullness of his truth continues to unfold the beauty of his plan for his people.

Seven months after our third child was born, Tom had a vasectomy. Now that we reflect on this decision, we can only come to the conclusion that we thought the Church's stand on contraception was outdated.

Not long after we had the surgery, God began his work in us in this particular area. I'm not exactly sure how we came to realize the horror of what we had done through sterilization.

We began to wonder if we should have a reversal. We both confessed our sin in addition to the use of birth control pills in the early years of our marriage and were both given absolution. As we continued our hunger in search of truth, our discovery of the beauty and truth of the

Catholic Church began to turn into a love story of our Lord and the splendor of his Church.

[We heard testimonies] of many couples who had had a sterilization reversal and that God had blessed and graced this decision abundantly in each couple. These blessings and graces didn't just stop with the couple, but also were passed down to the children the couple had before the reversal and, of course, to new children.

A priest said no one ever quite asked the question that way: What would be most pleasing to our Lord? Most asked our old way: Does the Church require reversal?

He said of course we were not required to have a reversal, that our sin was forgiven and forgotten. To have a reversal would be heroic, going above and beyond what we are called to do, and would be a martyrdom of sorts. But to specifically answer our question: he felt the reversal would be most pleasing to our Lord and that he would grace the decision to reverse.

Our greatest desire in this decision is to be in complete obedience to God's perfect and pleasing will. We also feel peace as to whether or not we will have more children, as God alone is the Author of life, and he works his will regardless of successful reversal statistics. We are finding since the surgery, as we are finding in so many areas of our lives, that there is freedom in obedience.

The worldly view is that there would be freedom through the use of contraception, when actually there is bondage. We have found a peace since our decision that can only be that peace that surpasses all understanding.

There is not only a lack of knowledge among Catholics as to what the Church really teaches but almost an avoidance of the teaching. Once we realized what we had done, we had great difficulty finding direction as to whether or not to reverse. We do feel as if our Lord brought us on a beautiful journey, but it was not without great struggle, much opposition, and misguided direction.

In addition it required perseverance in prayer and seeking God's direction on our part. It also required much prayer to discern even where to find godly direction in this area.

This story is an inspiration to us all.

Reversals can be prohibitively expensive. Anne, from Pittsford, New York, investigated the costs involved.

It was through much prayer that we came to this decision. Unfortunately, insurance paid for the vasectomy but not the reversal. Though it was very expensive, we relied on God and NFP to keep chaste and God provided for a windfall of money to reverse the vasectomy. We did reverse it and are open to life.

The exorbitant cost has led some priests to suggest that the couple remain infertile and donate the money to a good cause as their penance. One priest said, "There are other ways to have a baby." However, the couple's goal should not be to have another baby. It should be to undo the damage they have done, to set things right, to be whole again and to have the act of marriage be whole again.

When the expense of reversal is too great, some couples practice NFP to express their sincere sorrow for their sin. Since a woman continues to exhibit signs of fertility, she and her husband can know when fertile times would have occurred and can abstain during those times. This protects the couple from *enjoying* the benefits of their sin after they have gone to Confession.

To be truly sorry, they would have to have a change of heart so that if they could do it over, their serious reasons would lead them to NFP rather than sterilization. So they act the way they should have. Otherwise, the danger exists that in having sex during what would have been fertile times, they might enjoy the benefits of sterilized sex and be tempted to continue a contraceptive intention.

One couple in their fifties have benefited from this idea. The wife reports: "We thought of it [sterilization reversal], but it's too late. My current husband and I practice NFP anyway now because we figure it's the least we can do—better late than never."

Sometimes the biggest obstacle to a reversal is not the expense, but a spouse's unwillingness to undergo another operation. A couple from Whittier, California, initially debated the issue of reversal.

My husband had a vasectomy after our third child (1991). We regretted the decision almost immediately. We had to work toward unity on whether we had a moral obligation to reverse sterilization. Finally we had the vasectomy reversed two months ago. The cost involved kept us from doing it earlier, although as Catholics we felt a moral burden that helped motivate us to afford the surgery.

Timm, from Prairie du Chien, Wisconsin, expected questions from his doctor when he approached him about a reversal, but the first question surprised him. "The doctor we settled on had done several reversals on men who were in second marriages. The doctor asked me if I had had a change of wives. 'No, just a change of convictions!' I told him."[17]

After one couple realized their sin in sterilization, they not only went to a priest for Confession; they approached an infertile couple in their family. The husband asked his brother and sister-in-law to forgive them for spurning the gift of life they had enjoyed, all the while knowing that other family members were struggling with being unable to receive life. It was a step toward inner healing for the infertile couple, and it strengthened the friendship between the couples.

Sometimes it takes a couple a while to come to a conviction against sterilization; other times it occurs quickly. Here is the story of Dr. and Mrs. Paul Mungo from their separate vantage points.

Cathy: After our fourth child I was so out of balance (chemically, emotionally, and physically) that I basically said, "No fixing, no sex!" (*God forgive me!*) He went in for a vasectomy.

Paul: Our family physician did the operation, and one hour later I realized I had made a big mistake. Then the depression began. I went to my confessor about a week later, and he told me how he had seen some men get very depressed and mentally unstable after a vasectomy. (I did not tell him at that point that I had already had a vasectomy!)

Cathy: Our marriage went ("plummeted" is a better word) downhill from there. We were on the verge of divorce (literally) when we had an awesome experience from our Blessed Mother. We were suddenly brought to the *light* about many things in regards to our faith, our lives together, God, the Church—everything. She is so wonderful and amazing and loving!

Paul: As my walk toward Christ led by his Blessed Mother continued, I found that I too was going crazy about having had this vasectomy. I talked to many priests and some said to confess and forget; others said to abstain for part of the month as if we were using NFP; but I felt I was committing a mortal sin every time I was intimate with my wife.

I went to a weekend at Franciscan University while trying to decide what God wanted me to do in regard to reversing my vasectomy. I [went] in the chapel.

I have never been there alone. I proceeded to the tabernacle. At once I broke out into deep tears and then into a sob and collapsed before Christ. No one else was there but me and God.

I left and went to Confession to Fr. Koseki for forgiveness of my vasectomy, for going against the will of God. I asked him if I should go ahead with the operation. He simply said, "Yes." God filled me with peace and courage.

I went to a urologist finally and told him I wanted a vasectomy reversal (vasovasectomy). He asked why, and I told him for religious reasons, to do the will of God. He kind of looked at me funny and said OK. I must say here also that I felt like I was not only cheating on God but on my wife, due to the fact that I was selfish and not open to life.

Cathy: Eventually, after much prayer and good Catholic counseling from holy priests, Paul had a reversal of the vasectomy. It brought both of us great peace, and great healing and freedom in our marriage. We have left it up to the Lord in regard to more children. Whew! What a load that is off my mind! He's in charge—not me, not Paul, but *God!* And that means it's *perfect!*

Paul: My wife was in full accord through this entire ordeal. Several weeks later I reversed the vasectomy, in August 1993. A twenty-minute vasectomy took three and a half hours to undo.

There was lots of pain afterward to offer up for atonement. I thank God the Father, the Son, and the Holy Spirit, and the Blessed Mother for helping me to have this operation that I so badly wanted yet was frightened to have. I asked the Blessed Mother to hold my hand while I had the operation, and I just knew I could feel her hand in mine.

I am now free of the chains that I dragged. I feel free to pursue Christ more freely. The peace of mind and soul in union with Christ after the reversal has changed my life.

Paul and Cathy: Please, please, please tell people not to sterilize themselves!

Reversal of Fortune

What can it mean to a couple to reverse a sterilization? Anne declares: "It is so beautiful to be walking in the moral universe again. The freedom and joy are astounding. Also, God has been using us to witness to other couples about these issues." Judith describes spiritual awakenings: "Deeper faith, deeper love, deeper realization of the consequences of sin." Sandra concludes: "On October 13, 1992, I regained my womanhood."[18]

Another woman who hoped for a reversal wrote, "Inquiries revealed my tubes had been cauterized many times, in many different places, and that the chances of finding enough healthy tissue to succeed were extremely slim." Sadly, reversal was not an option.

Healing comes from sharing life and love. The Dickensons discovered this reality.

We learned the truth about God's plan to bless us, and at the age of forty-six, I consulted with a physician about ligation reversal. When I entered the Catholic Church, a wonderful priest gave me the courage to reverse it, but at forty-seven years old, it was too late—hormone level was down a bit, and it was at least fifteen thousand dollars!

Because of the age risk and the potential price tag, we opted to adopt. God sent us three beautiful sons. Adoption helped fill the hole in my heart. I have, as a pro-life woman and as a devout Catholic, become increasingly aware of and deeply saddened at how little (if at all) *adoption* of those little ones *p* aborted is mentioned or embraced. We now have five girls and three boys and are praying about adopting more in the future.

In some cases, the Lord restores the life-giving capacity once couples have reversals. Bob and Lori from Wisconsin share their story:

Influenced by worldly desires and not really seeking any direction from the Church, we felt that three children were enough for our family. We justified to ourselves the use of barrier methods of birth control. We considered ourselves pro-life and didn't want to use any abortifacients; but looking back we realize that we were not pro-life. We were really just anti-abortion.

Since we were done having children, we thought Bob should get a vasectomy, the "responsible" thing to do. Although we loved our children very much, our attitude from the beginning was not really one of children being a blessing from God. This led us toward the contraception mentality, and it ended in sterilization.

Through the prayers of countless people and by the grace of God, we came back spiritually to the Catholic Church. Within two years we realized the severity of our mistake and found ourselves in the confessional with much regret and sorrow. As reparation, we elected to abstain for one week a month to try to imitate other couples in the Catholic Faith.

Despite the knowledge that our sins were forgiven, it was hard to speak about the truth and convince others that the teachings of the Church were correct when we had failed to follow it ourselves. Our friend read an article from the Couple to Couple League about vasectomy reversal surgeries [including] a place to send for more information on inexpensive reversal doctors. We obtained the list, and through some research and prayer, we decided that this was something we needed to do in reparation for our sin, regardless of the cost and its success.

Through all this we realized (something we should have known from the first day of our marriage) that children are a blessing and we should welcome them as a gift from God. Our hope was that God would give us more children, but deep down we did not feel worthy and would have accepted the failure of surgery as the continued consequences of our actions. We would accept God's will.

The doctor indicated that he could only repair one side. We elected to attend the Couple to Couple League's NFP class with our desires set on determining when [my wife] would be fertile. As we participated in the classes, we observed how much this tied into the teachings of the Church and wished we could have taken this class before we were married.

Our marriage has been greatly enhanced by our understanding of the Church's teaching on openness to life. We have a greater respect for each other and are less selfish about our own wants and desires. We also have a strong desire to share the truth with young couples preparing for marriage and married couples who are in situations similar to ours.

We are even more dedicated to passing on these truths to our children and making sure they understand why the Church teaches it. It is our prayer that they will not have to suffer through the same mistakes we did.

It is with great joy that we close this letter by saying that God has since blessed our family with two little boys, one age two and the other five months, to join their three big sisters on a journey to heaven.

Like Bob and Lori, many couples are changing their minds about sterilization, repenting, and then, when possible, restoring their bodies to wholeness.

Several couples from Our Lady of Mount Carmel, Carmel, Indiana, have encouraged each other in sterilization reversals. We met Hank and his family when they hosted us the weekend we spoke in their parish. He wrote to us: "I had a vasectomy reversed. Several years passed by, and it seemed the reversal was not successful. We moved to St. Louis, and miraculously my family has been blessed with the gift of Rachel, a beautiful little girl who is very talented."

Hank and his wife became an encouragement to other couples. One of their friends, Tom, recounts the impact of their decision on other parish families who had become spiritually and physically closed to life. "One friend's wife had the reversal, and their son Danny (the only boy in a family of five kids) is the miracle that God sent them. Think of Danny's wonderful witness (as well as Rachel's) when they grow up and understand what their parents went through, spiritually and physically, to bring them into the world."

Though sterilization advocates appeal to couples to simplify their lives, the procedure actually increases the complexities, as sin always does. Sterilization is dangerous to their health, their marriage, and the life of their souls. Instead, let's encourage couples on their journey of faith to embrace the Lord, the truth, and each other in fruitful, life-giving love.

VI.

LIVING AND LEAVING
A LEGACY

CHAPTER THIRTEEN:

GOD'S CALL FOR MARRIAGE

We all come from families. Many of us have or will have families of our own. *"The future of humanity passes by way of the family,"*[1] according to Pope John Paul II.

How do we receive our legacy of the faith and live it in such a way that we leave this legacy to those who come after us? We answer God's call on our lives: to faithfulness, to fruitfulness, to holiness, and to heroic virtue.

The Call to Faithfulness

Learning the Faith

Learning the faith is not the same as joining a class at our parish, though classes can help us. It is our ongoing study and application, day by day, of the faith.

After fifty years of marriage, one couple talks about how they continue to grow in the faith in a variety of ways.

> We have kept our education going throughout our marriage. We nave an extensive library in our home of Bible commentaries, excellent books, etc. We teach Bible studies and attend conferences. We never stop praying, learning, and, we hope, growing. Prayers of others and a Christian community are important to help us get through the rough times in life. A close, prayerful, personal relationship with Jesus, the Father, and the Holy Spirit is the most important aspect in our lives.

Faithfulness to Christ means continually learning about him.

No matter what portion of the legacy of the faith we received, we can always give more to our children as long as we are willing to make the effort to learn. Monica from LaCrosse, Wisconsin, writes:

> I was afraid of being a mother—fear of the unknown. I was spiritually very immature. I attended a Catholic school for twelve years—it was not much of an education in living the Catholic faith. We never heard of *Humanae Vitae* or any of the Church's teaching on love, life, or family. My children will study papal writings on family life.

Tina, a recent convert to the Church, shared what it has meant to her and her husband to learn more about marriage.

> Our whole attitude toward the meaning of marriage has changed. We now feel and know that God wants all marriages to be a work of grace—sanctified and holy. The privilege of being the one whom God uses to bring an eternal human soul into his kingdom is extremely wonderful, awe-inspiring, and holy. Marriage has taken on a whole new dimension and meaning. We are eternally grateful.

Priority Living

Faithfulness to Christ means living with right priorities within our family: God first, marriage second, children third. Don and Mary, from Leesburg, Florida, said, "We began our marriage with unconditional trust in God. Fifty years, eight pregnancies, thirteen grandchildren, four greats later, we are more in love than ever! Praise the Lord!"

Though the challenges of raising a family in terms of time and energy can sometimes feel as if the order is inverted—children first, husband second, and God third—we must continually struggle to maintain the right order of our love and commitment.

Marital Chastity

Faithfulness to Christ means desiring his will above our own. "For this is the will of God, your sanctification: that you abstain from unchastity; that each one of you know how to take a wife for himself in holiness and honor, not in the passion of lust like heathen who do not know God" (1 Thes 4:3-5). God's will for us is to live a chaste life, whether unmarried or married, because we know him and want to be like him in holiness.

Our whole family was gathered at the rehearsal dinner for my youngest brother's wedding. Dad stood to speak. "I want to testify before all of you," he said, "and especially our seven oldest grandchildren, of the goodness of God and the faithfulness of my children and their spouses. Mimi and I were virgins when we married. And now all five of our children have been virgins when they wed, and they have married virgins, all because of their commitment to Christ and to purity. This is an amazing heritage!"

What a great grace—for this kind of purity comes from hearts submitted to the Lord. No one can remain pure without the strength of God. What spiritual capital to give the grandchildren: a legacy of purity and self-control.

God calls us to be faithful to this precious spouse he has given us. Chastity within marriage is essential. Fidelity to our spouse is an expression of our fidelity to Christ.

Consider God's words through the Old Testament prophet Malachi. When married priests during the time of Malachi were unfaithful to their wives of many years, the Lord refused to hear their prayers. Malachi told them that faithlessness in their marriage was faithlessness toward God. But if the priests would repent and be faithful to their spouses because of their faithfulness to God, they would receive the blessing of godly offspring (see Mal 2:13-16).

Faithfulness to God and His Church
God calls us to place our trust in him. When we entrust ourselves to God, we bless our families. "In the fear of the Lord one has strong confidence, and his children will have a refuge" (Prv 14:26).

Faithfulness to God involves faithfulness to his Church. Rather than distrusting the teaching of the Church, especially in the area of openness to life, we need to see the Church's teaching as an extension of the love and concern of our heavenly Father. Jim and Nancy from Omaha, Nebraska, put it so beautifully: "Why does the Church give us boundaries? Because she is the guardian of our souls and loves us so deeply."

The Call to Fruitfulness

Living the Faith

We not only learn *about* the faith, but we learn to *live* the faith. We are to "walk as children of light" (Eph 5:8). One mother is offering her children more than she received as a child: "I wish I had grown up in a Catholic family where the faith was loved, practiced, obeyed, taught, and shared. Through the grace of God, that is our goal for our children."

When we open our hearts and minds (and bodies) to physical fruitfulness, we experience the blessing of spiritual fruitfulness as well.

Priority Loving

What are the right priorities in loving? First, we receive God's gift of divine love through the person of Jesus. Then Jesus calls us to receive the gift of love through our spouse.

When we receive our spouse as gift and give ourselves to our spouse as gift, our relationship is fruitful—spiritually for all, physically for many. Then our children embody our love, receive our love, and reciprocate our love for each other and for God. Our communion of love in our family is rooted and grounded in God's love first.

To live a fruitful life of faith, we need to be deeply connected to the Lord.

Abide in me, and I in you. As the branch cannot bear fruit by itself, unless it abides in the vine, neither can you, unless you abide in me. I am the vine, you are the branches. He who abides in me, and I in him, he it is that bears much fruit, for apart from me you can do nothing. ... By this my Father is glorified, that you bear much fruit, and so prove to be my disciples.

JOHN 15:4-5, 8

He is the source of our life.

Within the vocation of marriage, our spouse is our primary channel of grace. We need to keep this channel free of the debris of sin by fidelity and openness to life. We must love people and use things, rather than use people and love things. If we maintain the right perspective, we will understand that material goods or earthly success cannot compare with the value of a child. God calls us to love him and our spouse in such a way that love will issue forth in new life.

Embrace Children With Joy

We have to be more than anti-abortion; we have to be pro-life. "Generous, open-to-life parenthood should be the norm and not the exception. Babies are a joy!" says Anne from Fairview Park, Ohio. The norm is living marital love.

Older brothers and sisters in the Lord can help us appreciate how fragile this gift of fertility is from their years of experience. They can give us the long perspective of the brevity of time from teaching our children to walk until we watch them walk out the door to begin their own families. They can remind us that God is faithful to provide when he is generous in giving us children.

Children are gifts to be received. "Whoever receives one such child in my name receives me; but whoever causes one of these little ones who believe in me to sin, it would be better for him to have a great millstone fastened round his neck and to be drowned in the depth of the sea" (Mt 18:5-6). We receive Christ when we receive a little one in his name.

Each year the Kirk clan gathers in Hilton Head, South Carolina, for a weeklong family reunion. Each adult couple updates the rest of us on the blessings and challenges they have faced in the last year and then asks for prayer.

One year, a day after one couple had shared, most of us were milling about, getting ready to play games. My brother Stephen broke into the conversation with an announcement: "We wanted to tell you all how to pray for us: We're having a baby!" The scene was utter pandemonium! Many of the grandchildren were there as well; everyone was cheering and laughing.

One of my sisters turned to me and said, "With a response like that, it's almost enough to make you want to get pregnant just to share the news!"

I responded, "And with joy like this, we are going to have crops of great-grandchildren!" I truly believe we will.

This kind of joy is contagious. It's so much bigger than rejecting contraception. It is all about embracing the Lord, his truth for our lives, our spouse, and our children in one ever-enlarging circle of life-giving love.

Not only parents but also grandparents need to embrace the children. Grandparents need to welcome each child, no matter how many there may be, and see them as God does: "Grandchildren are the crown of the aged, and the glory of sons is their fathers" (Prv 17:6). The fact that grandchildren even exist is a fulfillment of God's blessing on a godly couple: "May you see your children's children!" (Ps 128:6).

Grandparents' faith is part of their grandchildren's heritage. "But the steadfast love of the Lord is from everlasting to everlasting upon those who fear him, and his righteousness to children's children, to those who keep his covenant and remember to do his commandments" (Ps 103:17-18).

The Importance of Prayer
Living the faith fruitfully means communicating daily with the Lord of life, for prayer is the breath of the soul. Far too many of us are overworked and under-prayed; it is difficult to imagine carving time out each day for a good time of prayer. However, if we say an act of consecration for the day, we can turn all the joys and trials of the day into a prayer. This means that even ordinary, mundane activities of the day can be extraordinary means of grace for us and for our families.

Spiritual Fruitfulness for All
The call to fruitfulness is for everyone. All of us are called to spiritual motherhood and spiritual fatherhood regardless of the possibilities of physical fatherhood or motherhood. We all need ways to impart life, to nurture faith, to encourage spiritual growth.

The key to fruitfulness is remaining connected to Christ. As long as we receive his life, it will flow through us to others, whether in formal ministries within the Church or informally through mentor relationships of older women to younger women, older men to younger men, big sister to little sister, or big brother to little brother.

The Call to Holiness

Teach the Faith

To teach the faith, we have to know it. A great motivation to learn the faith is to offer instruction to others. This is especially true with our children, since our wedding vow included being open to life and being committed to their education.

God's covenant is extended through us to our children, as St. Peter preached at Pentecost. When people asked how they could be saved, he replied, "Repent, and be baptized every one of you in the name of Jesus Christ for the forgiveness of your sins; and you shall receive the gift of the Holy Spirit. For the promise is to you and to your children and to all that are far off, every one whom the Lord our God calls to him" (Acts 2:38-39). As Pope John Paul II reminds us, "As you beget children on earth, never forget that *you are also begetting them for God.*"[2]

Both parents and grandparents must teach the faith to children in order to avoid the sins of the past and to remind them of the saving power of God.

> He established a testimony in Jacob, and appointed a law in Israel, which he commanded our fathers to teach to their children; that the next generation might know them, the children yet unborn, and arise and tell them to their children, so that they should set their hope in God, and not forget the works of God, but keep his commandments; and that they should not be like their fathers, a stubborn and rebellious generation, a generation whose heart was not steadfast, whose spirit was not faithful to God.
>
> PSALM 78:5-8

As the saying goes, those who do not know the mistakes of the past are destined to repeat them. Every generation is to be given the chance to understand that the path of holiness is followed one small step at a time, one good decision at a time, one act of sacrifice and charity at a time. This seems especially true when their grandparents know and love the faith.

Train Young People in Chastity

In addition to all that has been shared in this book, here is some of the advice we give our children.

Physical intimacy is like fire—when it is kept in the fireplace of marriage, it produces heat and light that benefits the whole family. Outside of the fireplace, fire damages and destroys, produces scars on those we love, and does irreparable (though not unforgivable) harm. When St. Paul says, "Shun immorality" (1 Cor 6:18), he does not mean see how close you can get to it without being burned.

When you court, treat the other the way you would want your future spouse to be treated. Avoid the near occasions of sin by watching the amount of time you spend alone and how late you stay out. Don't do anything you would be embarrassed to tell your future spouse. Wear a sacramental— it's a great reminder in the heat of the moment to cool down.

Think of the person you are with as a holy vessel, made holy by God. As we noted before, would you ever think of taking your can of soft drink into the sacristy and emptying it into the communion cup? No!

Why not? Because that vessel has been made holy by being set apart for a special use. So has your body and the body of the man or woman you are courting been set aside in service to God either through marriage or religious life. Don't desecrate that vessel!

Beware of sexual intimacy that can follow spiritual intimacy, such as praying intensely together. Seek to honor the one you date, and if a lack of honor is shown to you, "ditch the loser," as the saying goes, because dating is premarriage. Pursue purity.

When it comes to openness to life, we need to place the *why* in our children's hearts, not simply the *what*. Theresa from Illinois says, "I teach them the importance of respecting their sexuality and that of others, and how vital prayer is to maintain a state of chastity." Another mother wrote, "I want all my children to know the Church's teaching and why the Church teaches it. If I would have followed the world's wrong view, then I would have robbed myself of a lot of joy that I now know as a mother of eleven children."

There are many opportunities to teach the faith, especially the Church's teaching on openness to life, within the Church. Some couples help their priests prepare people for marriage with pre-Cana courses or Engaged

Encounter. Others help couples prepare for baptism—another critical time in a couple's life—to explain their role in teaching their child the faith (and thereby learning it better themselves). Sometimes deacons or lay people involved in apologetics offer instruction within the RCIA program—the Rite of Christian Initiation of Adults—to prepare adults to be received into the Church.

Paul from California offers this testimony of his own faith journey.

I am in the diaconate formation program and am a catechist in our parish's RCIA. I have had occasional pangs of conscience over birth control. Up until now it was dealt with by rationalization, or by not thinking about it. I simply avoided discussing it, and none of the catechumens or candidates have ever brought up the subject in my three years of teaching. I pray now that I will be as bold as Peter after the first Pentecost, and impart the important values I have learned.

Paul's change of heart—his growth in holiness—has resulted in a change of practice. And it will result in a better RCIA program as well.

Another outlet for teaching within the Church is small group Bible studies. Nancy, now a grandmother, from Lafayette, New York, says, "I teach young mothers the peace and joy that come from accepting and living the Church's teaching on life." She has much wisdom to offer these young moms, week by week, to help them live their vocation day by day.

This is the kind of teaching that Sue wishes she had had access to when she was first married.

I wish I had heard, "God has a plan for you." "Your body is the temple of the Holy Spirit, so keep that temple pure." "You are a sacred being meant for holiness."

To me, holiness was always for special people—priests and religious— not [ordinary] men and women. I wish the Church's documents were explained instead of explained away.

I definitely intend to teach my children why we wait till marriage, why that gift of total self-giving is meant exclusively for a spouse, and about the sacredness of their commitment to God and to a spouse, if they choose marriage for their vocation.

I want them to know that through their sharing of love, they cooperate with and imitate God through life-giving love and that there is no greater honor than to be given the blessing of a child to nurture and care for—that only in giving yourself fully can you truly know the love of God. I never want my child to be ashamed to be "holy" (something I was always afraid to be!). I want that to be the most natural thing, just like breathing!

By the mercy of God, Sue and her husband will be able to teach their children these rich truths about marriage.

The Power of Obedience
Both our sins and our righteousness possess an intergenerational power. As part of the Ten Commandments, Moses recorded this prophecy of curse or blessing, depending on whether or not people rightly worshiped the God who had saved them.

> I am the Lord your God, who brought you out of the land of Egypt, out of the house of bondage. You shall have no other gods before me. You shall not make for yourself a graven image, or any likeness of anything that is in heaven above, or that is in the earth beneath, or that is in the water under the earth; you shall not bow down to them or serve them; for I the Lord your God am a jealous God, visiting the iniquity of the fathers upon the children to the third and the fourth generation of those who hate me, but showing steadfast love to thousands of those who love me and keep my commandments.
>
> EXODUS 20:2-6

Our actions have positive or negative consequences spiritually for generations to come. We must choose to love and obey the Lord for their sake. We must choose to live holy lives for their sake.

Obedience leads to understanding. There is a difference between inquiring why we should believe and demanding an explanation before obedience is considered. As parents, we know the difference instinctively, as does our heavenly Father.

Like the father who brought his son to Jesus for healing, we can pray,

"Lord, I believe; help my unbelief" (Mk 9:24). This kind of prayer has an authenticity that our children can respect, as opposed to our teaching them one thing but living another.

Children look for the connection between our words and our actions. They will accept a certain amount of failure if, along with the failure, there is humility and repentance. But they quickly reject what they perceive as lip service to faith when our hearts are far from it. If we persist, by the grace of God, we will become more and more like our heavenly Father; our lives will reflect a greater continuity between our beliefs and our actions.

Spiritual Friendship

Part of our prayer life is developing spiritual friendship with the saints who have gone before us. They have become holy like Christ. They have a holy desire to see us become holy. We need to harness heaven to help us.

One of the ways we learn about our faith is to learn about the saints. As the saying goes, "Love can inspire more than law can require." They were (are) real people who developed the virtues all of us, including our children and grandchildren, need in order to live lives of holiness.

Another part of our prayer life is spending time before the Blessed Sacrament, being in his presence. Most towns have at least one daily Mass offered; many areas have a number of options. Growing numbers of churches are making Eucharistic adoration a possibility.

We also want to spend time in mental prayer every day. To become like the Holy One of Israel, we need one-on-one time with him. For our relationship with our Lord to develop, we need to speak to him from our heart daily: offer him our day, review the challenges we face, thank him for all he is doing in and through us, and ask him for the strength to serve him as we should.

Every morning my mom and dad pray together for our entire clan, family by family, one person at a time. Part of their prayer includes the future spouses and children of the grandchildren to the tenth generation and beyond. Dad bore witness at the baptism of one of our sons that he had a new awareness of the possible meaning of his prayer. He said, "When I pray for the spouse of one of my Catholic grandchildren, I realize it might be the Church." What a powerful testimony to all who were there!

The Call to Heroism

Love the Faith

Soak in the truth, goodness, and beauty of God. In the context of this book, thank God for the truth that we image the Triune God through our act of life-giving love. Thank God for the goodness we can express in the marital act as an act of total self-donation. And thank God for the beauty of his gift of fertility and the child(ren) who can be created through our act of love.

We not only accept the faith; we love it. We embrace the faith wholeheartedly, though our society does not do likewise. We celebrate the mystery of the faith, though our culture is skeptical of anything empirically unprovable. And we long for deeper communion with the Lover of our souls, regardless of the criticism (or worse) that we face for love of God.

The Lordship of Christ

Too often people have the impression that if they give God an hour at Mass on Sundays, they have fulfilled their religious obligation. He ought to be satisfied. However, God is not looking for a meager offering to satisfy the demands of his awesome love. As he says throughout the Old Testament, "To obey is better than sacrifice" (1 Sm 15:22).

The Lord wants *all* our heart, *all* our mind, *all* our soul, and *all* our strength (see Dt 6:4-5). He wants Sunday—but he also wants Monday, Tuesday, Wednesday, Thursday, Friday, and Saturday. He wants *all* our talents, *all* our time, *all* our possessions—and yes, *all* our fertility, too. This is the kind of heroic call that teens need to hear. They are dying because they don't know there is Someone worth dying to themselves and living for!

Not only do we give God everything we are, but we also entrust our family to him. We trust him when we are not being blessed with children; we trust him when he blesses us with many children. He is faithful to work in and through us to accomplish his holy will.

God's will is to be lived God's way. St. Paul teaches powerfully in Ephesians chapter 5 how a husband and wife can reflect the mystery of Christ's relationship to the Church for the whole world, should they live the will of God using his blueprint for marriage.

A married man is to imitate Christ by laying down his life for his spouse. He is to embrace holiness through self-sacrifice. Some of these sacrifices are unique to the husband, different from the sacrifices his wife is called to make. As the head of the home, he is called to servant leadership rather than dominating authority over the family. The more responsive a husband is to the heart of the home—his wife—the more the wife will respect her husband's leadership.

St. Paul admonishes each husband to cherish his wife as his own body (see Eph 5:28-29). Physical affection sometimes, more than the act of marriage, can help his wife feel the depth of his love. (The children feel so loved when they see mom and dad "snitchin' in the kitchen"!) When a husband treats his wife's body with dignity and respect, he honors the gift of his spouse and the One who made her. This is true of each wife toward her husband as well.

Marriage is the fountain relationship from which flows the sacramental grace to meet the needs of our children. We have to keep the balance between the urgent needs of the children versus the important needs of both husband and wife in the core relationship of the family.

A young married woman with children becomes the master juggler of her children's needs, but sometimes she can forget the very real needs of her spouse. Perhaps her husband is not open to another baby because he feels as if he never has the bed alone with his wife. Maybe he does not feel as if he is getting attention. That's a valid concern.

Though the children's needs seem to press in, demanding immediate attention, a husband should tune in to his wife's individual needs and pray for her. She needs adult conversation without interruption, feeling as though her thoughts matter, too. She needs time for prayer and for play so she can be refreshed in spirit and body to give even more of herself to her family. The more a husband really loves his wife as Christ loves the Church, the more he will see his wife's heart open to more children.

Another key to living God's will God's way, according to St. Paul, is through the husband's service as a faithful priest in their domestic church. The more a husband leads his wife to understand the Scriptures and the Church's teaching ("washing her with the water of the Word," see Eph 5:26), the more both spouses will form their consciences according to God's truth.

Our marriage relationship is foundational: We were together alone before there were children, and we will be together alone when the children are gone. Now is the time to tend this relationship so that our love will flourish long-term. To do that, we need some time without the constant interruptions of wee ones.

Wives need this kind of refreshment as much as husbands do to be the best parents we can be. We also need prayer time, alone and together. We need to come apart to be with the Lord for strength, or we'll come apart emotionally and relationally.

Both husband and wife are called to lay down their lives for Christ and for each other. This kind of dying to self requires quiet, invisible heroism, especially since so many of the sacrifices go unnoticed. Even though many of the little ways each spouse dies to self are repeated week after week (cleaning, laundry, car care, yard work, office work), we can grow closer to God through those mundane tasks. The responsibilities may stay the same, but we change: We grow in holiness by choosing Christ and choosing our spouse each day.

Heroic Generosity

God will not be outdone in showing generosity. Heroic generosity flows from heroic virtue. Having children demands growth in virtue by parents and the other children alike.

It is so good for us all to wrestle with our selfishness. Is it possible that one of the reasons we have a crisis of vocations is the lack of generosity of Catholic couples to be open to life? For someone to give himself or herself to God in consecrated life, he or she must be raised with generosity of spirit. The pope speaks of the heroic generosity of some parents to receive many children from the Lord, though certainly a small family can have a beautiful spirit of generosity as well.

Grandparents are also called to continue the heroic generosity they have hopefully developed in their family. There is no such thing as retirement from Christian service. And no matter how much rugged individualism a mother or father might have, their adult children (daughters and sons-in-law, sons and daughters-in-law) will always need their generous love, support, and encouragement. This spirit of service does not have a limit, though there is an important difference between parenting and grandparenting.

Men and women who are older must resist the culture that is trying to draw them back into a selfishness from which they have matured through the challenges of family life. They are to continue to be mothers and dads who love their married children (and in-laws and grandchildren) in sacrificial ways. Though the relationship is altered as children grow older, the responsibilities of motherhood and fatherhood do not end.

We should not underestimate the importance of our relationship as grandparents when we invest our time and energy into the formation of our grandchildren. Are we alert to the opportunities we have for impacting their spiritual and emotional well being, for leaving a legacy of faith? How often have people testified to the fact that their grandparents' involvement in their lives, though limited by time or distance, was very significant.

Generosity from grandparents includes planning ahead to leave an inheritance to grandchildren as well as children. This is a godly goal. But how much greater a goal is it to leave a legacy of faith to grandchildren?

Grandparents need to prepare their hearts to receive every grandchild as the total gift he or she is. Their children want to share their joy with their parents. They need words of encouragement and assurance of prayer support.

Embrace the Cross

We are called to imitate Christ, the ultimate Hero. He said, "If any man would come after me, let him deny himself and take up his cross and follow me. For whoever would save his life will lose it, and whoever loses his life for my sake will find it" (Mt 16:24-25).

We have been called to live heroic lives in openness to life. That still does not mean we will have large families, as a number of couples today are discovering. (All we can do is be open; God decides the number of children we will have.) What it *does* mean is that we embrace all that God has for us—the challenges, the blessings, the suffering—through he vocation of marriage and particularly through the act of marriage. Let's pray for each other to be faithful.

Let the Lord Build Your Home

The Lord wants to build our home—our family. He has to be the One to build it, or else the labor is in vain (see Ps 127). We want our marriages and our families built God's way so that they will last. If we live God's will God's way, we will bear rich fruit for him; we will be faithful witnesses to our world through our marriage of the intimate and fruitful relationship God desires with every person.

Let's respond to the challenge before us:

Yes to the Lord with all our being, including our body, including our fertility;

Yes to our spouse in total self-donation to reflect our true love for each other;

Yes to our life-giving Lord who blesses our marital communion as life-giving lovers.

Like the Father, Son, and Holy Spirit who gave us life, let's be life-giving lovers and life-loving givers!

APPENDIX

Ideas for Ministry to Moms

Mary went to her kinswoman Elizabeth to minister to her needs during her pregnancy with John the Baptist (see Lk 1:39-56). We can imitate Mary's kindness and generosity by finding ways to help mothers we know who are expecting, who have newborns, or who have miscarried. Consider these ideas:

Early Pregnancy

Food
- Make gifts of herbs or groceries rich in nutrients that aren't easily affordable.
- Take over a meal so she doesn't have to smell the cooking.
- Offer to cook a meal at her house so she doesn't have to cook it.
- Invite her to your home for a meal—then she won't even have to do the dishes.
- Desserts take extra effort—they make a nice surprise for everyone.
- Offer to take her out to lunch alone.
- Pick up groceries for her when she gets easily nauseous in the store.

Sleep
- Take the children out so she can nap.
- Watch the children in the house so she can nap.
- Help her do tasks (such as ironing) that are usually set aside when she can't get to them until late at night. That way she will go to bed earlier because the tasks are done.

Encouragement
- She may be conscious of her looks (for example, she may feel fat). A compliment can help a lot.
- Praise her for her sacrifice for the Lord. Remind her of the truths that sustain.
- Enable her to contact *her* mom. Arrange a visit; watch the children; give her money for phone calls; buy postage stamps for her.

Mid-Pregnancy

Project Orientation
- Offer to assist her in a project.
- Take her children so she's free to do things in her home.
- Offer her the use of your car so she can go somewhere to get things needed for projects.
- If she sews, encourage her to make something for herself while she has the energy to do so. That way she can enjoy it after she has the baby.

Clothing
- Give or lend her your maternity clothes.
- Help her find clothes at yard sales, thrift shops, or stores.
- Watch the children so she can sew some clothes for herself.

Special Outings
- Watch the children so she can go on a retreat or attend a conference while she feels good.

Late Pregnancy

Dates
- Offer to watch the kids so she and her husband can have time out alone before life becomes more complicated.

Clean

- Scrub floors, iron, deep clean—all the tasks that are difficult with a big belly.

Exercise

- Join her in a walk to help her get in shape or to bring on labor.

Food

- Help her make a number of meals to fill her freezer.

Encouragement

- She may need something new (and *big*) to wear for the new season.
- Flowers might be nice because they aren't easily affordable.
- Be positive in talking about delivery to counter horror stories others may be recounting.
- Offer to pray with her during labor if she wants to call you.
- Help her walk through getting the home ready for the baby. Perhaps do something that she may have overlooked or didn't have the time or energy to do, such as painting the crib.

Bed Rest

- Watch the kids so she can keep her feet up to stop early labor or diminish water weight gain.
- Offer meals so they don't have to pay a lot for fast food.
- Offer a bedroom in your home for a rest on a hot summer day if you have air conditioning and she doesn't.

After Birth

Food

- Provide a meal.
- Coordinate meals so calls don't disturb her at home.
- It might be good to offer meals every other day. That way leftovers aren't wasted and the help lasts longer. This is more possible if she has some meals in her freezer already.

- Desserts are such a treat.
- Drop by with extra milk and bread.
- Give her a quick call before doing your grocery shopping to see if she has small items you can pick up for her.
- Help her with gardening, especially if she has had a C-section.

Cleaning
- Do general cleaning for her to help keep some sense of order.
- Help with laundry and ironing.

Sleep
- Take the children during the baby's nap so she can rest, too.
- Take the colicky baby on a walk so mom can rest.

Encouragement
- Have a shower (baby or personal) for every baby (before or after birth).
- Be with a mom who's going through postpartum depression. Find out what help is available to her.
- Lend her tapes or books for encouragement, especially if she can't be a part of Bible study at that time. She may have more reading time while she nurses than she had during pregnancy.
- Give her a new skirt or jumper (one in which she can nurse), one size bigger than normal.
- Ask for specific prayer concerns and follow through—sometimes every hour on the hour.
- Offer her a ride to Mass.
- Offer to sit with her and the children at Mass.
- Offer to baby-sit so she can go to Confession, pray, or go to Mass alone.
- Baby-sit so she can do something fun such as reading, playing an instrument, sewing, or cooking alone.
- Cut her hair or do a perm, if you can.
- Make going to yard sales possible for her. Go with her and help her, or baby-sit so she can go alone.
- Visit when the children are in bed so she has some good adult conversation.

- Baby-sit so she can go hear a stimulating talk at church or the local university.
- Jot down a verse of encouragement on a note card so she can read it throughout the day.
- Lend or give her a tape of beautiful worship music to lift the mood of the home.

Errands
- Offer to carpool older children.
- Offer to go to the post office or dry cleaners for mom.
- Take her kids for a haircut if they need it.
- Give her unusual gifts (wrapping paper, postcards, stamps, tape).
- Take the older kids to the pool and let her stay home.

When She's Moving to a New Home
- Take the children to your home so she can pack.
- Help her pack, especially when the children are in bed (less confusing, more good conversation).
- Help her fix up the house for sale.
- Provide meals in your home so she doesn't have to clean up to fix supper or clean up after.
- Help her move.
- Take children the day of the move to someplace fun.
- Baby-sit several days so she can organize her home.
- Help her unpack.

After a Miscarriage

- Cry with her. Don't offer meaningless answers such as "The baby probably wasn't healthy" or "Just be thankful for the children you have."
- Offer a meal or two.
- Give her a small memento to remember the child by, such as a Christmas ornament with the child's name on it.
- Note the due date, and give her a special card on that day.

- It's usually not helpful to take the children, because they bring so much comfort to Mom, but check with Mom about it.

When Dad Travels

- Baby-sit so Mom can have some time to herself, get work done, or go out with a friend.
- Join her and the children so there's another adult at the table.
- Offer baby-sitting when Dad gets home so that Mom and Dad get time alone.
- Assist her in gardening or housekeeping projects, such as painting, that Dad may not have time to do.
- Encourage her to maintain regular family life with the children (meals, bedtimes) even though Dad's not there.

Anytime

- Encourage financial or postmarital guidance through good reading materials, seminars, or even counseling.
- Suggest the couple go on a Marriage Encounter Weekend; perhaps you could baby-sit.
- Offer a small group Bible study for young mothers, including baby-sitting, for spiritual refreshment.
- Offer resources on time management and home organization.

Ideas for Husbands

- Converse with your wife. She thinks great thoughts, too, though the little ones don't know it yet.
- Remember that low-energy times for everyone are just before supper and at bedtime.
- Be available half an hour before supper to be with the children so Mom can be alone in the kitchen.

- Assist in bedtime routines.
- Free her to go to Confession, Mass, Bible study, talks, and a retreat.
- Remember that a spiritually refreshed wife is a content wife.
- Go with her to Mass.
- Make dates a priority. Regularly plan time together.
- Bring her flowers, cards, candy when appropriate, and let her know how much she is appreciated
- Tell her of her beauty. Even stretch marks and scars are reminders of how much she has loved you.
- Pray for her!

After Adoption

- Celebrate with cards, flowers, and a gift.
- Have a shower for the joy of it as well as the practical help.
- If the baby is not a newborn, find out what equipment is still needed. Perhaps larger size clothing or cloth diapers are best.
- Offer meals. Just because a mom is not recovering from delivery does not mean that mealtime help would not be appreciated.

Notes

Chapter One
My Testimony

1. National Right to Life, using current (1997) statistics from the U.S. Centers for Disease Control, verifies that 19 percent of abortions in the U.S. are performed on married women. This statistic has been constant for more than ten years.

2. Throughout this book I quote many people from all over the country who are identified simply with first names or hometowns to protect their privacy. This information was given to me through a survey I conducted and through personal correspondence. Quotations without accompanying endnotes are from this survey.

3. I am unaware of any other Christian body that maintains a stand against contraception.

4. See Charles Provan, *The Bible and Birth Control* (Monongahela, Pa.: Zimmer, 1989), for a variety of quotes from Protestant leaders from the Reformation to the present who were unequivocal in their opposition to contraception.

5. Mary Pride, *The Way Home* (Westchester, Ill.: Crossway, 1985), 81.

6. David Lord, S.J., *Five Great Encyclicals* (New York: n.p., n.d.), 92; cited by Alfred M. Rehwinkel, *Planned Parenthood and Birth Control in the Light of Christian Ethics* (St. Louis: Concordia, 1959), 37–38.

7. See Pope Paul VI, *Humanae Vitae* [hereafter cited as "HV"] (Boston: Daughters of St. Paul, 1968).

Chapter Two
Triune Family

1. Pope John Paul II, *Puebla: A Pilgrimage of Faith* (Boston: Daughters of St. Paul, 1979), 86.

2. *Gaudium et Spes* [hereafter cited as "GS"], n. 24 (available on-line at www.vatican.va).

3. GS, n. 48; cited in *Catechism of the Catholic Church,* 2nd ed. [hereafter cited as "CCC"] (Citta del Vaticano: Libreria Editrice Vaticana, 1997), 1603.

4. Scott Hahn, *First Comes Love* (New York: Doubleday, in preparation).

5. Congregation for the Doctrine of the Faith, *Donum Vitae* [hereafter cited as "DV"] (February 22, 1987), Introduction, n. 1. (Available on-line at www.vatican.va.).

6. CCC, 1609.

7. Pope John Paul II, *Letter to Families* [hereafter cited as "LF"] (Boston: Pauline Books and Media, 1994), n. 12.

8. Henry V. Sattler, "Sacramental Sexuality I," *Communio* (Winter, 1981): 340–57.

9. GS, n. 48.

10. See CCC, 1661.

11. LF, n. 13, quoting his "Homily for the Closing of the Holy Year" (December 25, 1975).

12. GS, n. 49.

13. Pope John Paul II, *On the Dignity and Vocation of Women,* (Boston: St. Paul Books & Media, 1988), n. 5.

14. GS, n. 50.

Chapter Three
Cherish the Child

1. Valerie Takahama, "No Kidding! More Couples Remain Childless by Choice," *Lincoln [Nebraska] Journal-Star,* 5 November 1999.

2. LF, n. 17.

3. LF, n. 13.

4. Pope John Paul II, homily on the Washington Mall, Washington, D.C., 7 October 1979; quoted in John F. Kippley, *Sex and the Marriage Covenant: A Basis for Morality* (Cincinnati, Ohio: Couple to Couple League, 1991), 73.

5. GS, n. 50.
6. CCC, 2366.
7. LF, n 20.
8. Beth Matthews, *Precious Child* (Steubenville, Ohio: Emmaus Road Publishing, in preparation).

Chapter Four
Contraception = Reject the Child

1. Kippley, *Sex,* 309.
2. Provan, 17.
3. William Arndt and F. Wilbur Gingrich, ed., *A Greek-English Lexicon of the New Testament* (Chicago: Chicago University Press, 1957), 861.
4. See John Hardon, *Catholic Catechism* (Garden City, N.Y.: Doubleday, 1975), 367.
5. For a useful explanation of natural law, see Kippley, *Sex,* 8, 26, 48.
6. HV, n. 11.
7. Sigmund Freud, *A General Introduction to Psycho-Analysis,* trans. Joan Riviere (New York: Liverwright, 1935), 277; quoted in Kippley, *Sex,* 39.
8. HV, n. 12.
9. Pope John Paul II, *Familiaris Consortio* (1982), n. 32 [hereafter cited as "FC"], available on-line at www.vatican.va.
10. FC, n. 32; quoted within the Pontifical Council for the Family's *Vademecum for Confessors Concerning Some Aspects of the Morality of Conjugal Life* [hereafter cited as *"Vademecum"*] (Citta del Vaticano: Libreria Editrice Vaticana, 1997), n. 11.
11. *Vademecum,* n. 11.
12. LF, n. 12.
13. Steve Habisohn, Founder of the GIFT Foundation, in "Why This Conference Now?" address to the Pandora's Pillbox Conference in 1999, Chicago.
14. Michael McManus, "Pope Paul VI: Right on Contraception," *Scranton [Pennsylvania] Times,* 24 October 1999.
15. LF, n. 14.

16. *Vademecum,* 16.

17. GS, n. 50.

18. LF, n. 12.

19. Christopher West, "Historical Man," audiotape from the series *Naked Without Shame: Sex and the Christian Mystery.* Available from the GIFT Foundation.

20. Pope John Paul II, *Evangelium Vitae* (1995), n. 13 [hereafter cited as "EV"], available on-line at www.vatican.va.

21. Dale Oesterling, M.D., "Following the Holy Spirit," in Cleta Hartman, ed., *Physicians Healed* (Dayton, Ohio: One More Soul, 1998), 95.

22. Couple to Couple League, "The Pill: How Does It Work? Is It Safe?," 2.

23. Couple to Couple League, "Pill," 4.

24. See Chris Kahlenborn, M.D., *Breast Cancer: Its Link to Abortion and the Birth Control Pill* (Dayton, Ohio: One More Soul, 2000).

25. Pope John Paul II, "Interpreting the Concept of Concupiscence," General Audience of 8 October 1980, in *Blessed Are the Pure in Heart* (Boston: St. Paul, 1983), 145.

26. Christopher West, *Good News About Sex & Marriage: Answers to Your Honest Questions About Catholic Teaching* (Ann Arbor, Mich.: Servant, 2000), 28.

27. Pope Pius XI, *Casti Connubii* (1930), n. 56 [hereafter cited as "CC"], available on-line at www.vatican.va.

28. Quoted in *L'Osservatore Romano* [hereafter cited as "LOR"], 6 July 1987.

29. Quoted in LOR, 3 December 1979.

30. See CCC, 1777.

31. FC, n. 34.

32. Molly Kelly used this phrase in a presentation at the Franciscan University of Steubenville, Steubenville, Ohio.

33. LF, n. 13 (emphasis in the original).

34. Mark Shea, "Interference vs. Cooperation: The Wisdom of Catholic Sexual Theology," unpublished paper.

Chapter Five
Holy Communion and Intimate Union

1. CCC, n. 1621.
2. Paraphrase of a story from Kippley, *Sex*, 33.
3. CCC, 1642, quoting Ephesians 5:21.
4. See CCC, 1409.
5. CCC, 1624.
6. CCC, 1392, including a phrase from *Presbyterorum Ordinis*, n. 5.
7. LF, n. 12.
8. See CCC, 366.
9. Bob McDonald, "The Two Shall Be One: What Contraception Does to Marriage," audiotape from the Pandora's Pillbox Conference in 1999 in Chicago, Illinois. Available from the GIFT Foundation.
10. See Archbishop Fulton Sheen, *Three to Get Married* (New York: Appleton-Century-Crofts, 1951).
11. HV, n. 13.
12. CCC, 1644.
13. LF, n. 11, including a phrase from *Centesimus Annus*, n. 39.

Chapter Six
Embrace the Truth

1. CCC, 1785.
2. CCC, 1783.
3. LF, n. 14.
4. HV, n. 27.
5. John Hartman, M.D., "The Stone Which the Builders Rejected," in Hartman, *Physicians Healed*, 51–52.
6. See Kahlenborn, 262–64.
7. *Rite of Marriage*, n. 24; quoted in John Kippley, *Marriage Is for Keeps* (Cincinnati: Foundation for the Family, 1994), 136.
8. CC, n. 54.
9. CC, n. 57.
10. *Vademecum*, n. 19.

11. *Vademecum,* n. 19.

12. HV, n. 14.

13. According to a phone conversation on July 10, 2001, with a member of the National Right to Life staff, regarding the percentage of married women procuring abortions. The statistic was based on information from the Center for Disease Control's reports over the last ten years.

14. See D. Mishell, "Current status of oral contraceptive steroids," *Clinical Obstetrics and Gynecology* 19 (December 1976):, 746–47.

15. See L. Cvetkovich, M.D., DDP/NFP report, "Contraceptives and the Menstrual Cycle."

16. "The Shot" by Joan Appleton, R.N., published by Pro-Life Action Ministries.

17. See HV, n. 14.

18. *Sterilization in Catholic Hospitals* [hereafter referred to as "Sterilization"], in *Vatican Council II,* vol. 2, *More Post-Conciliar Documents,* ed. Austin Flannery (Collegeville, Minn.: Liturgical Press, 1982), 454–55, n. 1.

19. Sterilization, n. 1.

20. HV, n. 14.

21. John Paul II, "The Church's teaching on contraception is not a matter for free discussion among theologians," LOR, 6 July 1987.

22. Bob McDonald, audiotaped remarks.

23. Project Rachel, National Office of Post-Abortion Reconciliation and Healing, P. O. Box 070477, Milwaukee, WI 53207-0477. Check out their website: www.marquette.edu/rachel.

Chapter Seven
Embrace the Truth in Love

1. *Vademecum,* n. 12.

2. LF, n. 10 (italics in the original).

3. GS, n. 47.

4. Joseph Cunningham, "The Complete Gift of Self," Canticle 6 (Autumn 1999): 32–35.

5. See their website at www.sidelines.org.

6. LF, n. 17 (emphasis in the original).

7. The Cardinal Mindszenty Foundation, P.O. Box 11321, St. Louis, MO 63105.

8. St. Paul refers to the Christians of Corinth as "living epistles" or letters, "written not with ink, but with the Spirit of the living God" (2 Cor 3:2-3). Likewise, Scott and I refer to our children as the most important letters we'll write, trying to keep our writing projects in the correct perspective.

Chapter Eight
Natural Family Planning (NFP)

1. HV, n. 16.

2. John Paul II, "Pope calls spouses to a sense of responsibility for love and for life," LOR, 17 December 1990.

3. John Kippley, "What Does the Catholic Church REALLY Teach about Birth Control?" (Couple to Couple League pamphlet), 10.

4. Thomas Hilgers, *Creighton Model Fertility Care System* (Omaha, Neb.: Pope Paul VI Institute, 1997), i (emphasis in the original).

5. See John and Sheila Kippley, *The Art of Natural Family Planning,* 4th ed. (Cincinnati: Couple to Couple League International, 1996), 139ff.

6. Archbishop Charles Chaput, *Of Human Life: A Pastoral Letter* (Denver: Office of Marriage and Family Life, Archdiocese of Denver, 1998), 13 (emphasis in the original).

7. HV, n. 16.

8. FC, n. 32.

9. John Paul II, "Educational Guidance in Human Love: Outlines for Sex Education," LOR, 5 December 1983.

10. GS, n. 50.

11. See Kippley, *Art,* 245. Also, look for a fascinating new study, soon to be published, requested by Mercedes Wilson and her organization, Family and the Americas.

12. CCC, 2368.

13. HV, n. 10.
14. GS, n. 50.
15. John Paul II, "Pope Calls Spouses." The Holy Father quotes here from GS, n. 50.
16. Pope John Paul II, "Spouses are called to live the entire truth of *Humanae Vitae*, pastors are to teach it without calling it into question," LOR, 11 April 1988.
17. *Vademecum*, 15.
18. EV, n. 97 (emphasis in the original)
19. *Vademecum*, 21.
20. *Vademecum*, 21.

Chapter Nine
Can We Be Open to One More Soul?

1. Kippley, *Sex*, 217 (emphasis in the original).
2. Nanci Hellmich, "Losing Sleep May Lead to Weight Gain and Diabetes," *USA Today*, 28 March 2001. Ongoing study by Eve Van Cauter at the University of Chicago on the relationship between sleep deprivation and weight gain.
3. Suzanne Fowler, *The Light Weigh* (Leawood, Kans.: Suzanne Fowler, 1998).
4. Robert Sassone, *Handbook on Population*, 5th ed. (Stafford, Va.: American Life League, 1994) is filled with documentation. Available online at www.all.org/world/po03.htm.
5. For more information, listen to Laurel MacLeod's audiotape "No Room at the Inn: The Truth about World Population," Pandora's Pillbox Conference in Chicago, 1998; an outstanding resource available through the GIFT Foundation.
6. GS, n. 50.
7. The Christian organization Focus on the Family has a wide range of materials to assist parents in our daunting task of nurturing children.
8. Pope John Paul II, "Homily at Capitol Mall," 7 October 1979, in *The Message of Justice, Peace and Love* (Boston: St. Paul Editions, 1979),

281–82; quoted in Kippley, *Art*, 230.

9. CC, n. 57.

10. E. Michel, *Eine Anthropologie der Geschlechtsgemeinschaft* (1948), 127, 189, 196; cited in Helmut Thielicke, *Theological Ethics: Sex* (Grand Rapids, Mich.: Eerdmans, 1964), 210.

11. Blessed Josemaría Escrivá, *Christ Is Passing By* (Princeton, N.J.: Scepter, 1973), 212.

12. *Vademecum*, 22–23.

13. Kippley, *Sex*, 220.

14. *Vademecum*, 23.

15. EV, n. 74.

Chapter Ten
Miscarriage and Stillbirth

1. "Silent Loss," *Herald-Star* (Steubenville, Ohio), 2 May 1993.

2. "Silent Loss."

3. SHARE is a support network for pregnancy and infant loss. They can be contacted at the St. Joseph Health Center, 300 First Capitol Dr., St. Charles, MO 63301.

4. "Silent Loss."

5. For more information, contact Dr. Thomas Hilgers, Pope Paul VI Institute, National Center for the Treatment of Reproductive Disorders, 6901 Mercy Road, Omaha, NE 68106.

6. Reprinted by permission from Karen Edmisten.

7. Pregnancy and Infant Loss Center, 1421 East Wayzata Blvd., Suite #30, Wayzata, MN 55391.

8. Resource Team: Fr. Keith Wallace (pastor, St. Mary Star of the Sea Parish) and Bernadette Zambri (a bereaved parent). Morning Light Ministry offers, once a year, a seven-week series that explores the question "Where is God in all of this?" This is an opportunity to share your experience with other bereaved parents and to discover how God has not abandoned you as you travel on your faith and grief journeys. In the last week of the program the group celebrates a special Mass in loving memory of their babies who have died.

9. Morning Light Ministry, c/o St. Mary Star of the Sea Church, 11 Peter Street South, Mississauga, Ont. L5H 2G1.

10. For more information, contact Msgr. James Telthorst at (314) 533-2824.

11. CCC, 1261 (emphasis in the original); quote includes Mark 10:14.

12. "Silent Loss."

13. "Silent Loss."

Chapter Eleven
Infertility

1. See Roger W. Miller, "Infertility, and How It's Treated," *FDA Consumer* (June 1983): 31–36.

2. Marilyn M. Shannon, *Fertility, Cycles and Nutrition* (Cincinnati, Ohio: Couple to Couple League, 1990), 60–61.

3. Kippley, *Sex*, 304.

4. W. Harris, T. Harden, and E. Dawson, "Apparent effect of ascorbic acid medication on semen metal levels," *Fertility and Sterility* 32 (1979): 456–57; cited in Shannon, 113.

5. Shannon, 113. See Harris, et al., 457, and E. Dawson, W. Harris, W. Rankin, L. Charpentier, and W. McGanity, "Effect of ascorbic acid on male fertility," *Annals of the New York Academy of Sciences* 498 (1987): 312ff.

6. Shannon, 68. See A. Wilcox, C. Weinburg, and D. Baird, "Caffeinated beverages and decreased fertility," *The Lancet* (December 24/31, 1988): 1453ff; also R. Christianson, F. Oechsli, and B. van den Berg, "Caffeinated beverages and decreased fertility," *The Lancet* (February 18, 1989): 378.

7. Shannon, 115 (emphasis in the original). See P. Weathersbee and J. Lodge, "A review of ethanol's effects on the reproductive process," *Journal of Reproductive Medicine* 21 (1978): 63.

8. Kippley, *Art*, 310; see "Smoker impotence cited," *Cincinnati Enquirer*, 2 December 1994.

9. Kippley, *Art*, 307; see Associated Press report, "Women smokers at risk," *Cincinnati Enquirer*, 24 May 1985, reporting on an article in

the *Journal of the American Medical Association,* 24 May 1985. S.L. Laurent et al., "An epidemiologic study of smoking and primary infertility in women," *Fertility and Sterility* 57 (1992): 565–72.

10. Kippley, *Art,* 311.
11. Christine de Stoop, *Contraception: The Hidden Truth* (Castle Hill, Australia: Christine de Stoop, 2000), 110.
12. Kippley, *Art,* 305.
13. Kippley, *Art,* 305–6.
14. Pope Paul VI Institute, *Creighton Model* Fertility *Care System.* 14 November 2001. Available on-line at www.creightonmodel.com.
15. DV, II, n. 8.
16. CCC, 2376, including a quote from DV, II, 1.
17. CCC, 2377.
18. DV, II, n. 5.
19. National Catholic Bioethics Center, 19 Washington St., Boston, MA 02135.
20. DV, Introduction, n. 2.
21. Chaput, n. 16 (emphasis in the original).
22. See DV, n. 8.
23. DV, n. 8.
24. GS, n. 50.
25. Lynda Stephenson, "New Ways to Help Childless Couples," *Virtue* (May/June 1985): 31–32, 75.
26. CCC, 2379.

Chapter Twelve
Sterilization

1. CCC, 2297 (emphasis in the original).
2. A woman is sterilized by tubal ligation, in which the fallopian tubes are rendered incapable of passing an egg, or by hysterectomy, in which a woman's generative organs are removed. A man is sterilized by vasectomy, in which each of the vas deferens is rendered incapable of passing sperm.
3. "Sterilization," 454.

4. Joseph Stanford, M. D., "My Personal and Professional Journey With Regard to Moral Issues in Human Procreation," in *Physicians Healed*, 114.

5. Pam and Burnie Zercher, "Absence of Sperm," in *A Change of Heart*, ed. Nancy Campbell (Franklin, Tenn.: Above Rubies, 1997), 19.

6. "Sterilization," 455.

7. Habisohn, "Why This Conference Now?"

8. CCC, 2399.

9. CareFirst Blue Cross/Blue Shield Insurance, *Employee Benefit Guide*, 13.

10. "Sterilization," 454.

11. These long-term health risks are documented in "Tubal Ligation: Some Questions and Answers," a pamphlet from the Couple to Couple League.

12. Sherrie Peterson, "Post-Tubal Problems," in Campbell, *Change*, 73.

13. H. Whit Oliver, M. D. "First Do No Harm," in *Physicians Healed*, 88.

14. Campbell, *Change*, 2–3; see J.J. Roberts, M.D., *Is Vasectomy Worth the Risk? A Physician's Case Against Vasectomania* (West Palm Beach, Fl.: Sunshine Sentinel Press, 1993).

15. Roberts, *Vasectomy*, 35, cited in Campbell, *Change*, 3.

16. Campbell, *Change*, 3; see also Roberts, *Vasectomy*.

17. Timm and Ann Brom, "God Is in Charge," in Campbell, *Change*, 47.

18. Sandra Smith, "Joy Unspeakable," in *Change*, 88.

Chapter Thirteen
God's Call for Marriage

1. FC, n. 86 (emphasis added).

2. LF, n. 22 (emphasis in the original).

Resources

Church Documents

Catechism of the Catholic Church, 2d ed. Citta del Vaticano: Libreria Editrice Vaticana, 1997.

Chaput, Charles J. *Of Human Life.* Denver: Office of Marriage and Family Life, Archdiocese of Denver, 1998.

Congregation for the Doctrine of the Faith. *The Gift of Life (Donum Vitae).* Citta del Vaticano: Libreria Editrice Vaticana, 1990.

Flannery, Austin, ed. *Vatican Council II.* Vol. 1. *The Conciliar and Post Conciliar Documents.* Northport, N.Y.: Costello, 1975.

———. *Vatican Council II.* Vol. 2. *More Post Conciliar Documents.* Collegeville, Minn.: Liturgical Press, 1982.

Pontifical Council for the Family. *The Truth and Meaning of Human Sexuality.* Citta del Vaticano: Libreria Editrice Vaticana, 1995.

———. *Vademecum for Confessors Concerning Some Aspects of the Morality of Conjugal Life.* Citta del Vaticano: Libreria Editrice Vaticana, 1997.

Pope John Paul II. *The Gospel of Life (Evangelium Vitae).* New York: Time Books, 1995.

———. *Letter to Families.* Boston: Pauline Books and Media, 1994.

———. *Letter of Pope John Paul II to Women.* Boston: St. Paul Books & Media, 1995.

———. *On the Dignity and Vocation of Women (Mulieris Dignitatem).* Boston: St. Paul Books & Media, 1988.

———. *Puebla: A Pilgrimage of Faith.* Boston: Daughters of St. Paul, 1979.

———. *The Splendor of Truth (Veritatis Splendor).* Boston: St. Paul Books & Media, 1993.

———. **Pope Paul VI.** *Human Vitae.* Boston: Daughters of St. Paul, 1968.

Pope Pius XI. *Christian Marriage (Casti Connubii).* London: Catholic Truth Society, 1930.

Books

Arnold, Mary. *Pregnancy Diary, A Christian Mother's Reflections.* San Francisco: Ignatius, 1996.

Bonacci, Mary Beth. *Real Love: Mary Beth Bonacci Answers Questions on Dating, Marriage and the Real Meaning of Sex.* San Francisco: Ignatius, 1996.

_____. *We're on a Mission from God: The Generation X Guide to John Paul II, the Catholic Church and the Real Meaning of Life.* San Francisco: Ignatius, 1996.

Burke, Cormac. *Covenanted Happiness: Love and Commitment in Marriage.* San Francisco: Ignatius, 1990.

Campbell, Nancy, ed. *A Change of Heart.* Antioch, Tenn.: Above Rubies, 1997. Stories of couples who have had reversals from vasectomies and tubal ligations. Available from the publisher, P.O. Box 351, Antioch, TN 37011-0351.

de Stoop, Christine. *Contraception: The Hidden Truth.* Castle Hill, Australia: Christine de Stoop, 2000. Available from the author, 31 David Rd., Castle Hill 2158, NSW, Australia.

Drogin, Elasah. *Margaret Sanger: Father of Modern Society.* Coarsegold, Calif.: CUL Publications, 1979.

Ford, John C., and Gerald Kelly. *Contemporary Moral Theology.* Westminster, Md.: Newman Press, 1958–63.

Fowler, Suzanne. *The Light Weigh.* Leawood, Kans.: Suzanne Fowler, 1998. Available from the author, 4701 College Blvd., Suite 102, Leawood, KS 66211.

Guste, Bob. *The Gift of the Church.* Santa Barbara, Calif.: Queenship, 1993.

Hahn, Scott. *First Comes Love.* New York: Doubleday, 2002.

Hahn, Scott, and Kimberly Hahn. *Rome Sweet Home.* San Francisco: Ignatius, 1993.

Hartman, Cleta, ed. *Physicians Healed.* Dayton, Ohio: One More Soul, 1998.

Hess, Rick, and Jan Hess. *A Full Quiver.* Brentwood, Tenn.: Wolgemuth and Hyatt, 1989.

Ilse, Sherokee, and Linda H. Burns. *Empty Arms: A Guide to Help Parents and Loved Ones Cope with Miscarriage, Stillbirth and Neonatal Death.* Long Lake, Minn.: Wintergreen, 1985.

Kahlenborn, Chris, M.D. *Breast Cancer: Its Link to Abortion and the Birth Control Pill.* New Hope, Ky.: One More Soul, 2000.

Keaggy, Bernadette. *A Deeper Shade of Grace.* Nashville, Tenn.: Sparrow, 1993.

Kiser, Keith, and Tami Kiser. *The Incredible Gift!* Huntington, Ind.: Our Sunday Visitor, 1996.

Kippley, John F. *Sex and the Marriage Covenant: A Basis for Morality.* Cincinnati, Ohio: Couple to Couple League, 1991.

_____. *Marriage Is for Keeps: Foundations for Christian Marriage.* Cincinnati, Ohio: Foundation of the Family, 1994.

Kippley, John F., and Sheila K. Kippley. *The Art of Natural Family Planning,* 4th ed. Cincinnati, Ohio: Couple to Couple League, 1996.

Kippley, Sheila K. *Breastfeeding and Natural Child Spacing: How "Ecological" Breastfeeding Spaces Babies,* 2d ed. Cincinnati, Ohio: Couple to Couple League, 1989.

Kreeft, Peter. *Making Sense out of Suffering.* Ann Arbor, Mich.: Servant, 1986.

La Leche League. *The Womanly Art of Breastfeeding.* New York: Plume, 1991.

Lafser, Christine O'Keeffe. *An Empty Cradle, A Full Heart: Reflections for Mothers and Fathers After Miscarriage, Stillbirth, or Infant Death.* Chicago: Loyola, 1998.

Lawler, Ronald, Joseph Boyle, and William May. *Catholic Sexual Ethics.* Huntington, Ind.: Our Sunday Visitor, 1985.

Lewis, C.S. *A Grief Observed.* New York: Bantam, 1961.

Linn, Matthew, Dennis Linn, and Sheila Fabricant. *Healing Relationships With Miscarried, Aborted and Stillborn Babies.* New York: Paulist, 1985.

Madrid, Patrick, ed. *Surprised by Truth.* San Diego: Basilica, 1994.

_____. *Surprised by Truth II.* Manchester, N.H.: Sophia Institute, 2000.

Matthews, Beth. *Precious Treasure.* Steubenville, Ohio: Emmaus Road, 2002.

Morrow, Judy Gordon, and Nancy Gordon DeHamer. *Good Mourning.* Dallas: Word, 1989.

Pope John Paul II. *Love and Responsibility.* San Francisco: Ignatius, 1993.

_____. *Original Unity of Man and Woman.* Boston: St. Paul Editions, 1981.

Pride, Mary. *The Way Home.* Westchester, Ill.: Crossway, 1985.

_____. *All the Way Home.* Westchester, Ill.: Crossway, 1989.

Provan, Charles D. *The Bible and Birth Control.* Monongahela, Pa.: Zimmer, 1989.

Quay, Paul. *The Christian Meaning of Human Sexuality.* San Francisco: Ignatius, 1985.

Rank, Maureen. *Free to Grieve: Healing and Encouragement for Those Who Have Experienced the Physical, Mental, and Emotional Trauma of Miscarriage and Stillbirth.* Minneapolis, Minn.: Bethany, 1985.

Roberts, H.J., M.D. *Is Vasectomy Worth the Risk? A Physicians' Case Against Vasectomania.* West Palm Beach, Fla.: Sunshine Sentinel Press, 1993.

Santorum, Karen Garver. *Letters to Gabriel: The True Story of Gabriel Michael Santorum.* Irving, Tex.: CCC of America, 1998.

Sassone, Robert. *Handbook on Population,* 5th ed. Stafford, Va.: American Life League, 1994. Available from the publisher, P.O. Box 1350, Stafford, VA 22555.

Schwiebert, Pat, and Paul Kirk. *When Hello Means Goodbye.* Portland, Ore.: Perinatal Loss, 1985.

Shannon, Marilyn M. *Nutrition, Cycles, and Infertility.* Cincinnati, Ohio: Couple to Couple League, 1990.

Sheen, Fulton J. *Three to Get Married.* New York: Appleton-Century-Crofts, 1951.

Smith, Janet E., ed. *Why Humanae Vitae Was Right: A Reader.* San Francisco: Ignatius, 1993.

Von Hildebrand, Dietrich. *Marriage: The Mystery of Faithful Love.* Manchester, N.H.: Sophia Institute, 1984.

Weber, James. *Grow or Die!* New Rochelle, N.Y.: Arlington House, 1977.

West, Christopher. *Good News About Sex & Marriage.* Ann Arbor, Mich.: Servant, 2000.

Willke, Jack, and Mrs. Willke. *Abortion: Questions and Answers.* Cincinnati, Ohio: Hayes, 1985.

Audiotapes and Videotapes

Hahn, Scott, and Kimberly Hahn. "Life-Giving Love." Available from St. Joseph Communications.

"Pandora's Pillbox Conference: The Twelve Myths of Contraception." Available from the GIFT Foundation.

Smith, Janet. "Contraception: Why Not?" Available from One More Soul.

West, Christopher. "Naked Without Shame: Sex and the Christian Mystery—

Reflections on Pope John Paul II's Theology of the Body." Available from the GIFT Foundation.

Organizations

Adoptive Families Magazine, P.O. Box 5159, Brentworth, TN 37024; (800) 372-3300.

AMEND (Aiding Mothers Experiencing Neonatal Death), 4324 Berrywick Terrace, St. Louis, MO 63128; (314) 487-7582; www.amendgroup.org.

American Academy of Natural Family Planning (AANFP), University of Utah, Department of Family and Preventive Medicine, 50 N. Medical Dr., Salt Lake City, UT 84132; (801) 581-7234.

Apostolate for Family Consecration, Catholic Familyland, 3375 County Road 36, Bloomingdale, OH 43910-9901; (740) 765-4301; www.familyland.org; info@familyland.org.

Billings Ovulation Method Association, USA, P.O. Box 16206, St. Cloud, MN 55116; (651) 699-8139; www.boma-usa.com.

Catholic Charities, 340 Columbia St., Suite 105, South Bend, IN 46601; (219) 234-3111 or (800) 686-3112 for information on adoption.

Catholics United for the Faith, 827 N. 4th Street, Steubenville, OH 43952; (740) 28FAITH or (800) MY-FAITH; www.cuf.org.

Coming Home Network International, P.O. Box 8290, Zanesville, OH 43702-8290; (800) 664-5110; fax (520) 752-2367; www.chnetwork.org.

The Compassionate Friends, Inc., P.O. Box 3696, Oak Brook, IL 60522-3696; (630) 990-0010 or (877) 969-0010; fax (630) 990-0246; www.compassionatefriends.com.

Couple to Couple League, 4290 Delhi Pike, Cincinnati, OH 45238; (513) 471-2000; www.ccli.org; ccli@ccli.org. Specializes in the sympto-thermal method of Natural Family Planning.

Diocesan Development Program for NFP, U.S. Conference of Catholic Bishops, 3211 4th St, NE, Washington, DC 20017; (202) 541-3240 or (202) 541-3054; www.usccb.org.

Empty Cradle, 4595 Mt. King Dr., San Diego, CA 92117; (619) 595-3887.

Endometriosis Association, P.O. Box 92187, Milwaukee, WI 53202; (800) 992-ENDO or (800) 426-2END.

Family Life Offices in every Catholic diocese.

Family of the Americas, Mercedes Wilson, Director, P.O. Box 1170, Dunkirk, MD 20754; (800) 443-3395; www.familyplanning.net; family-planning@yahoo.com. Specializes in the ovulation method of Natural Family Planning.

GIFT Foundation, P.O. Box 95, Carpentersville, IL 60110; (800) 421-GIFT; www.giftfoundation.org; info@giftfoundation.org. Tapes available at cost.

La Leche League International, 1400 N. Meacham Rd., Schaumburg, IL 60168-4079; (847) 519-7730 or (800) LA LECHE; www.lalecheleague.com.

Morning Light Ministry, c/o St. Mary Star of the Sea Church, 11 Peter Street S., Mississauga, Ont. L5H 2G1; (905) 278-2058.

National Adoption Information Clearinghouse, 330 C Street SW, Washington, DC 20447; (888) 251-0075; www.calib.com/naic.

National Catholic Bioethics Center, 159 Washington St., Boston, MA 02135; (617) 787-1900

One More Soul, 616 Five Oaks Avenue, Dayton, Ohio 45406; (800) 307-SOUL; fax (937) 279-2370; OMSoul@juno.com; www.OMSoul.com. NFP-only Physicians are listed in their Online Directory.

One More Soul National Sterilization Reversal Hotline: (800) 307-7685.

Pope Paul VI National Center for the Treatment of Reproductive Disorder (or Institute for the Study of Human Reproduction), Dr. Thomas W. Hilgers, Director, 6901 Mercy Rd., Omaha, NE 68106-2604; (402) 390-6600; fax (402) 390-9851; www.popepaulvi.com. "The center offers diagnosis and treatment for women who suffer from such reproductive disorders as infertility, premenstrual syndrome (PMS), hormonal and bleeding disorders, repetitive miscarriage, and endometriosis."

Population Research Institute, P.O. Box 1559, Front Royal, VA 22630; (540) 622-5240; www.pop.org.

The Pregnancy and Infant Loss Center of Minnesota, 1415 E. Wayzata Boulevard, Suite 22, Wayzata, MN 55391; (952) 473-9372. Publisher of *Loving Arms* newsletter.

Project Rachel—National Office of Post Abortion Reconciliation and Healing, P.O. Box 070477, Milwaukee, WI 53207-0477; (800) 5WE-CARE; www.marquette.edu/rachel; noparh@juno.com.

Real Love Productions (Mary Beth Bonacci), 6732 W. Coal Mine Ave., #228, Littleton, CO 80123; (303) 237-7942; fax (303) 703-4035; www.reallove.net; www.info@reallove.net.

St. Joseph Communications, P.O. Box 1911, Suite 83, Tehachapi, CA 93581; (800) 526-2151; www.saintjoe.com; richard@saintjoe.com.

St. Joseph's Covenant Keepers. Family Life Center International, P.O. Box 6060, Port Charlotte, FL 33949; (941) 764-7725; www.dads.org; sjck@sunline.net.

Sexaholics Anonymous (SA), P.O. Box 111910, Nashville, TN 37222; (615) 331-6230; www.sa.org; saico@sa.org.

SHARE, St. Elizabeth's Hospital, 211 S. Third St., Belleville, IL 62222; (618) 234-2120; www.stelizabeth.org.

Sidelines National Support Network National Office, P.O. Box 1808, Laguna Beach, CA 92652; (949) 497-2265; www.sidelines.org; wwwsidelines@sidelines.org. Supporting women who have to be on bed rest mid-pregnancy.

Sisters of Life, Our Lady of New York, 1955 Needham Avenue, Bronx, NY 10466.

Society of Blessed Gianna Beretta Molla, P.O. Box 59557, Philadelphia, PA 19102-9557; (213) 297-5940.